AF305314

Windo

Christopher Masters

Windows in Art

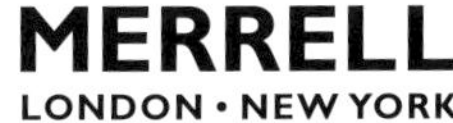

MERRELL
LONDON · NEW YORK

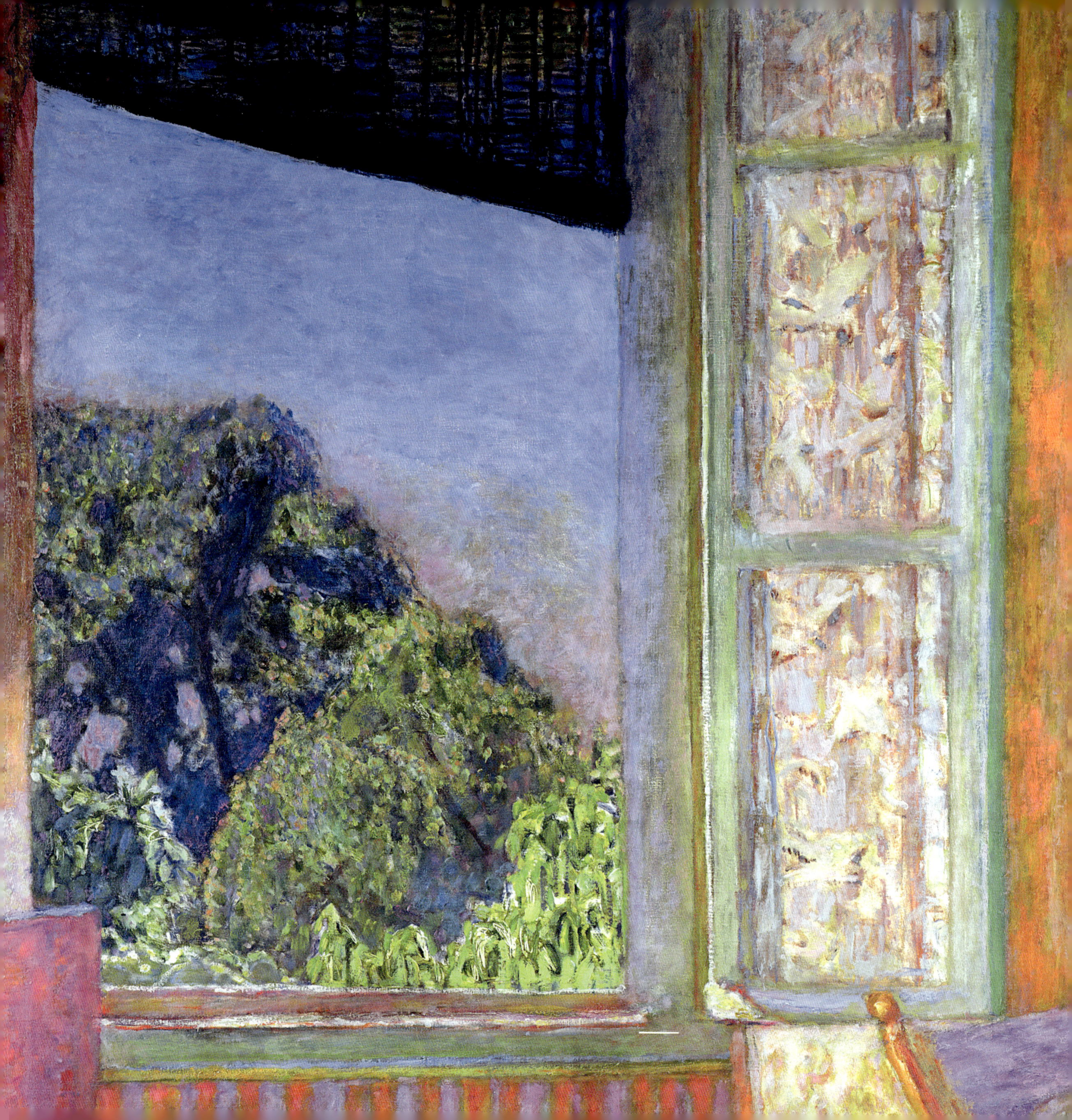

Windows in Art

Christopher Masters

Windows in Art

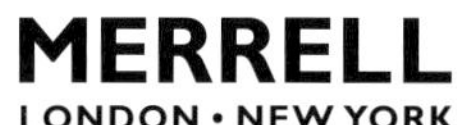

MERRELL

LONDON · NEW YORK

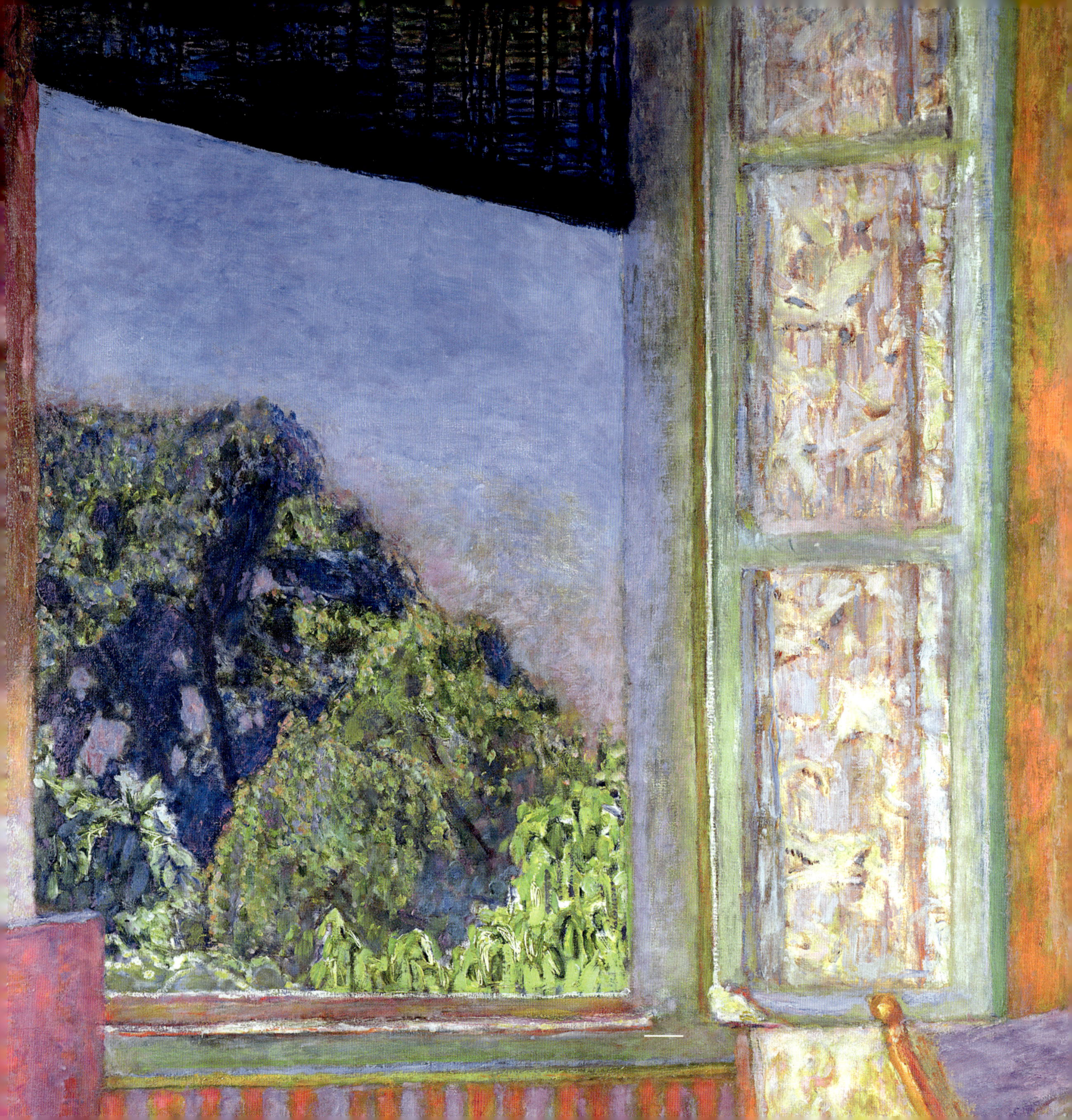

6   Introduction

23   Status and Style

47   Revelations

81   Windows on the World

125   Mirror of the Soul

153   The Architecture of Light

182   Notes

184   Further Reading

185   Index

Introduction

A window provides access to two of life's essentials: light and air. It can also be used to enhance a room's sense of space. However, it is more than just a means to an end. In addition to its practical functions, a window possesses symbolic, expressive and architectural qualities, many of which have for centuries furnished Western art with some of its most fascinating if overlooked subjects. This book celebrates the multiple roles of the window in art through five key themes that, it is hoped, will encourage a greater appreciation of this now ubiquitous artefact, as well as cast light on the significance of the paintings and sculptures in which it is featured.

The representation of windows is highly revealing of a culture's attitude towards the power and significance of light. Until quite recently, windows of any size were a luxury, enjoyed by wealthy people during periods of security and peace; indeed, in eighteenth- and nineteenth-century England and France they were subjected to heavy taxation. The window was, therefore, a status symbol, a way of proclaiming wealth and taste, as can be seen from the exceptional range of images in our first chapter, 'Status and Style'. Light itself has been regarded as having a metaphysical quality, and in the second chapter, 'Revelations', windows are shown as providing a metaphor for spiritual illumination. In many of the works a figure is bathed in light that pours in obliquely from the side. While the earliest of these paintings are religious in nature, similar effects can eventually be seen in secular pictures by such masters as Jan Vermeer (1632–1675).

Naturally, our third section, 'Windows on the World', demonstrates a variety of views of exterior reality, which can be contrasted with the inner landscapes that feature in 'Mirror of the Soul'. While offering very different images of worldliness or introspection, both these chapters also deal with the theme of the voyeur.

In many of the works illustrated in this book, the physical structure of the window is a marginal feature, subservient to the view it frames. In our final chapter, 'The Architecture of Light', we concentrate on the physical qualities of a window and its relationship to the building of which it is a part. This architectural element is, however, always complementary to the image's wider meaning and aesthetic qualities.

The book's thematic approach allows for some stimulating juxtapositions, as well as the identification of key issues and ideas. However, this introduction is intended to provide a sense of chronology, defining not only the physical transformations of the window but also its evolving cultural role. In doing so, it places particular emphasis on the Renaissance and

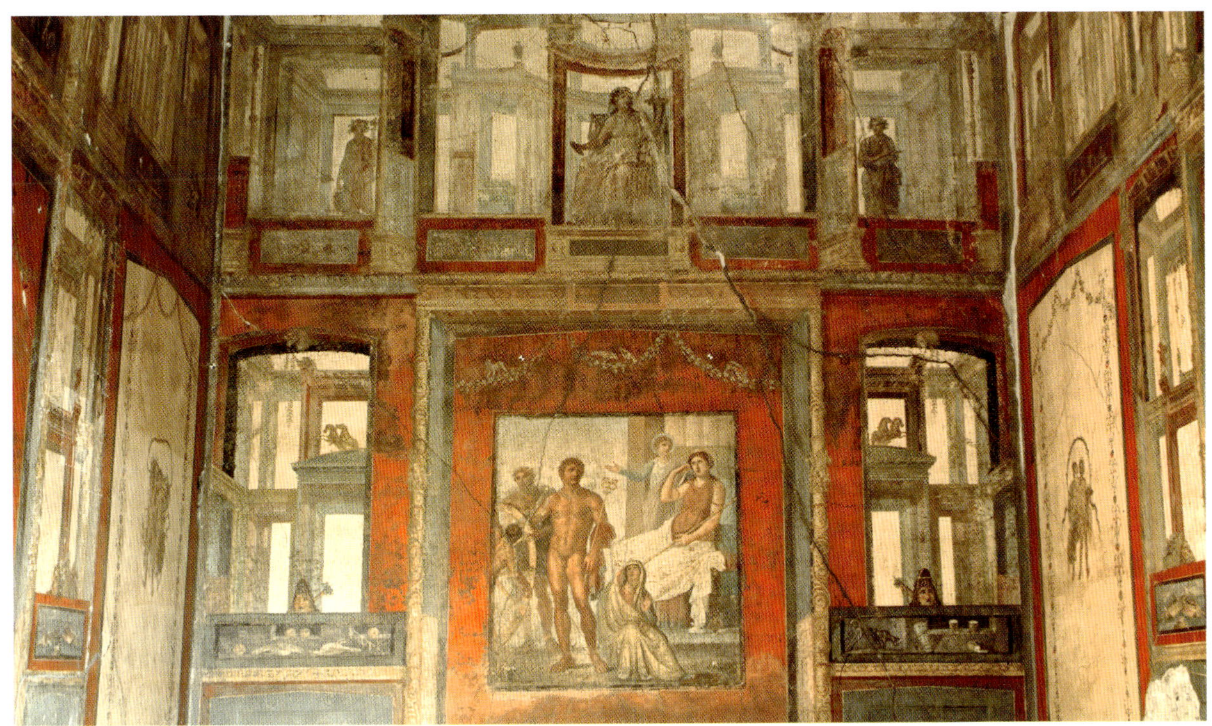

modern periods, when vital developments in the concept of art were powerfully expressed through the metaphor of the window.

———

'The men of old were born like the wild beasts, in woods, caves and groves, and lived on savage fare.'[1] With this pithy description of humanity's primitive state, the Roman architectural theorist Marcus Vitruvius Pollio (*fl.* late first century BC) began his account of the earliest dwellings, some made 'in imitation of the nests of swallows', soon to be succeeded by 'forked stakes connected by twigs' and 'walls of lumps of dried mud ... with reeds and leaves to keep out the rain and the heat'.[2] Mankind began its ascent from bestiality by creating a basic shelter, but the use of space, air and light was still some way off. The window would have to wait for an age of civilization.

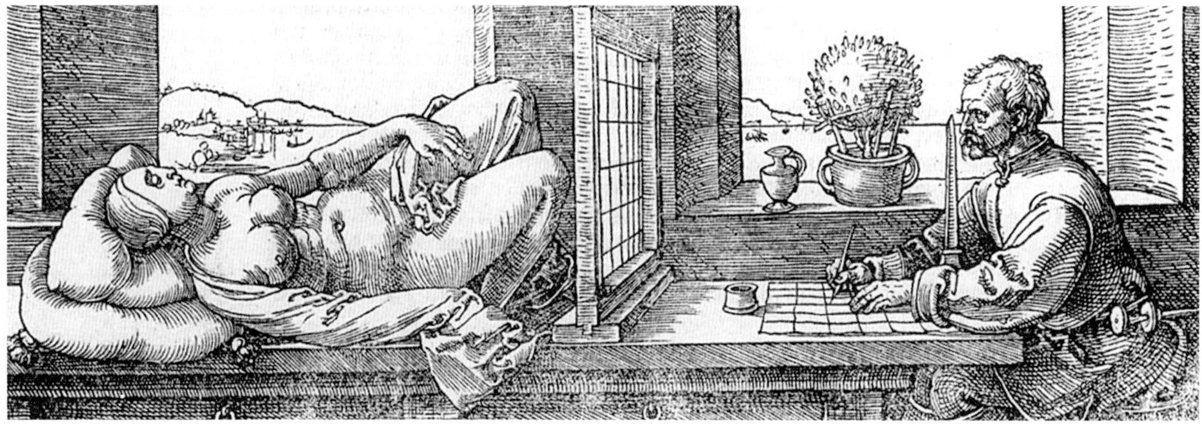

Even in Roman times, however, windows were far from ubiquitous. As Vitruvius recognized, rural buildings were much easier to light than houses in crowded cities, and, as a walk around Pompeii will demonstrate, even the grandest of homes had few external openings. It is not surprising, then, that Roman painters, using all their technical sophistication, often burst asunder the walls of houses with fictive windows and other openings, creating highly theatrical vistas, as in the frescoes at the House of the Vettii in Pompeii (page 7).

These decorations, with their extravagant perspective typical of the 'Fourth Style' of Roman wall painting (*c.* 20–79), are more scenographic than illusionistic. The artist has created not a credible reality but an antidote to the urban squalor outside, emphasizing both the luxury of the setting and his own skill. It is significant that the windows are interspersed with figurative images that manage to be naturalistic while also remaining obviously painted. Such classical authors as Pliny the Elder (23/24–79) enjoyed telling stories of artists who depicted grapes that the birds pecked or curtains that their colleagues tried to open, but no one could make such a mistake here. The principal function of these 'windows' may have been to indicate the patron's status, but they are also a spectacular display of the painter's artifice.

Although the window-turned-into-paint is essentially a chimera – a theatrical creation with just a suggestion of space and air – the painting-turned-into-window is one of the more consistent principles of European art. This concept was formulated by the Renaissance humanist and architect Leon Battista Alberti (1404–1472), who, in his treatise *De pictura* (On Painting; 1435), declared: 'Let me tell you what I do when I am painting. First of all, on the surface on which I am going to paint, I draw a rectangle of whatever size I want, which I regard as an open window through which the subject to be painted is seen.'[3] He then proceeded to explain not only how to make parallel lines appear to converge at a vanishing point on the horizon but also how to represent correctly the intervals between horizontal lines at progressively deeper positions.

Alberti's technique, which drew on the practices of such contemporaries as the architect and sculptor Filippo Brunelleschi (1377–1446), inspired later figures in both Italy and abroad, as can be seen in the sixteenth-century image of a perspective device (opposite) by Albrecht Dürer (1471–1528). However, 'one-point perspective' was by no means a comprehensive method of creating an illusion of reality, since it presents a static view of the world dependent on the image being viewed from a single position identical to that of the artist at the time the painting was made. Moreover, it ignores other optical factors determining our perception of reality, above all the atmospheric and light effects that fifteenth-century Netherlandish artists were able to explore thanks to their experiments with the medium of oil paint.

In the Annunciation Triptych (page 10) by the workshop of Robert Campin (*c.* 1375/79–1444), the central panel includes a tiny figure of Christ descending on the rays of light that penetrate the circular windows on the left. This use of light to symbolize the presence of divinity was a feature of art that was not unique to the Renaissance, as is demonstrated in the chapter 'Revelations'. However, the view through St Joseph's casement window in the right-hand wing of the triptych illustrates an innovation characteristic of early Netherlandish painting, namely, the depiction in minute detail of a cluster of handsome, and equally well-fenestrated, merchant houses. The pictorial space achieved in Joseph's room through the use of multiple vanishing points is enhanced by the cityscape, which also helps to create a link between the biblical character and the contemporary world of the worshipper.

Despite this element of continuity between interior and exterior, a clear boundary is created by the window frame. This essential division, emphasized by the disparity of scale between the room and the world outside, can be found in many of the images featured in this book. The view is of a narrow box-like space defined by the dimensions of the window, reflecting

Workshop of Robert Campin
(*c.* 1375/79–1444)

Annunciation Triptych (Merode Altarpiece)
c. 1427–32
Oil on oak
Central panel: 64.1 × 63.2 cm (25¼ × 24⅞ in.);
each wing: 64.5 × 27.3 cm (25⅜ × 10¾ in.)

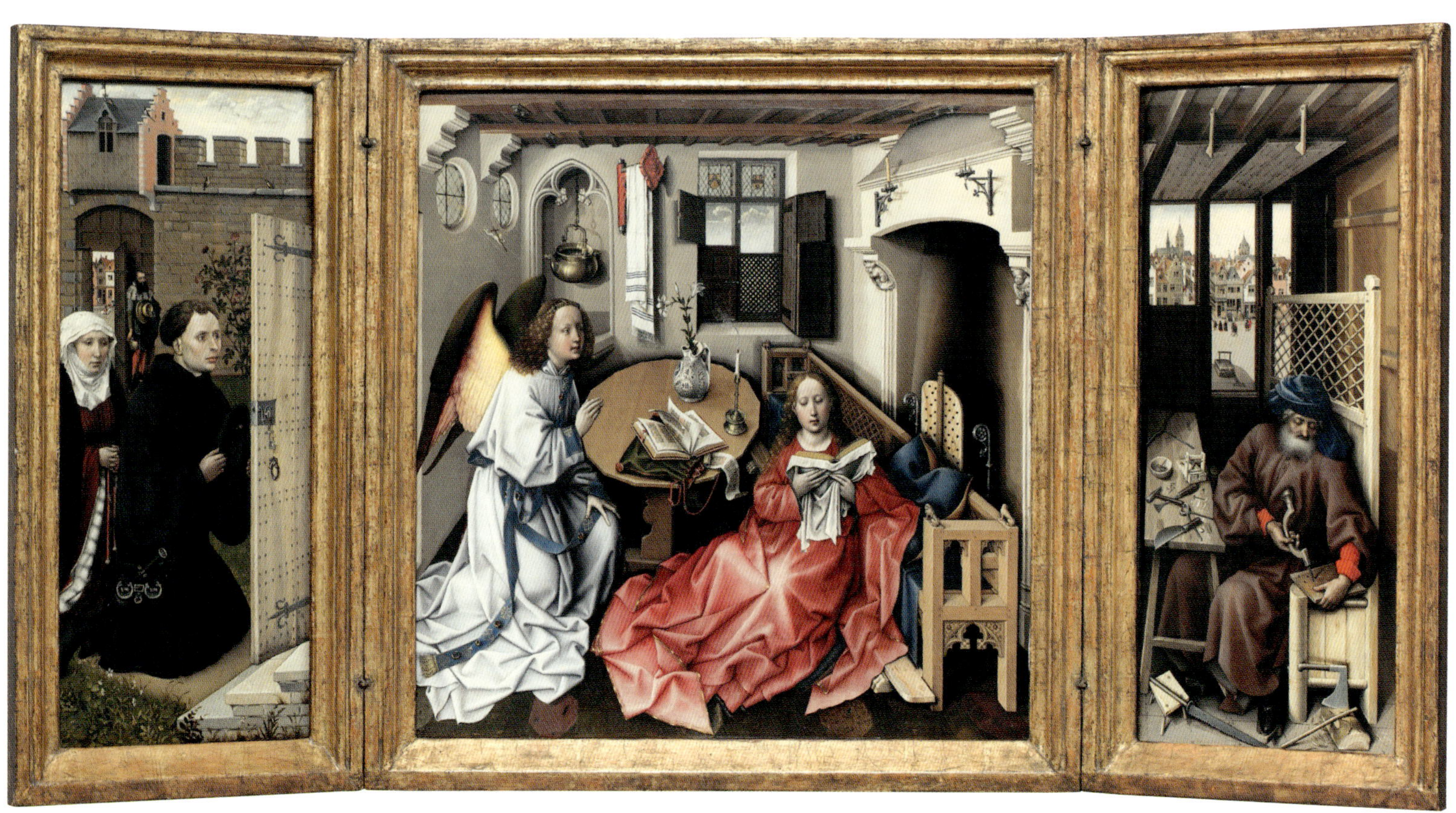

a conception of pictorial space that did not radically change for more than four hundred years. Certainly there are countless variations, exemplified here by such works as the seventeenth-century peepshow by Samuel van Hoogstraten (1627–1678; page 167) or the scene from the *Marriage à la Mode* series by William Hogarth (1697–1764; pages 82–83), executed almost a century later. Hogarth's view through a sash window, which shows a speculative building development that is part of the marriage negotiations, is relatively flat and linear, but the conceit of the painting as a window is emphasized by the numerous canvases adorning the adjacent walls.

It was not until the late nineteenth century that the painted window, both as a concept of art and as an actual motif, began radically to be transformed. As demonstrated by the painting of Eugène Manet on the Isle of Wight (page 100) by Berthe Morisot (1841–1895), the Impressionists' fresh approach to the depiction of light eroded conventional tonal distinctions between foreground and background and, in this case, between the room and the world outside. In contrast, *Melancholy (Laura)* (right) by Edvard Munch (1863–1944) exploits the interplay between warm and cool hues, but the effect is primarily expressive without any naturalistic intent. Munch juxtaposes the feverish reds and yellows

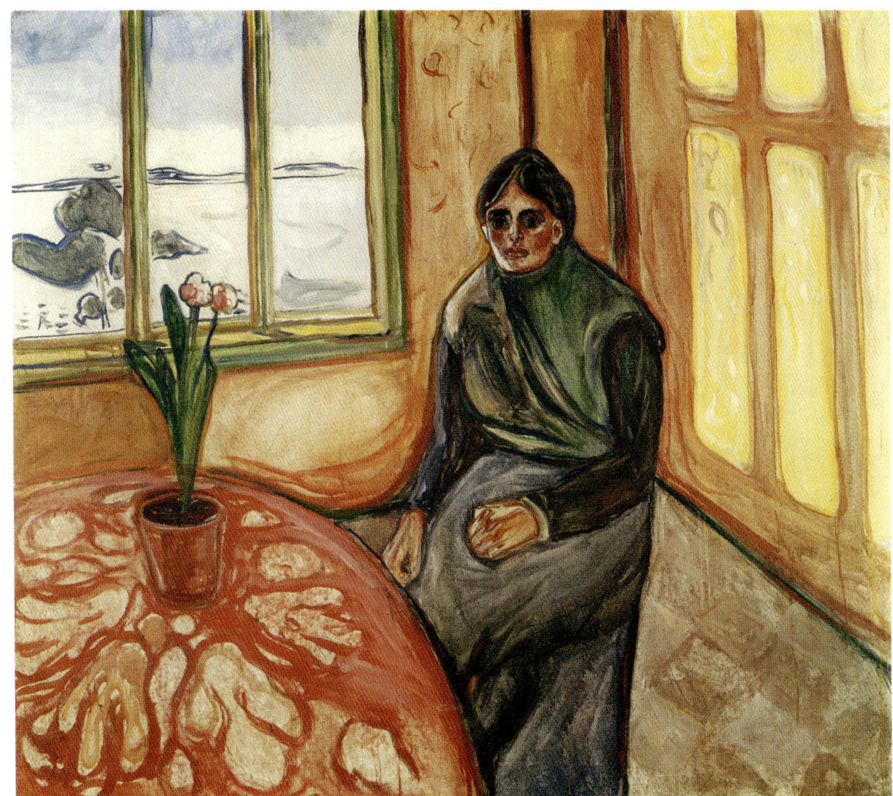

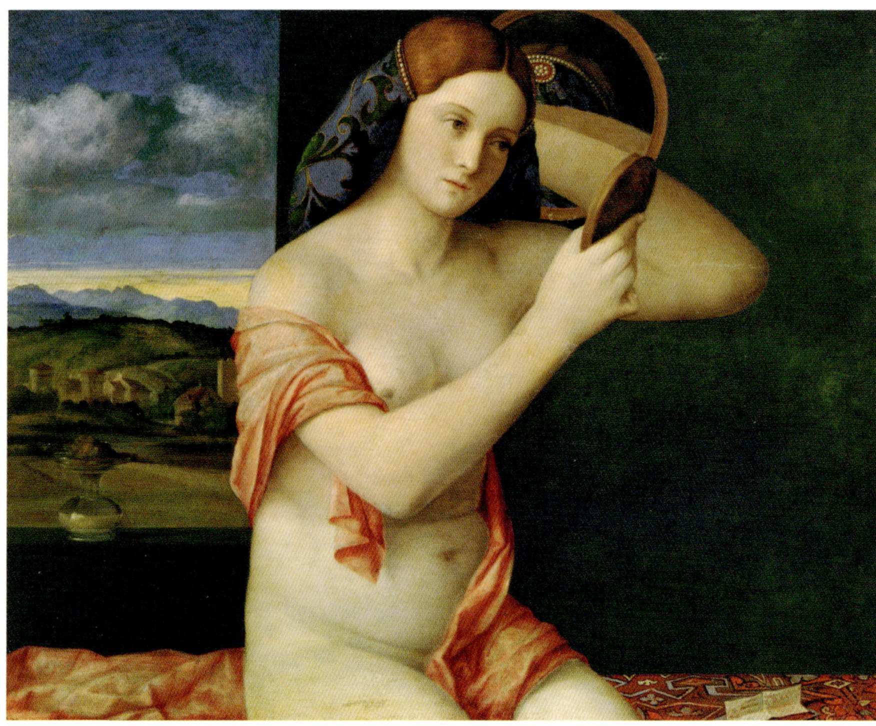

of the interior with a landscape that is presented as an opaque patch of blue paint – a denial of transparency that appears most spectacularly in the black, nocturnal window of Munch's *Moonlight I* (page 145).

The conventions of post-Renaissance painting were most audaciously challenged by the modernist movements of the early twentieth century. In *Red Room (Harmony in Red)* (opposite) by Henri Matisse (1869–1954), the complementary colours inside and outside the room create rhythmic effects that are, as the title of the work suggests, almost musical. There is also a strong decorative quality, an emphasis on pattern that was to some extent a feature of the Renaissance tradition; Giovanni Bellini (?1431/36–1516), for example, uses recurring hues to bind together the composition of *Woman (?Venus) at Her Toilet* (left). However, Matisse's emphasis on flatness and anti-naturalism is a striking innovation, developed throughout his career – with countless variations – in paintings that include views of ateliers and Mediterranean scenery or vegetation (pages 14 and 115).

It is significant to note that in the autumn of 1955 Pablo Picasso (1881–1973) responded to Matisse's death the year before by producing a dozen canvases of his own studio in which the palm trees seen through the window

Henri Matisse
(1869–1954)

Red Room (Harmony in Red)
1908
Oil on canvas
180.5 × 221 cm (71 × 87 in.)
THE STATE HERMITAGE MUSEUM, ST PETERSBURG

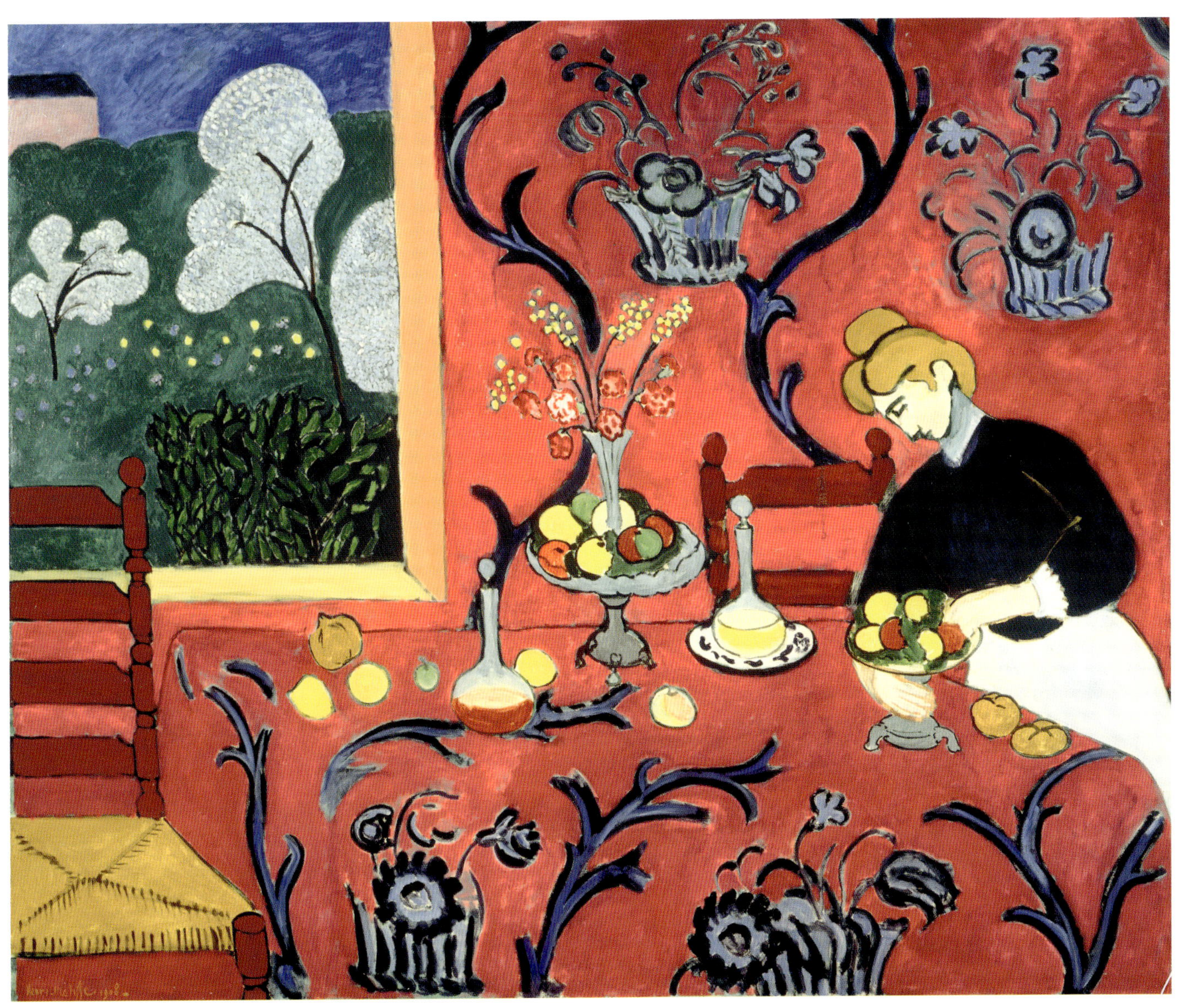

Henri Matisse
(1869–1954)

Red Interior: Still Life on a Blue Table
1947
Oil on canvas
116 × 89 cm (45⅝ × 35 in.)
KUNSTSAMMLUNG NORDRHEIN-
WESTFALEN, DÜSSELDORF

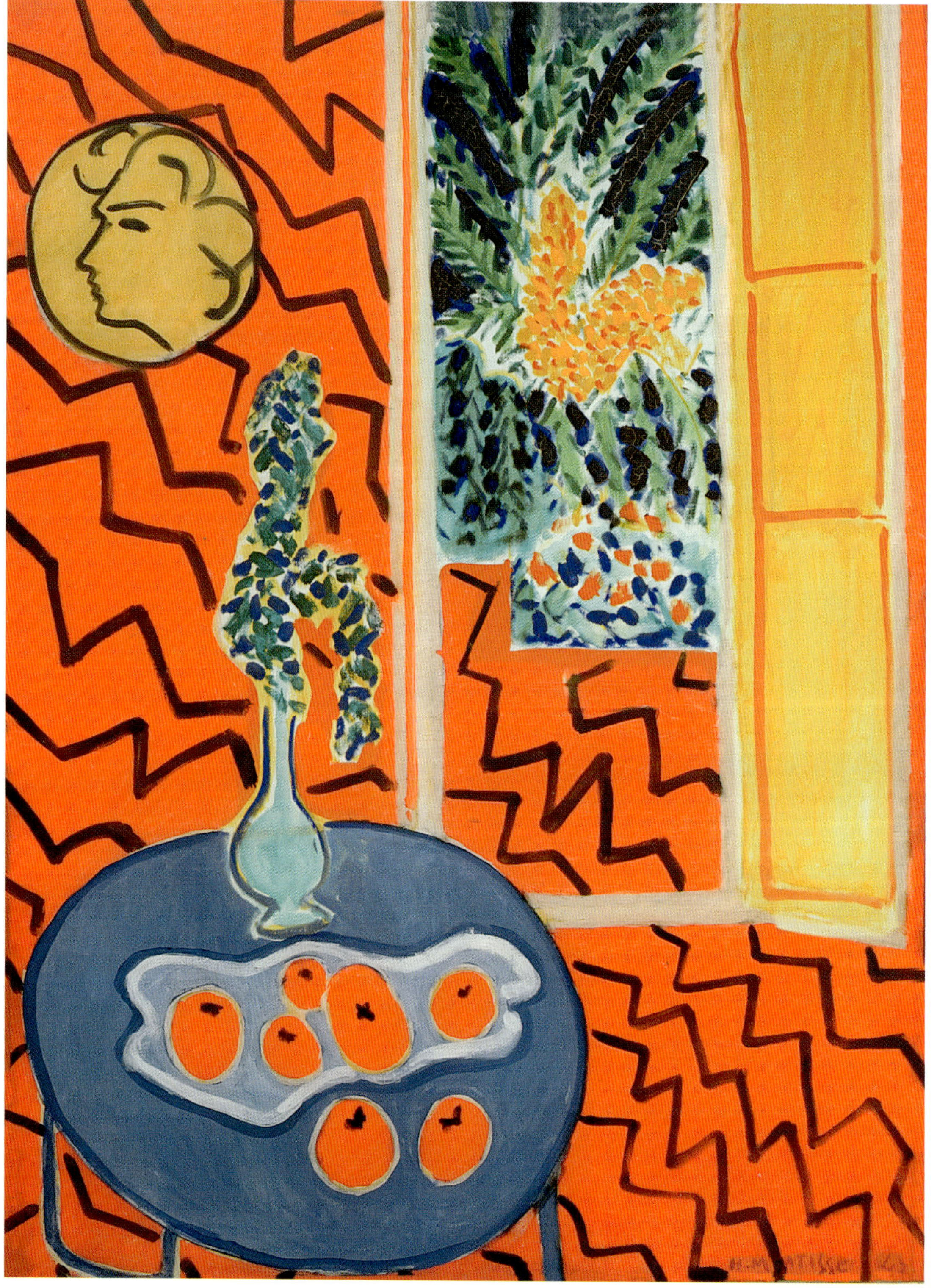

Pablo Picasso
(1881–1973)

The Studio
1955
Oil on canvas
80.9 × 64.9 cm (31 ⅞ × 25½ in.)
TATE, LONDON

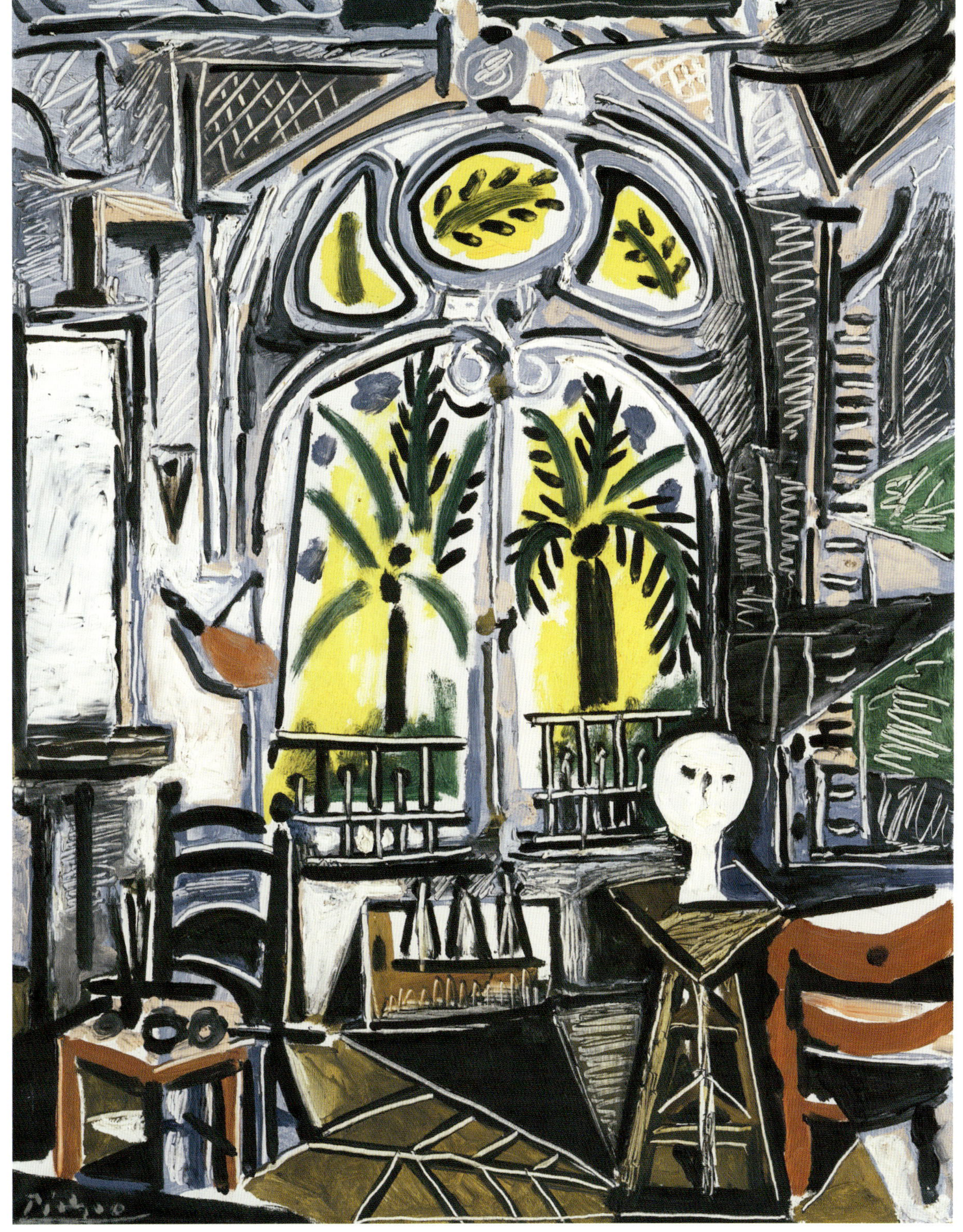

Marcel Duchamp
(1887–1968)

Fresh Widow
1920
Mixed media
78.9 × 53.2 × 9.9 cm (31 × 21 × 3 ⅞ in.)
THE MUSEUM OF MODERN ART, NEW YORK

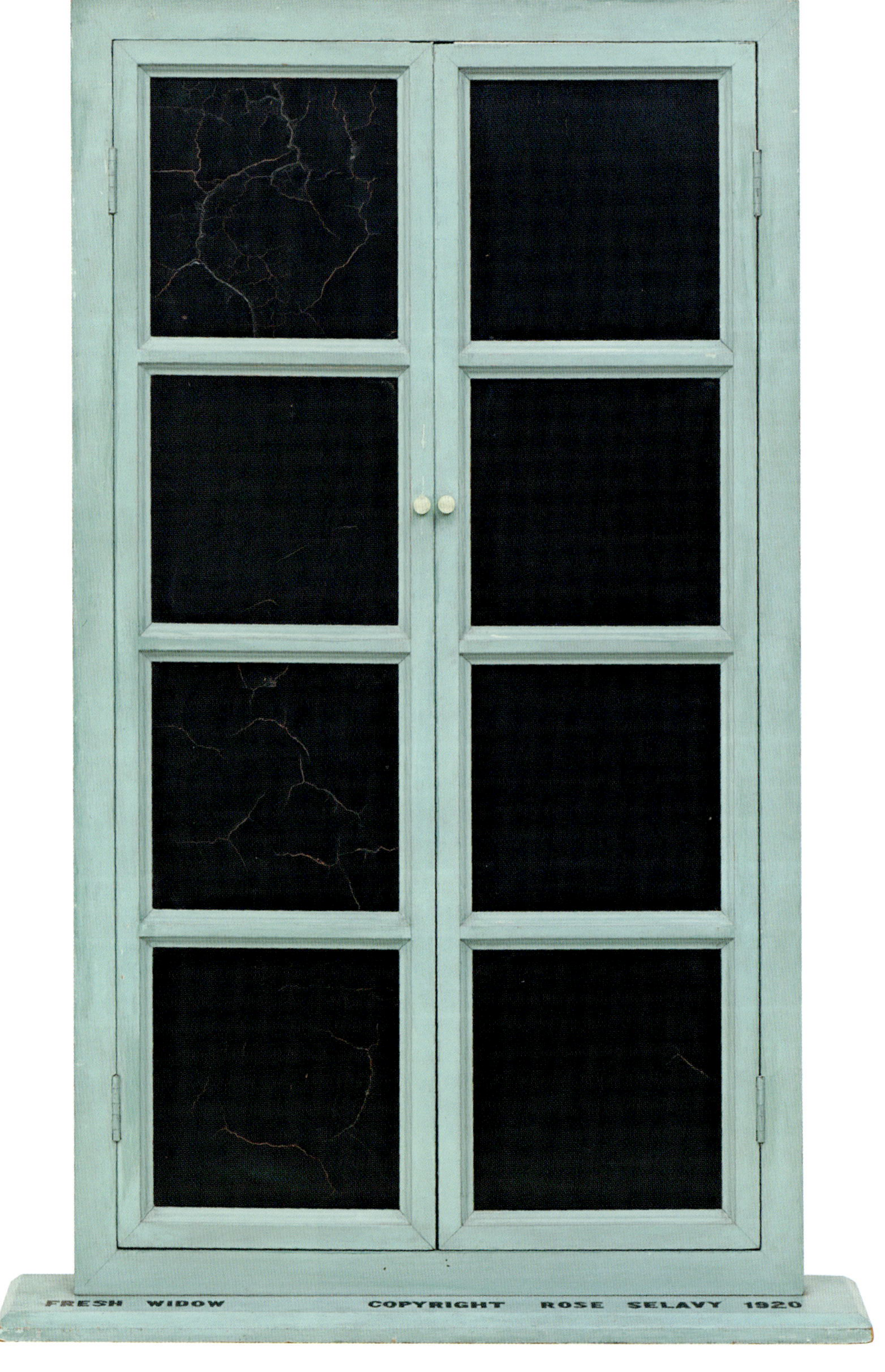

are incorporated into a rigorous interior composition, with suitably mournful hues (page 15). Despite this homage to Matisse, the florid art nouveau window is peculiar to Picasso, a feature of 'La Californie', the villa – near Cannes in the South of France – that he purchased in the summer of 1955.

Picasso's complex, sparring relationship with Matisse had begun at the time when the Spanish artist was pioneering cubism in the years leading up to the First World War. This new style soon produced some remarkable, and varied, window views, from the angular *Still Life before an Open Window, Place Ravignan* (page 117) by Juan Gris (1887–1927) to *Windows* (page 118) by Robert Delaunay (1885–1941), a lyrical work in which the outline of the Eiffel Tower delivers the picture from total abstraction.

In the 1920s the Dada and surrealist movements tackled the theme of the window through a variety of challenging, disorientating approaches. René Magritte (1898–1967), ostensibly working within the illusionist tradition, played with the concept of the painting as a window by depicting an easel-mounted canvas that conceals the view from a window while exactly replicating it (page 136). More daringly, *Fresh Widow* (opposite) by Marcel Duchamp (1887–1968) signified a rejection not only of Alberti's artistic model but also of

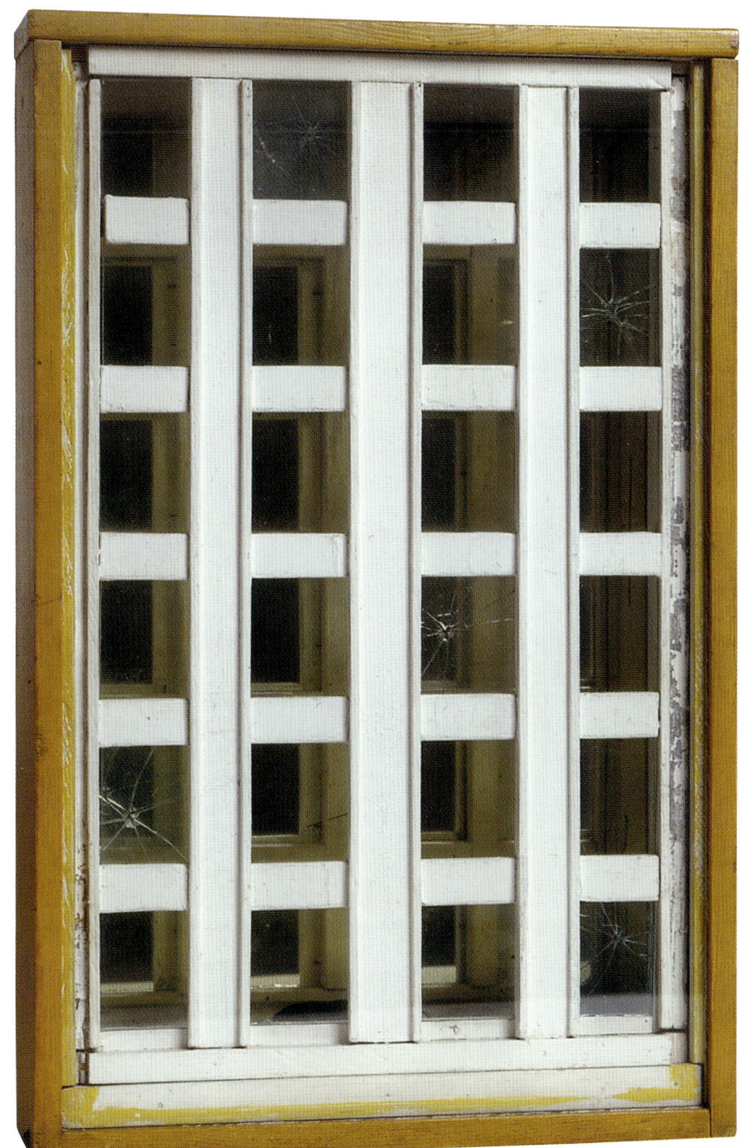

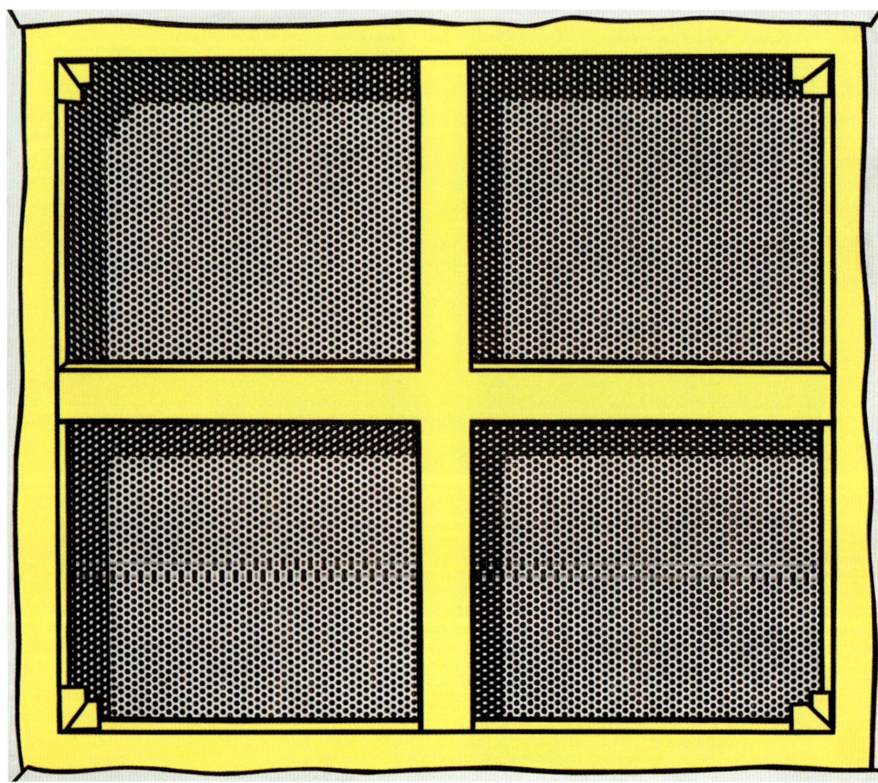

painting altogether. With its black leather and punning title, this seminal work ironically mourns the death of humanist art. The painting as a window has been replaced by an everyday object covered with opaque screens, and lacking any content other than a reference to the tradition that it has emphatically rejected.

The concept of the art object as a thing in itself was subsequently explored in a variety of ways. In 1949 the American abstract artist Ellsworth Kelly (born 1923) was inspired by a window in the Musée d'Art Moderne in Paris to create a non-illusionistic black-and-white pattern out of two canvases – one of which had been reversed – and their wooden frame. Two decades later the Pop artist Roy Lichtenstein (1923–1997) used his characteristic printers' dots to create a work that resembles both the stretcher at the back of a canvas and the frame of a window (left) – motifs anticipated by the German Romantic Carl Gustav Carus (1789–1869) as early as the 1820s, when he depicted his studio window with an inverted canvas placed against it (opposite).

Other artists have used another kind of inversion, turning window-like forms into reflective surfaces that throw back the viewer's image rather than revealing something beyond the frame. At first sight, *Untitled (Window Box Construction)* (page 17) by Joseph Cornell (1903–1972) seems to be about as blank as an

Carl Gustav Carus
(1789–1869)

Studio Window
1823–24
Oil on canvas
28.8 × 20.9 cm (11 ⅜ × 8 ¼ in.)
MUSEUM BEHNHAUS DRÄGERHAUS, LÜBECK

artefact can be, and yet the rows of mirrors concealed within the repetitive, rectangular structure represent fleeting experiences while evocatively expanding on them.

More recently, the Swiss artist Ugo Rondinone (born 1963) greeted visitors to the Institute of Contemporary Art in Boston with *Clockwork for Oracles* (page 20), fifty-two mirrored and brightly hued windows set in rough wooden frames against a background of whitewashed newsprint. The everyday materials were transformed by their juxtaposition, while visitors to the gallery saw altered images of themselves in the coloured glass. The installation was named after a poem by Edmond Jabès (1912–1991), an Egyptian-Jewish writer who fled to Paris following the Suez Crisis of 1956, and shares with its source what Rondinone has described as an essential quality of Jabès's work: 'a mystical attention to religious experience coupled with a real engagement with daily human conditions'.[4]

While many modern artists have ignored, derided or transformed traditional concepts of art, architects in the age of industrialization took advantage of new materials to reinvent the window. Apart from the tracery, or stone openwork, of the great structures of the Middle Ages (pages 51 and 159), windows in the past – however beautifully proportioned or adorned –

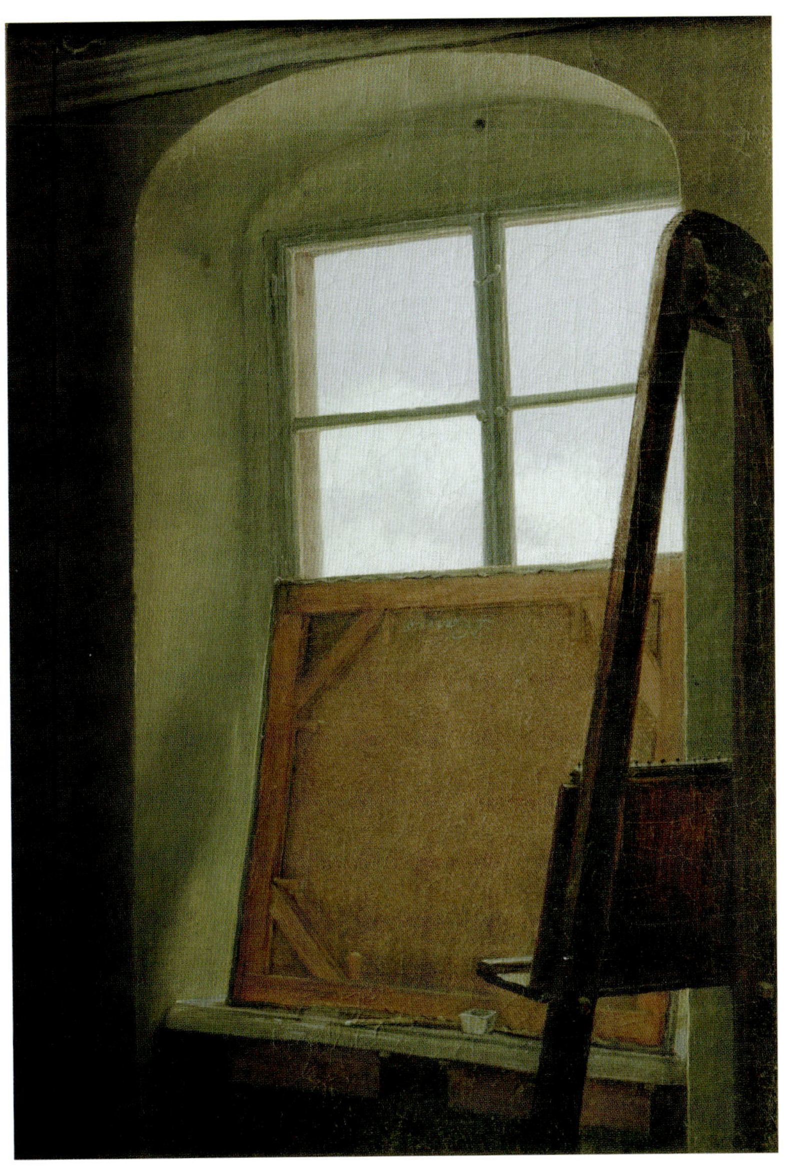

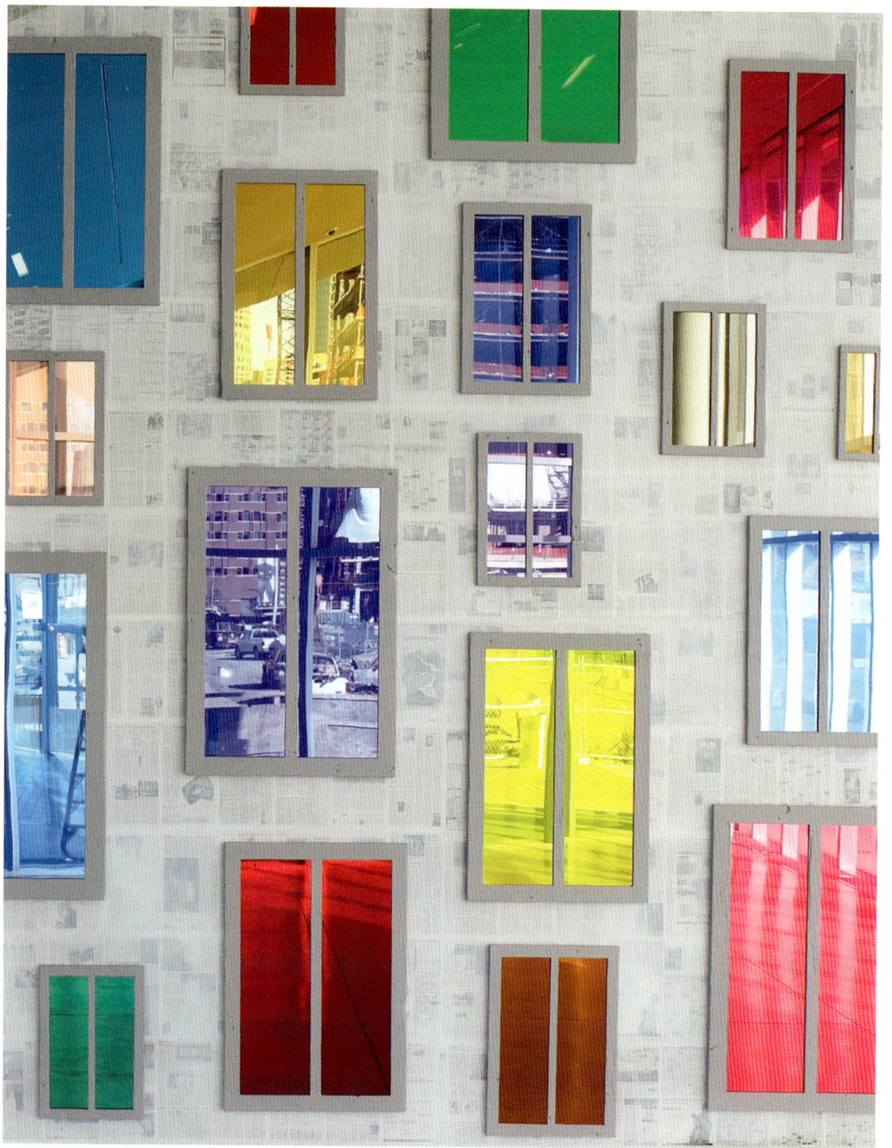

had tended simply to be holes in solid walls. While the development of the modernist window is a subject for another book, this volume includes some remarkable images of walls of glass, from the Precisionism of Charles Sheeler (1883–1965; page 181) to the more intimate paintings of Edward Hopper (1882–1967). In *Western Motel* (pages 178–79), Hopper's memorable canvas of his wife and car, he separates his prized possessions with a window that is so dominant because it is hardly perceptible. Here, as in Delaunay's *Windows* (page 118), the distinction between interior and exterior has been almost completely dissolved, even though the idiom in which Hopper was working was far closer to the Renaissance ideal that Delaunay had helped to shatter.

The post-industrial window has not simply been confined to oil on canvas. In recent decades artists have created installations and site-specific sculptures that have brilliantly exploited both the metaphorical and the aesthetic potential of windows – conventional and otherwise. *House of Windows* (page 151) by the Japanese artist Chiharu Shiota (born 1972) consists of a series of evocative structures made from the debris of demolitions in her adopted city of Berlin, while in 2007 the Danish-Icelandic artist Olafur Eliasson (born 1967) created a remarkable structure in the grounds of the VKR Holding campus – located to the north of Copenhagen – the subject of which

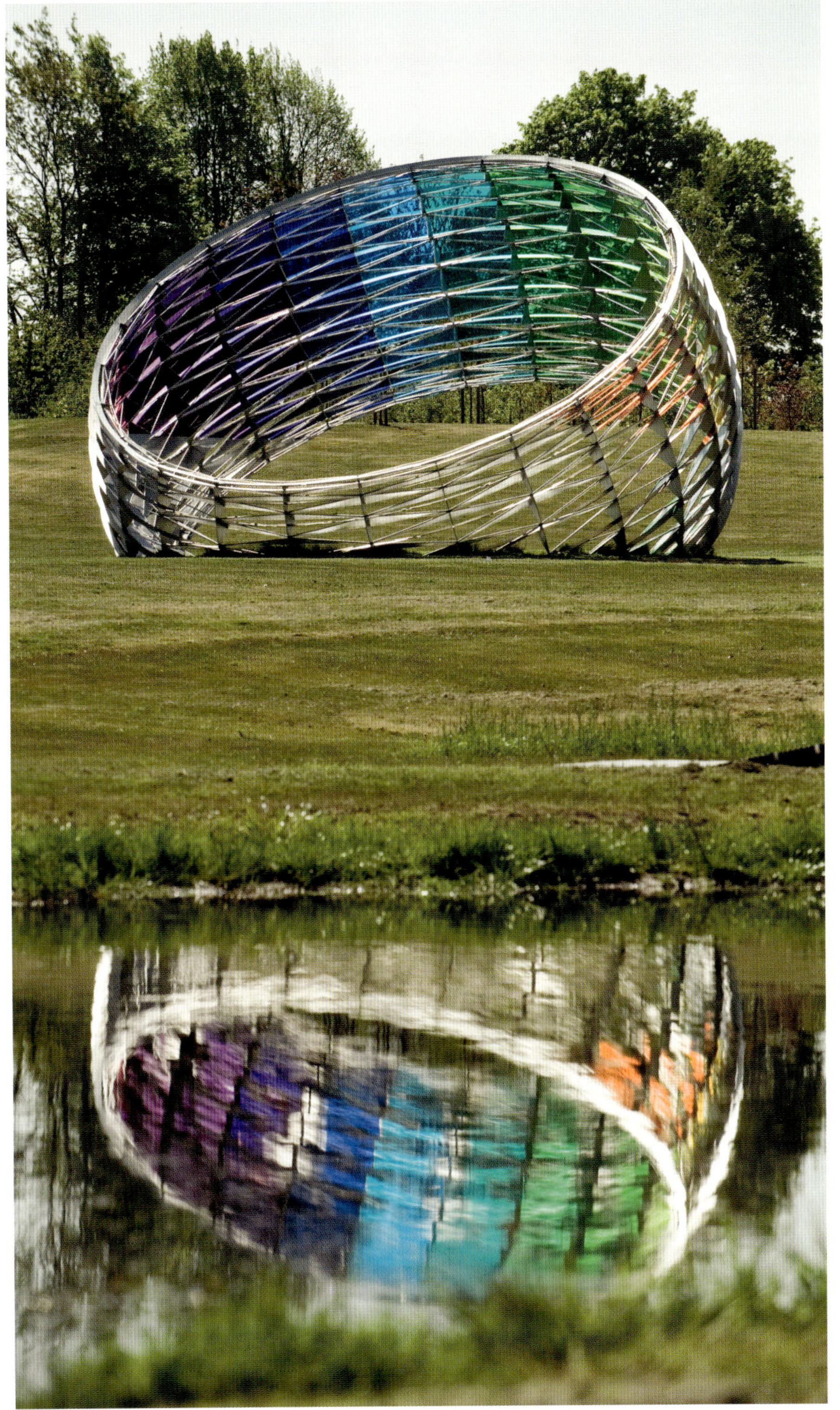

was no less than the Earth's movement around the sun. *The Daylight Pavilion* (right) is a monumental cylinder, partly sunk into the ground, made from metal and spectrum-coloured acrylic. Analogous to a VELUX roof window, VKR Holding's most famous product, the sculpture transmits light from above, casting it on to the ground in exquisite patterns that alter with the hour and season. The elements of the structure are aligned with the sun's movement through the sky at different times of the year, while the arrangement and relative sizes of the acrylic pieces reflect the changing hours of daylight and even the alterations in the rate at which the days increase or decrease in length.

In its formal qualities Eliasson's piece has little in common with the oil paintings and other conventional media that illustrate much of this book, or even with the aesthetic concepts with which they are associated. Yet, in its mastery of light and space, and interaction with its surroundings, it encapsulates the beauty that the window has bestowed on our environment over the centuries. As in the case of so many of the works here, *The Daylight Pavilion* intensifies our experience of the world and encourages us to think afresh about the very nature and role of art. It is hoped that, in presenting such a striking array of images and artefacts, this book will achieve a similar goal.

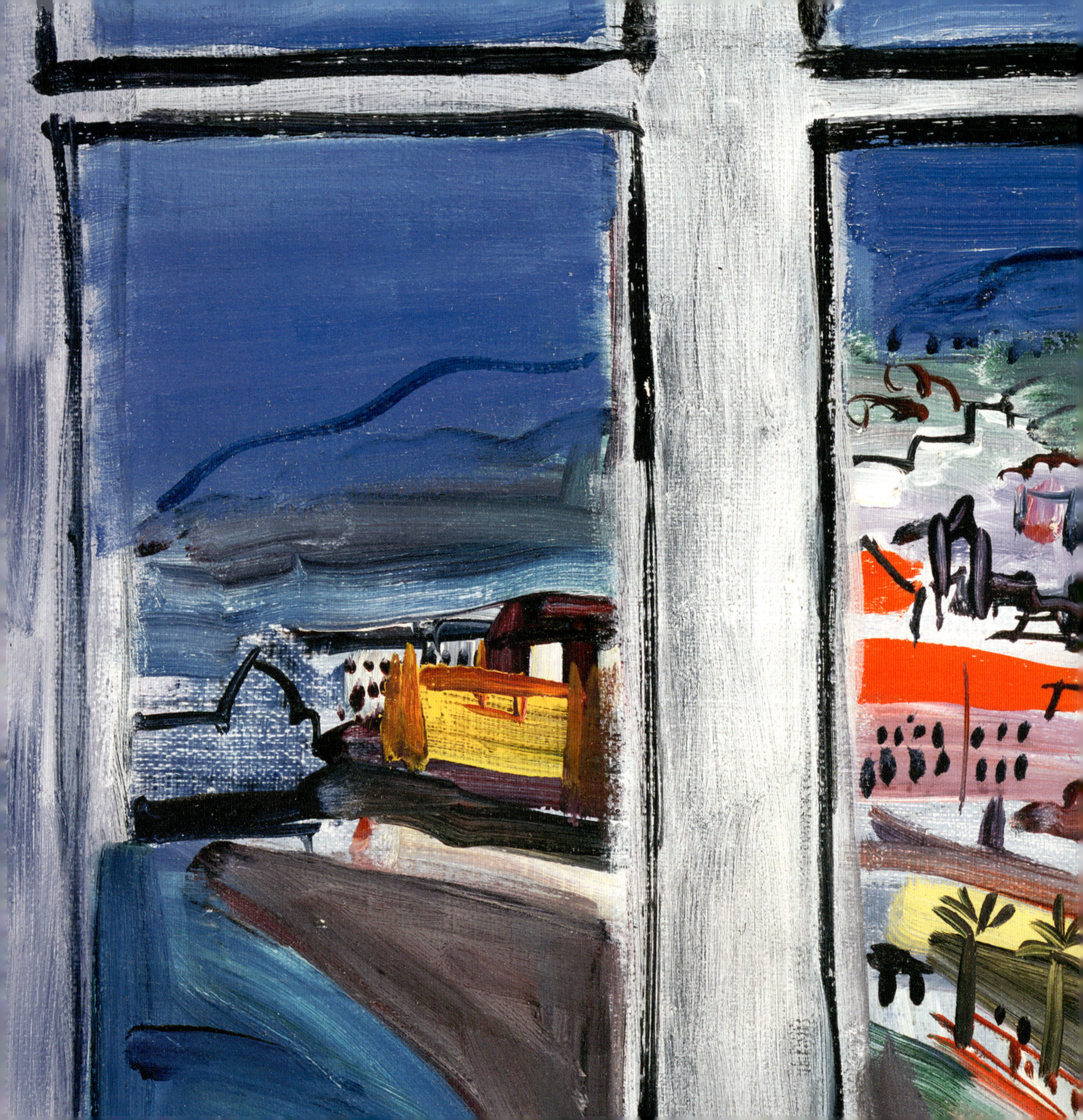

Status and Style

With its airy, uncluttered interior illuminated by light entering through open shutters, David Hockney's witty image of Ossie Clark and Celia Birtwell (pages 24–25) epitomizes a certain period and style. As well as inverting a convention of portraiture, whereby the man is often shown standing next to a seated woman, it brings the window – a common signifier of wealth and taste – out of the margins and into the centre of the picture.

Although there are precedents for awarding the window such prominence (see, for example, page 43), in most earlier paintings it appears at the side, as in the celebrated portrait of Giovanni Arnolfini and his wife by Jan van Eyck (page 27). As opposed to Van Eyck's extreme discretion, Titian (page 30) and, above all, Jan Vermeer (page 29) have included windows that attract attention through their colour and ornamentation, if not their position. Whatever their format, these examples relate very specifically to the characters' social status – and sometimes their morality as well.

Although size is not everything in the world of windows, it counts for a great deal, as demonstrated spectacularly by Paolo Veronese's full-scale, *trompe l'œil* fresco (page 33) and Francesco Guardi's painting of a banquet in honour of a Venetian doge (pages 34–35). In contrast to these grand aristocratic statements, the bourgeois *Zimmerbilder*, or 'room paintings', depict much more intimate spaces, which windows play a vital role in articulating. Adolph Menzel's emphasis on air and light (page 41) reflects evolving artistic interests in the decades prior to Impressionism, but also reveals contemporary ideas of domestic taste and comfort, in which ventilation was particularly important.

While the window is a more conspicuous pictorial feature in nineteenth-century interiors than in their predecessors, it remains just one component of the scene. Occasionally, however, artists have displayed a certain fixation with fenestration, as in the case of Raoul Dufy and his depiction of Nice (page 44), in which the window and its expensive view have taken over the whole image. In this instance, the window becomes the principal symbol of social standing, not so much through any quality of its own but by providing a glimpse of a particular lifestyle and location.

David Hockney
(born 1937)

Mr and Mrs Clark and Percy

1970–71
Acrylic on canvas
213.4 × 304.8 cm (84 × 120 in.)
TATE, LONDON

This stylish image of the British fashion
designers Ossie Clark (1942–1996) and Celia
Birtwell (born 1941) is dominated by the balcony
window in the centre of the composition.
The work is based on photographs that, as
Hockney has said, made him 'conscious of
the importance of the light source in a picture,
and what the light does to forms'.[1] Despite
the painting's brightness, Hockney moderated
the exaggerated tonal contrasts created by
photographing directly into the light, so as to
reveal the elegant balustrade and street that
were invisible in the original print. The
balcony – a prized feature in London life –
obviously enhances the sense of space and light,
but also lets in air, adding to the atmosphere
of indolent relaxation epitomized by the seated
Clark, not to mention his cat.

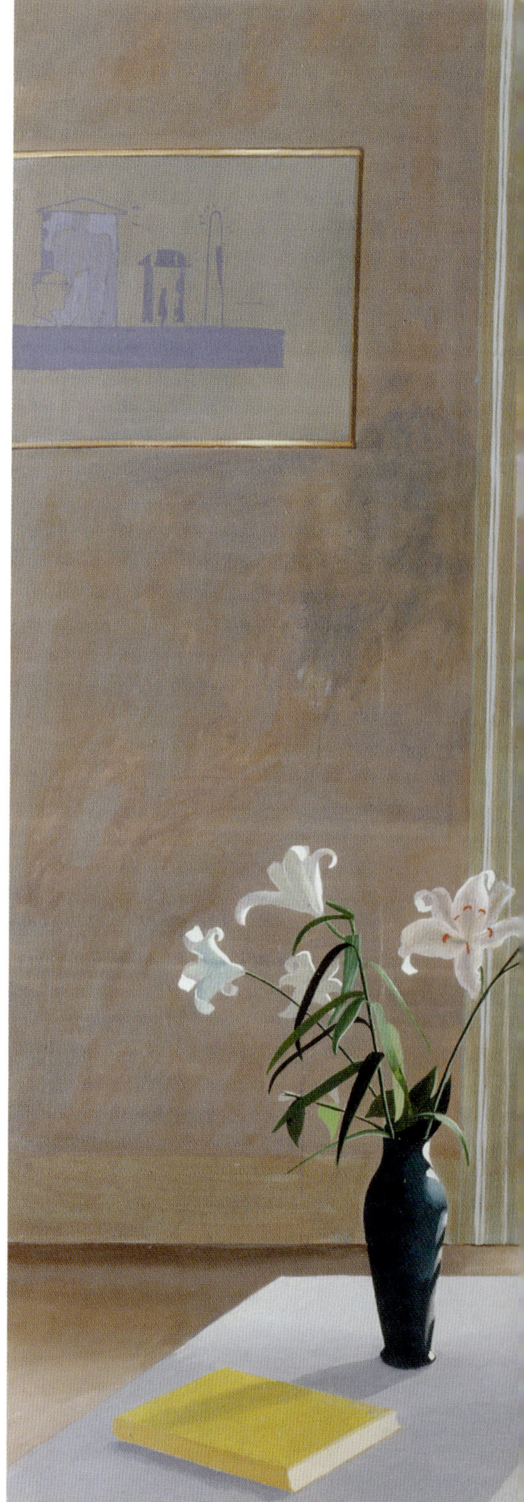

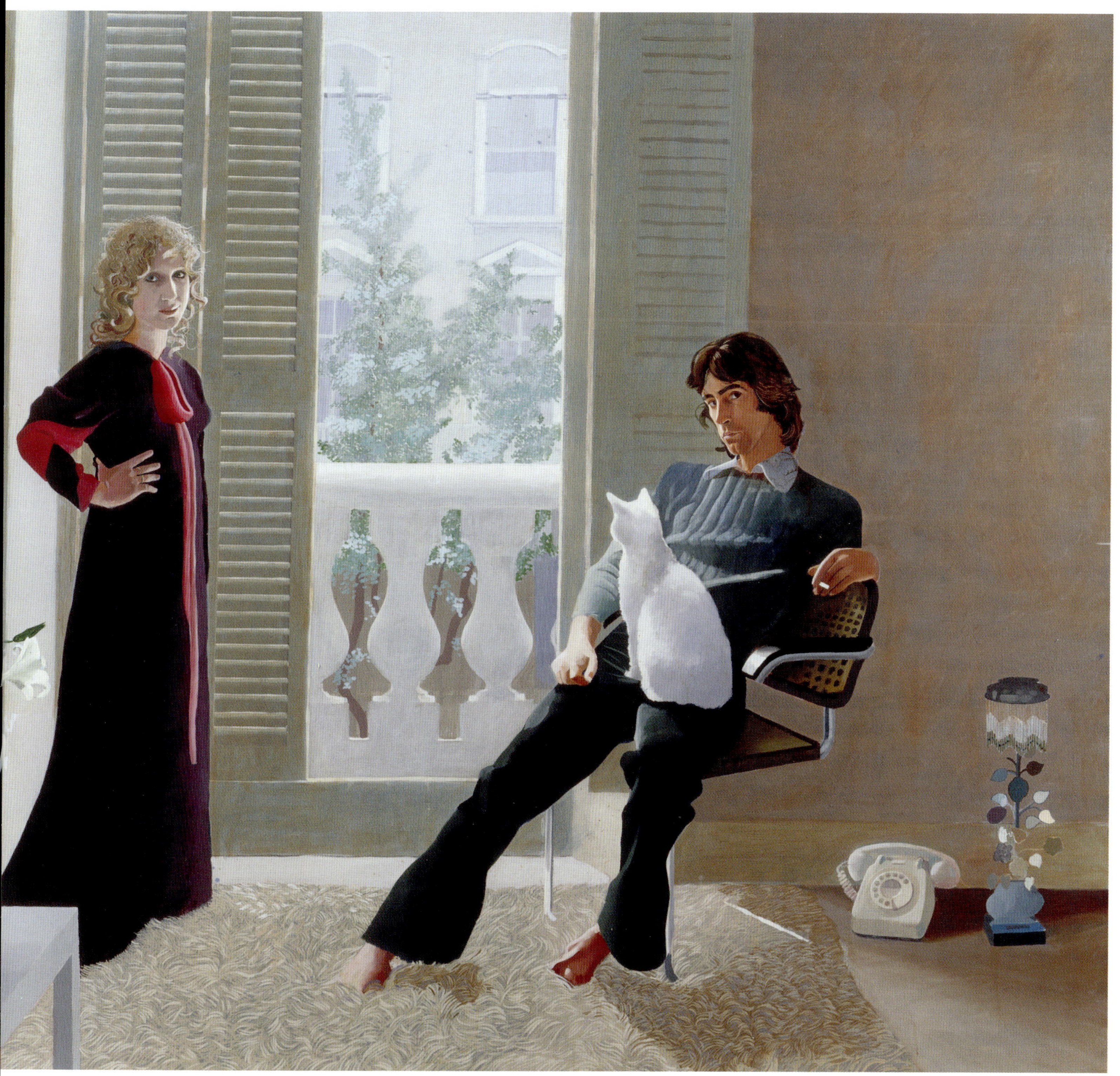

Jan van Eyck
(c. 1395–1441)

Portrait of Giovanni Arnolfini and His Wife

1434
Oil on oak
82.2 × 60 cm (32⅜ × 23⅝ in.)
THE NATIONAL GALLERY, LONDON

The window on the left-hand side of this famous, luminous portrait (see detail, right) is one of its more neglected features. Yet it reveals much about the painting's setting and the status of the mysterious couple – as well as providing the composition with its principal light source.

Although this window offers us only a sliver of a view, its brick surround and the cherry branches beyond demonstrate that we are looking at the upper floor of a prosperous merchant's house with a garden. Structurally, the window is typical of an affluent, even palatial home of the period, with its unglazed, shuttered lower part surmounted by an upper section consisting of clear bull's-eye panes (see page 62) and blue, red and green stained glass.

It is, however, the effects created by daylight that give the picture its distinction, from the gleaming orange on the sill to the extraordinary reflections in the convex mirror, including those of windows that are otherwise unseen. Ultimately, the patrons' status is proclaimed by the skill and fame of the remarkable painter whom they have managed to employ, hence the florid Latin inscription over the mirror: '1434 Johannes de Eyck fuit hic' (Jan van Eyck has been here).

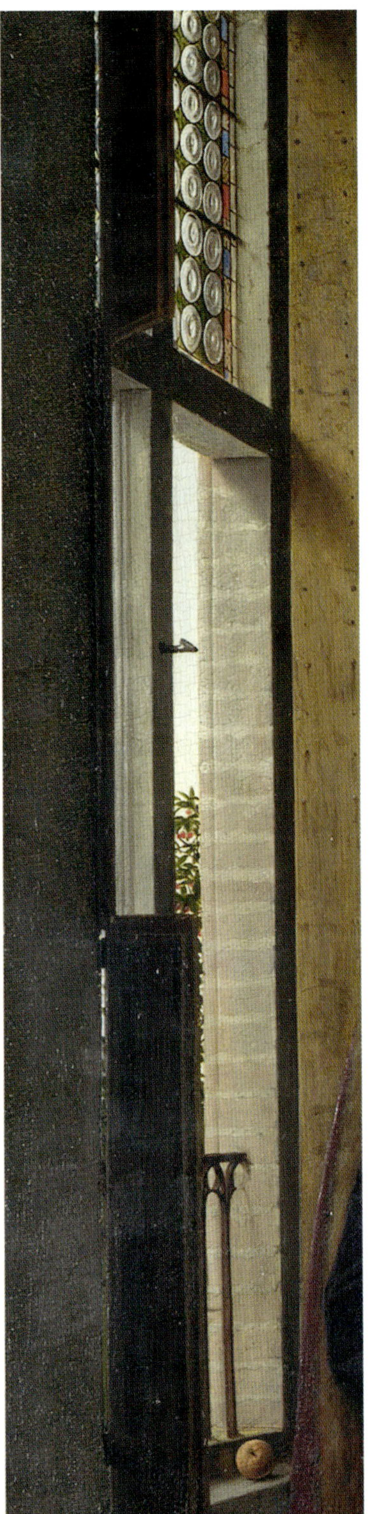

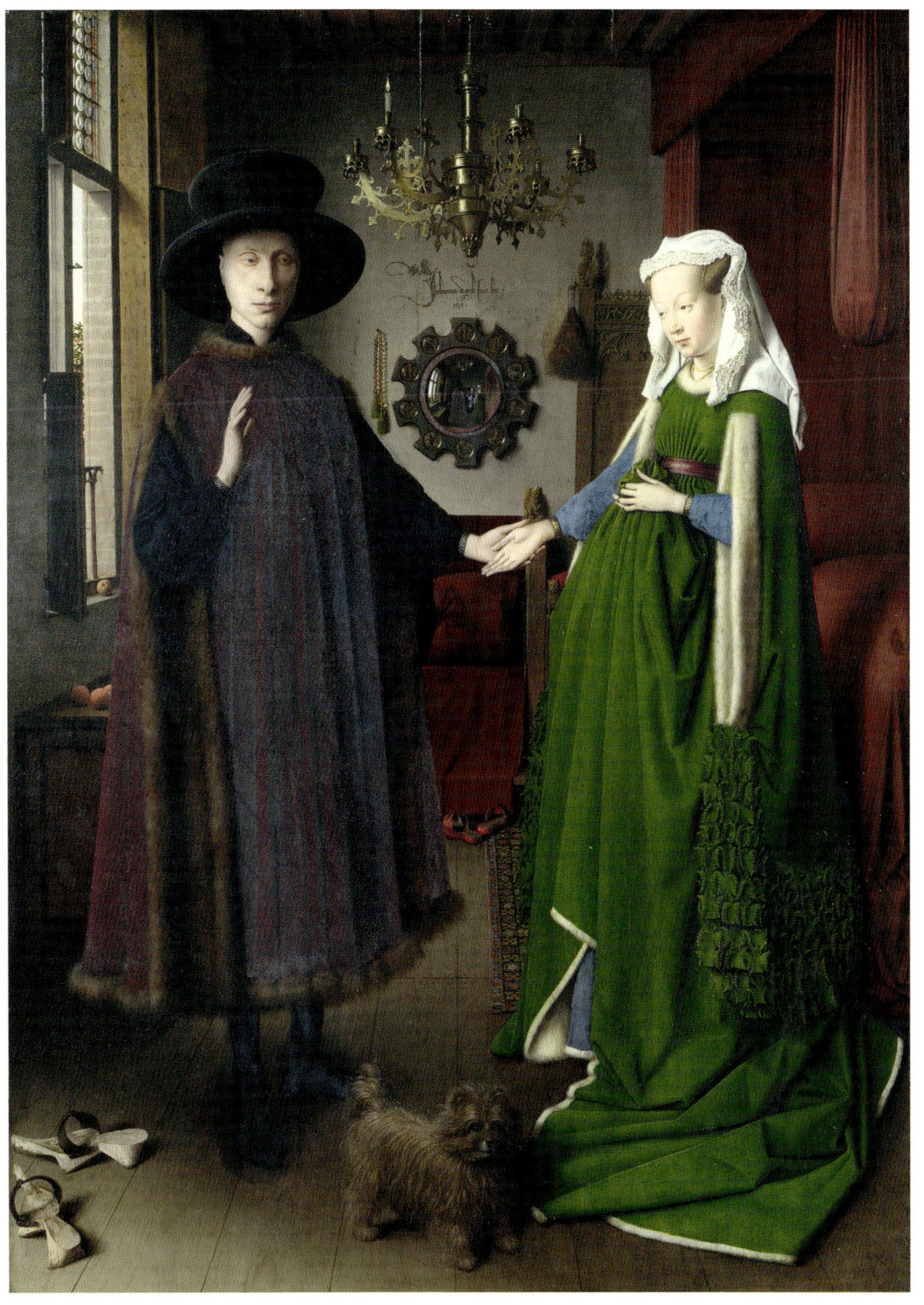

Jan Vermeer

(1632–1675)

The Glass of Wine

c. 1661–62
Oil on canvas
65 × 77 cm (25½ × 30⅜ in.)
GEMÄLDEGALERIE, STAATLICHE MUSEEN ZU BERLIN

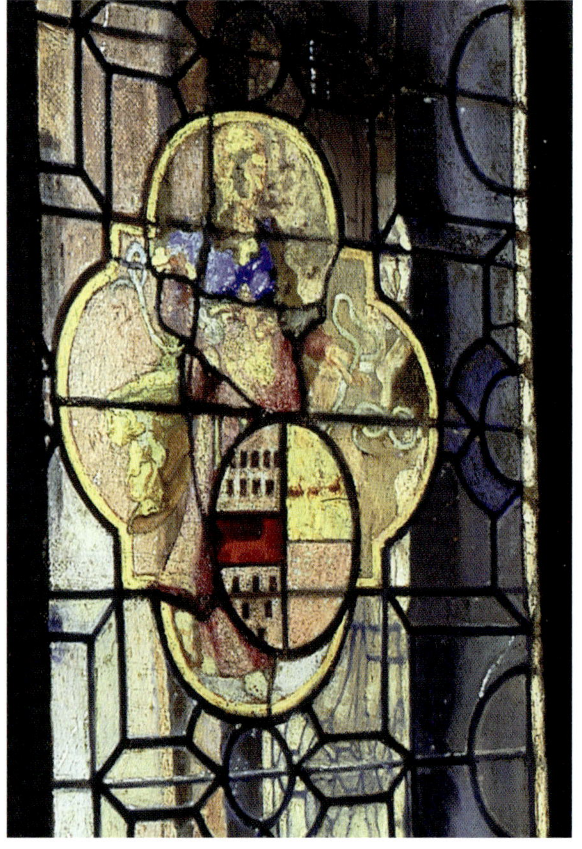

The apparent air of social distinction in Vermeer's painting is enhanced by the heraldry in the elegant leaded window (see detail, left), which includes an allegorical figure of Temperance holding a bridle and a carpenter's square. Yet it is unclear precisely what the coat of arms is doing here, since it belonged to a woman called Janetge Vogel, who died in 1624 and lived some distance away from Vermeer. Somehow the artist came across this motif, using it to enhance both this composition and *The Girl with the Wine Glass* (*c.* 1659–60; Herzog Anton Ulrich-Museum, Braunschweig). The warm hues in this painting, especially the reds, are picked up by the luminous colours of the glass, and yet the large, ornate casement window also adds an element of asymmetry, even disharmony. Perhaps this is deliberate. After all, it is swinging open to illuminate a scene that is a little unsavoury and far from temperate, as the woman in the satin dress drinks up her wine, watched intently by her fashionable companion.

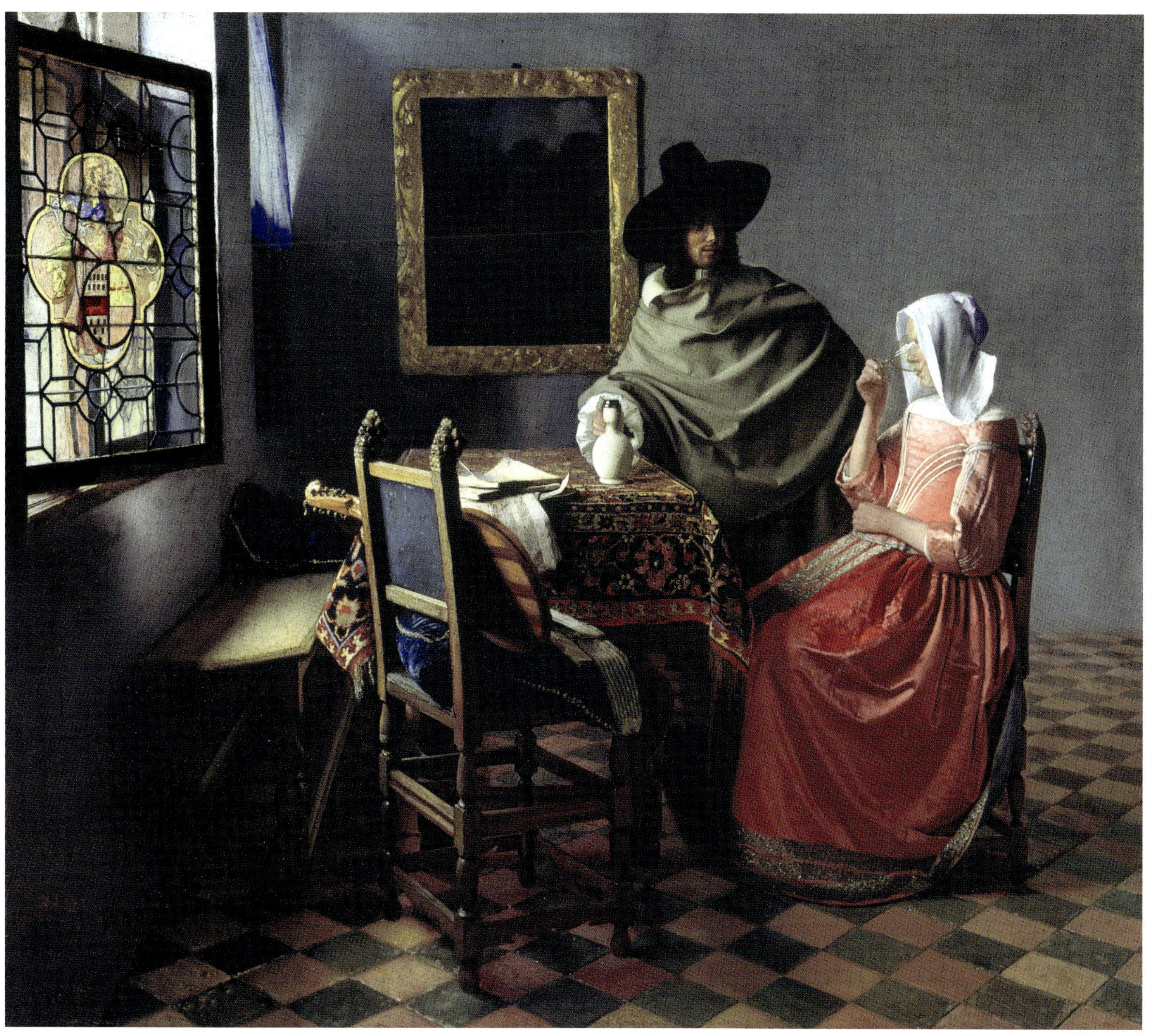

Venus of Urbino

1538
Oil on canvas
119 × 165 cm (46⅞ × 65 in.)
GALLERIA DEGLI UFFIZI, FLORENCE

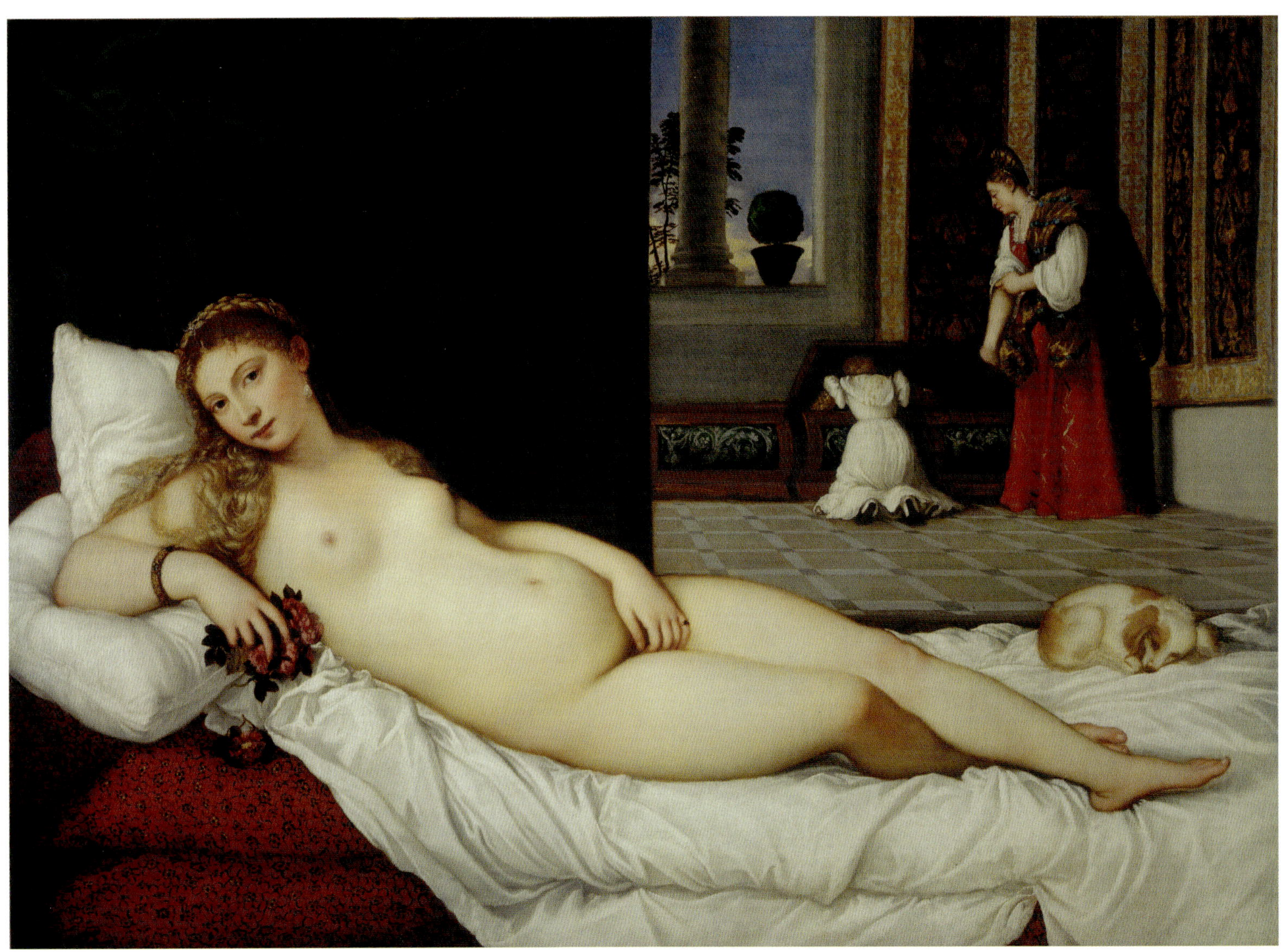

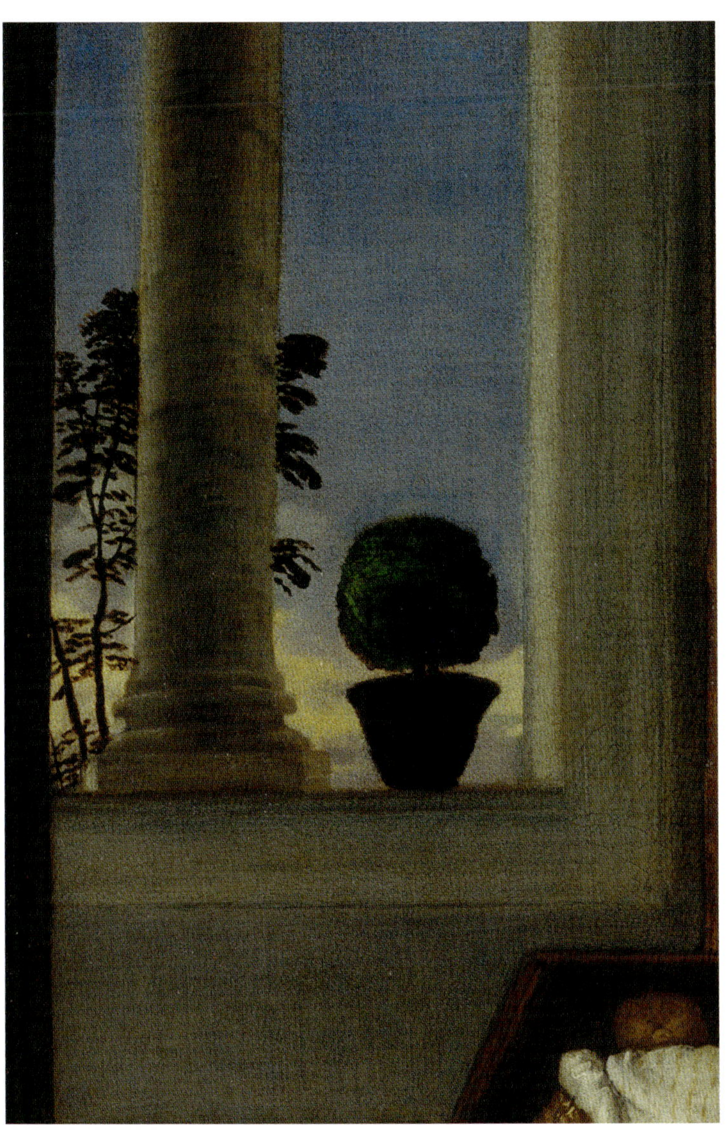

This beautiful canvas, delivered in 1538 to Guidobaldo della Rovere, Duke of Urbino, has long been known under its mythological title, although in the sixteenth century it was referred to simply as a 'nude woman'. While the precise theme remains a mystery, it is hinted at by particular features in the background. The palatial setting, with its bipartite classical window (see detail, left) reminiscent of certain buildings in Urbino, reinforces the link to the duke. The woman depicted may have been a courtesan, but other details suggest that, whatever the model's profession, the character she was playing had a higher status. The maids near the window are removing or replacing clothing in a *cassone*, or 'marriage chest', and the myrtle on the sill is associated with the marital state, as well as with Venus herself. Could the painting have been made for the duke's wedding, with the female figure representing love in its most elevated form?

Whatever the context of its commission, this is a supremely successful composition, in which foreground and background are tied together by their rectangular formats, their proportions and, above all, their colours. Nothing, however, can quite prepare the viewer for the cool dawn hues shining intensely through the window, which contrast spectacularly with the hothouse tones inside.

Paolo Veronese

(1528–1588)

Stanza del Cane (detail)

c. 1561
Fresco
VILLA DI MASER (VILLA BARBARO), NEAR TREVISO

Veronese's extraordinary fresco in the Stanza del Cane (Room of the Dog) at the Villa di Maser is a monument to wealth and taste, not to mention the artist's own brilliance. The idealized view of ancient ruins, sea and sky is framed by a richly ornamented Ionic window, a feat of *trompe l'œil* intended to harmonize with the architecture and the stucco decoration that surrounds it. The villa itself (completed by 1558) was designed by the great Italian architect Andrea Palladio for the brothers Daniele and Marc'Antonio Barbaro, who were themselves distinguished humanists. Daniele's achievements included a translation of *De architectura* (On Architecture) by the Roman architect Vitruvius, and he undoubtedly intended the villa to be, among other things, a demonstration of his erudition.

As well as its architecture and idealized image of nature, this room presumably unites some of the Barbaros' other preoccupations. Above the fictive window is an exquisite painting of the biblical story of the mystic marriage of Saint Catherine, while, as if to balance such piety, in front of the coloured marble parapet sits a vivid toy dog – the dainty domestic detail that gives the room its name.

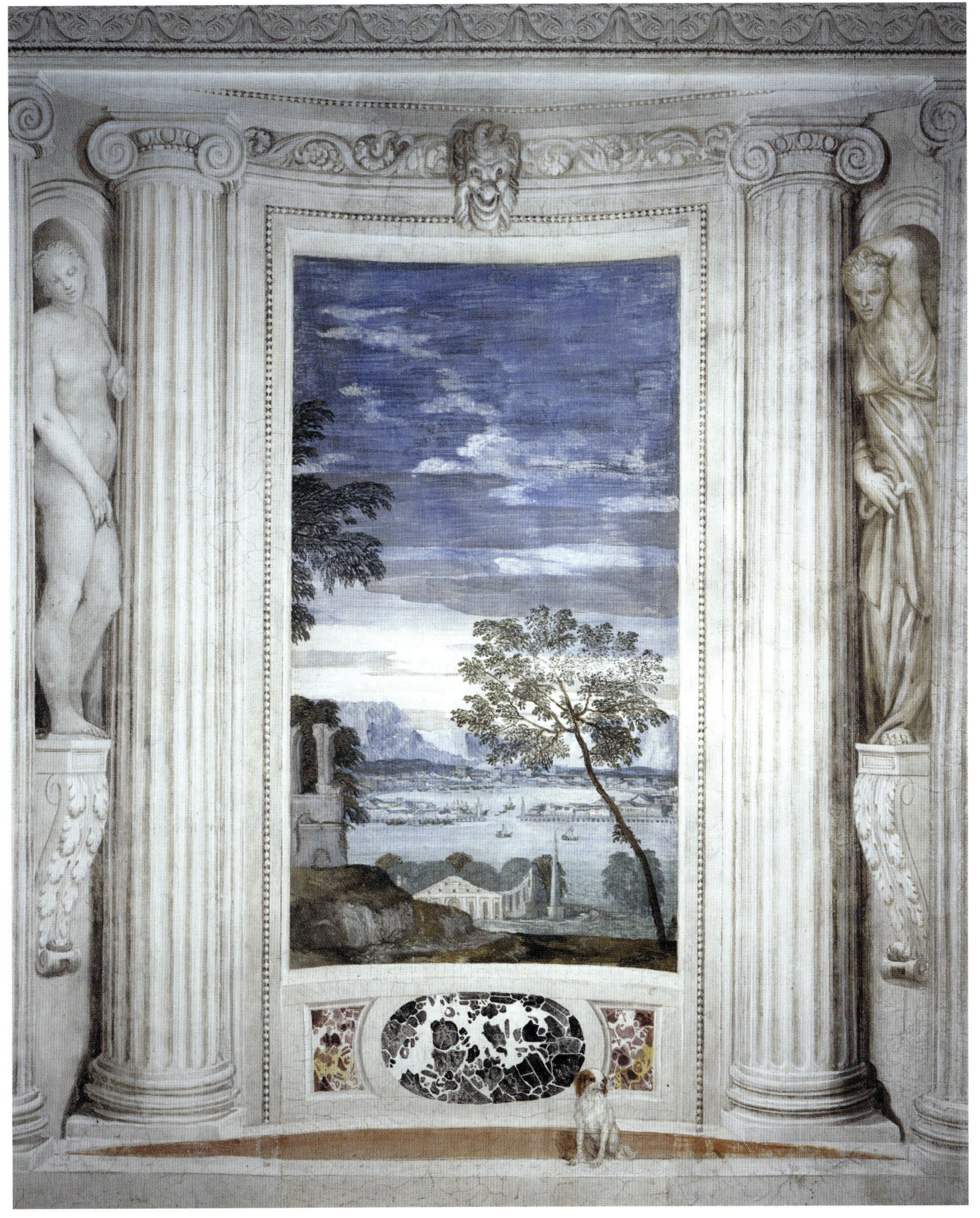

Francesco Guardi

(1712–1793)

The Doge Offers Dinner

1770/75
Oil on canvas
67 × 100 cm (26⅜ × 39⅜ in.)
MUSÉE DES BEAUX-ARTS, NANTES

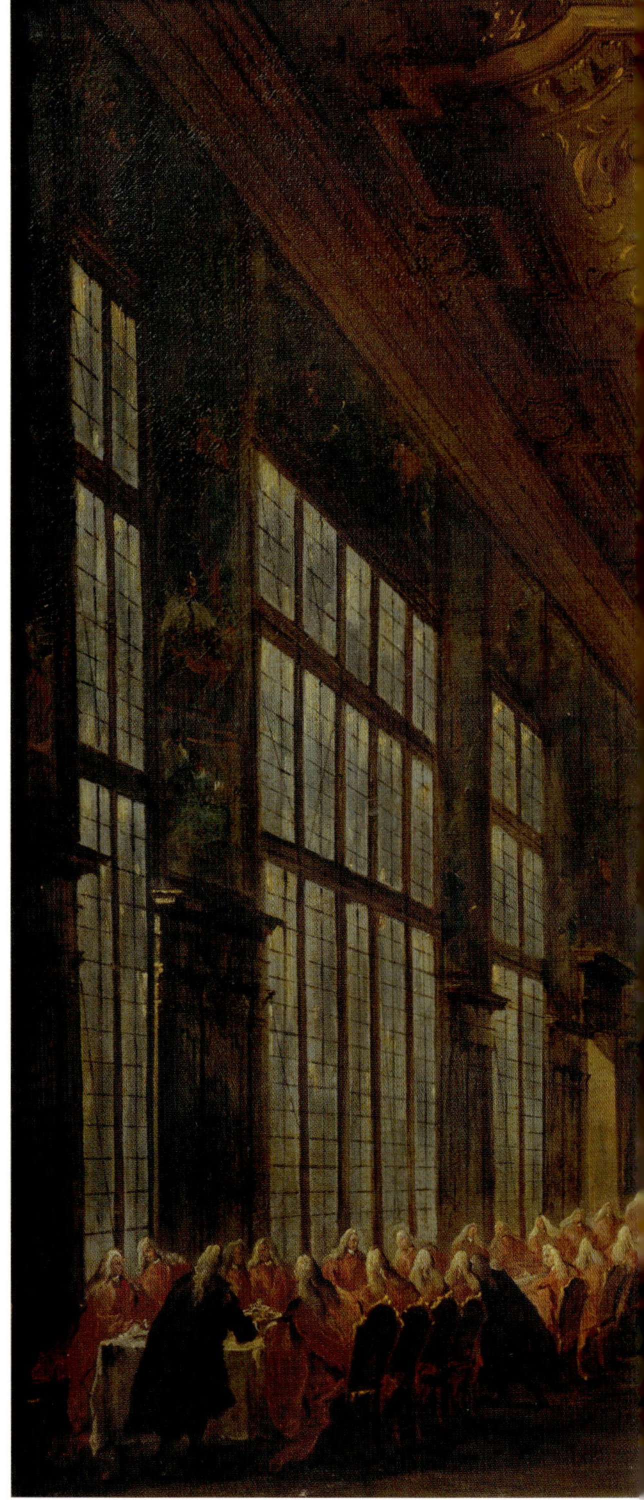

While the Doge's Palace, the former seat of government in Venice, is justly celebrated for its painted decoration created after a fire in 1577, the most remarkable features of its banqueting hall are the immense mullioned windows, here depicted in swooping perspective. They make the human figures, including the doge under his *baldacchino* (ceremonial canopy), look paltry and insignificant, even though in its magnificence this scene actually enhances the dignity of the Venetian state. As one of a series of twelve canvases celebrating the installation of Alvise Giovanni Mocenigo as doge in 1763, Francesco Guardi's painting is charged with political significance. All this, however, is achieved with characteristic Venetian gaiety: costumed guests enliven the centre of the room, while the whole scene is animated by patches of colour, well illuminated by natural light.

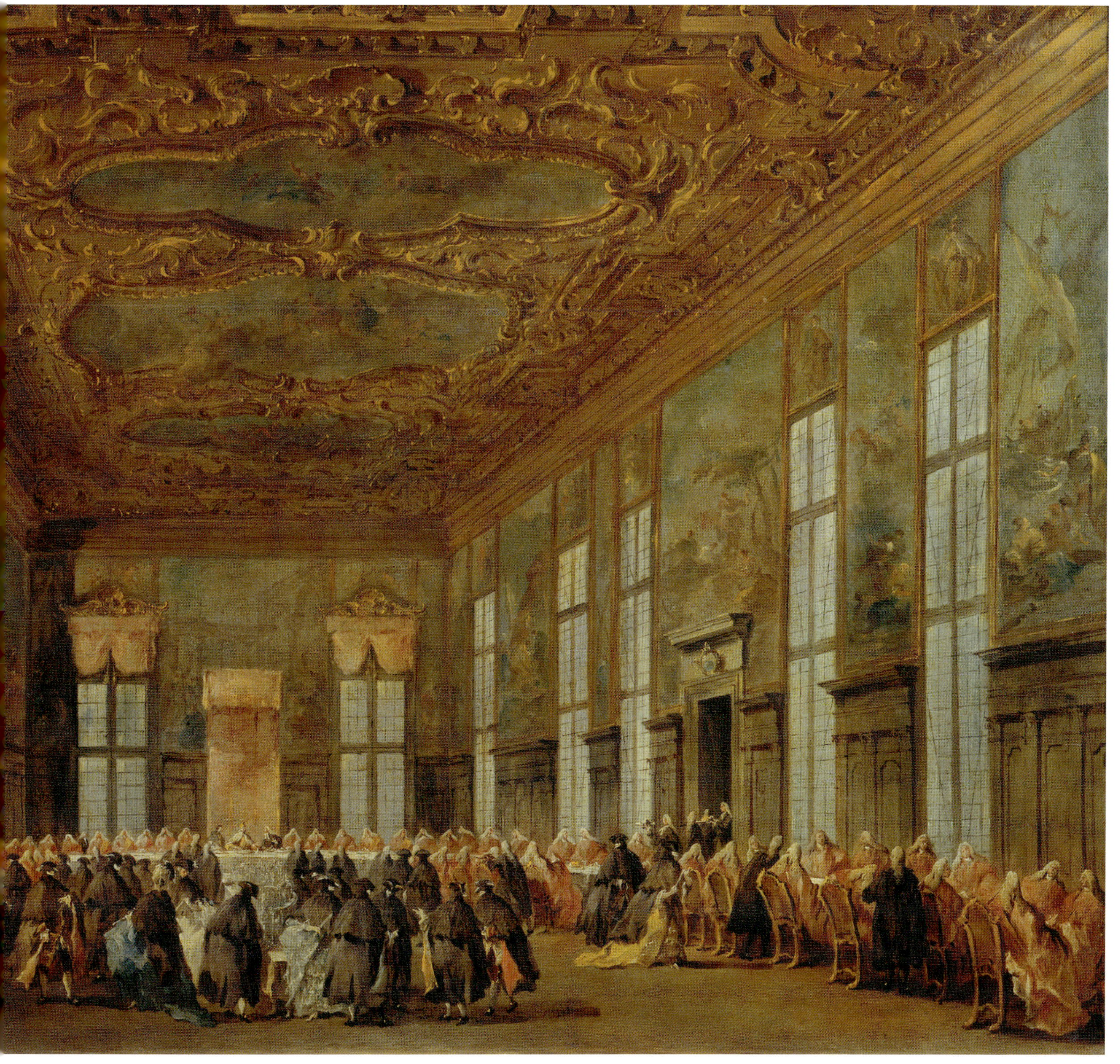

Carl Moll

(1861–1945)

My Living Room (Anna Moll at the Desk)

1903
Oil on canvas
100 × 100 cm (39⅜ × 39⅜ in.)
WIEN MUSEUM KARLSPLATZ, VIENNA

The private life of the bourgeoisie is the subject of this remarkable picture by the Austrian painter Carl Moll, set in the Viennese house that was designed for him by the Secession architect Josef Hoffmann. The canvas shows Moll's wife, Anna (whose daughter from a previous marriage was Alma Mahler, wife of the famous composer), engaged in an activity far removed from the passive roles associated with women in earlier painting. The style of the decoration is very distinctive, with crisp lines emphasized by the rectangular window bays and neatly arranged flowerpots. There is also an austerity about the cool light shining through the partly drawn curtains and reflecting off the polished floor. Good taste and restraint are perfectly combined.

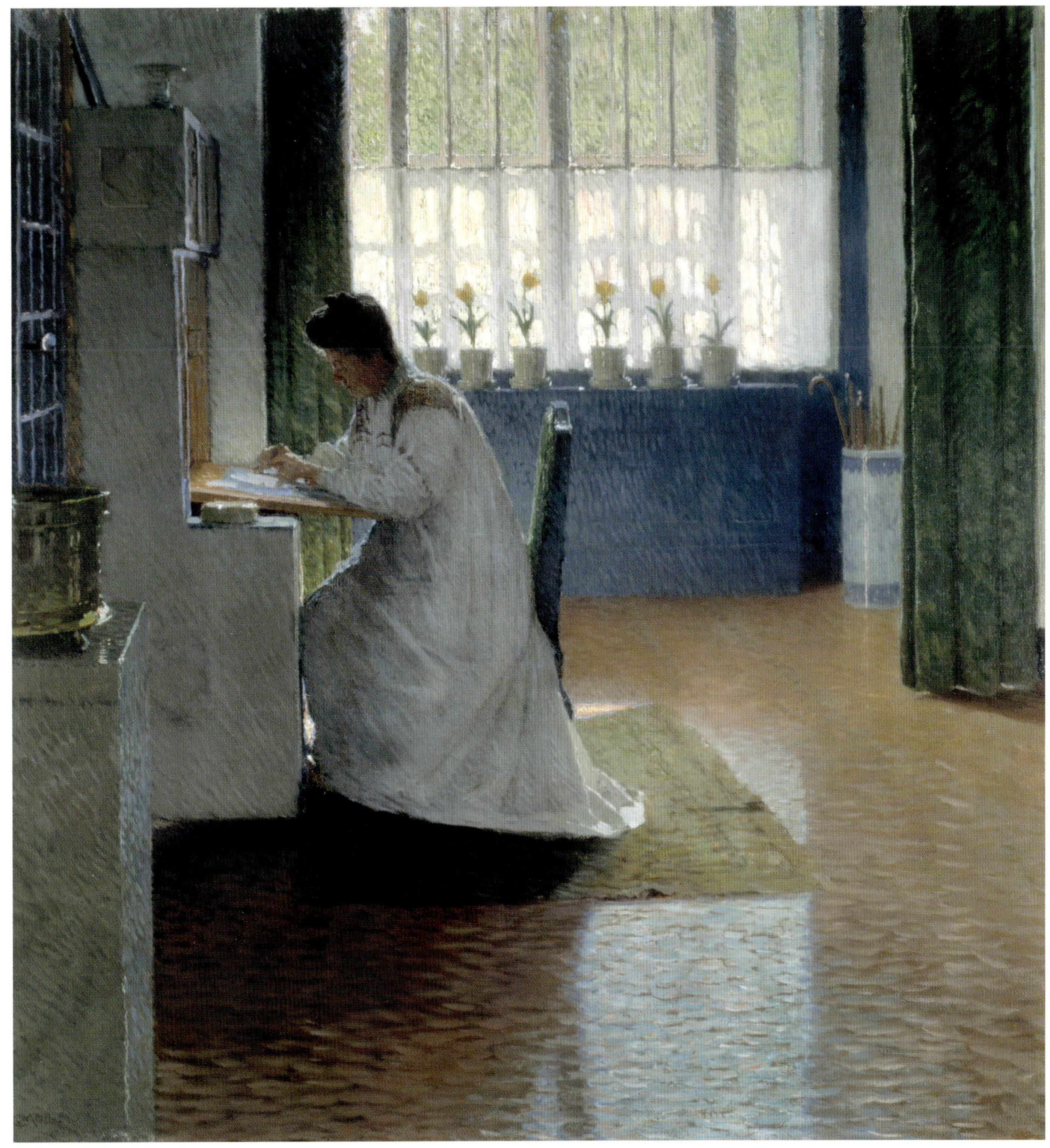

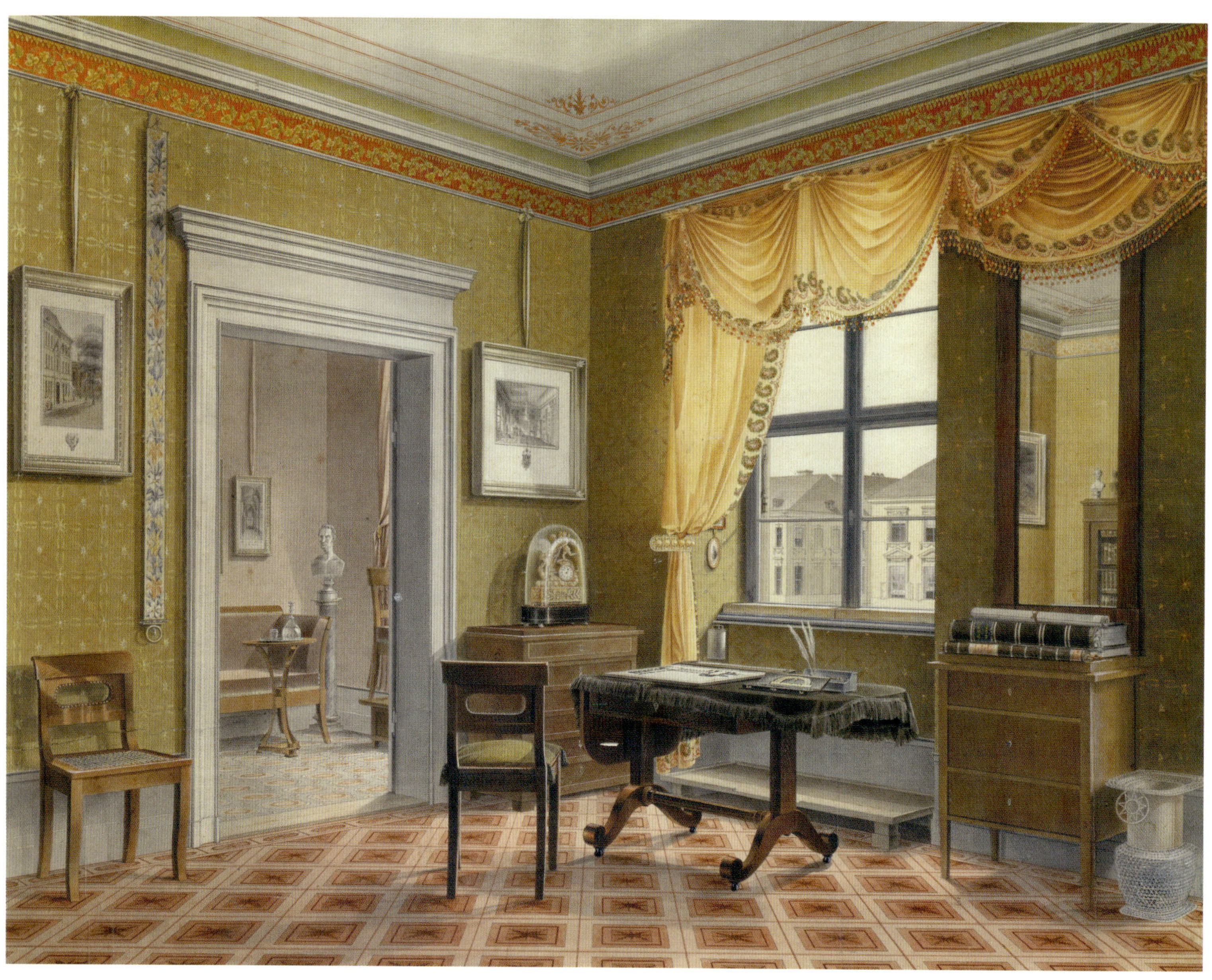

Leopold Zielcke

(1791–1861)

The Artist's Studio in His Apartment at Friedrichstrasse 228

c. 1825
Pen and black ink, watercolour and gouache
46.7 × 58.7 cm (18⅜ × 23⅛ in.)
GERMANISCHES NATIONALMUSEUM, NUREMBERG

This view of the artist's apartment in Berlin, minus its inhabitant, is angled so as to allow the eye to pass easily through the connected spaces and out of the window in the far wall. The dignified façades visible in the distance are external counterparts to the stylish Biedermeier interior, with its emphasis on high-quality materials and utility. The lucid, rational style of the furnishings is enhanced by the bright, natural light illuminating both chambers, which also brings out the striking colour of the walls.

Leopold Zielcke's image is a fine example of the *Zimmerbilder* (room paintings) that were so popular in Biedermeier Germany among both the aristocracy and the aspiring bourgeoisie, including Zielcke himself. They celebrate domestic pride, good taste and social status – qualities epitomized by the elegant fenestration at the heart of this picture.

Adolph Menzel

(1815–1905)

The Balcony Room

1845
Oil on board
58 × 47 cm (22⅞ × 18½ in.)
ALTE NATIONALGALERIE, BERLIN

Adolph Menzel, a German realist, continued
the genre of *Zimmerbilder* (see page 39) in his own
way. Empty of people, his room is almost devoid
of possessions, with a couple of randomly
placed chairs adding to the mood of informality.
In a truly modern way, style and comfort are
suggested by the sensations of space, air and
light. Sunshine falls across the floor and
illuminates the far wall – seen in various
degrees of finish – while, most importantly,
the centre of the composition is dominated by
a large white curtain billowing in the breeze
that passes through the open French windows.

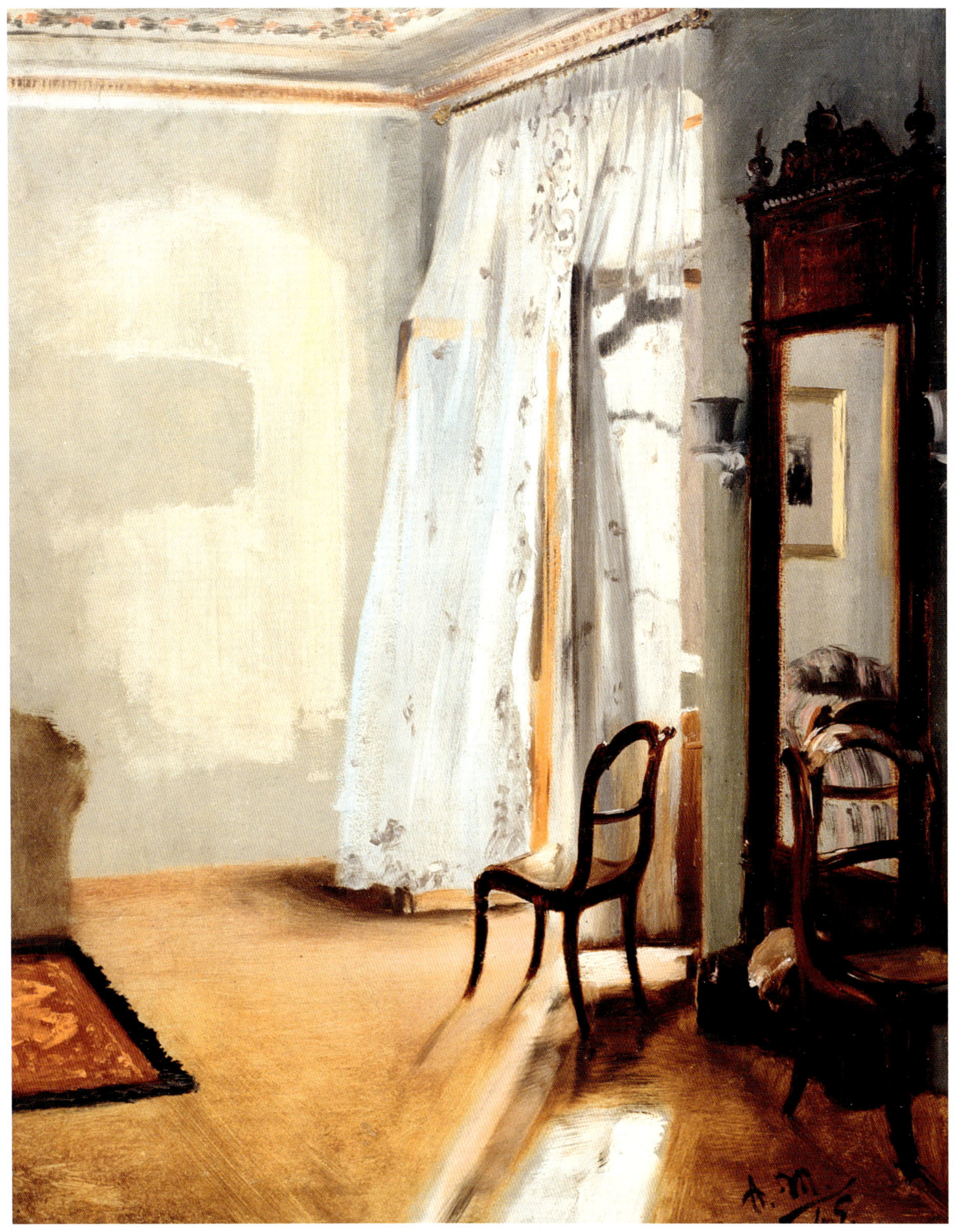

Augustus Leopold Egg

(1816–1863)

The Travelling Companions

1862
Oil on canvas
65.3 × 78.7 cm (25¼ × 31 in.)
BIRMINGHAM MUSEUM AND ART GALLERY

Augustus Leopold Egg's painting of two genteel young women travelling through the South of France in a railway carriage is dominated by the large window in the centre. A suggestion of movement is created by the swinging tassel hanging from the blind, while the world outside is kept at a distance and even ignored: the women are clearly absorbed in their own private reality.

The window's generous proportions also enhance the sense of comfort and luxury. The women are behaving as they might do at home, undisturbed by any fellow passengers. Identically dressed but engaged in contrasting activities, they occupy an ordered, symmetrical space, in which the window plays an essential compositional role.

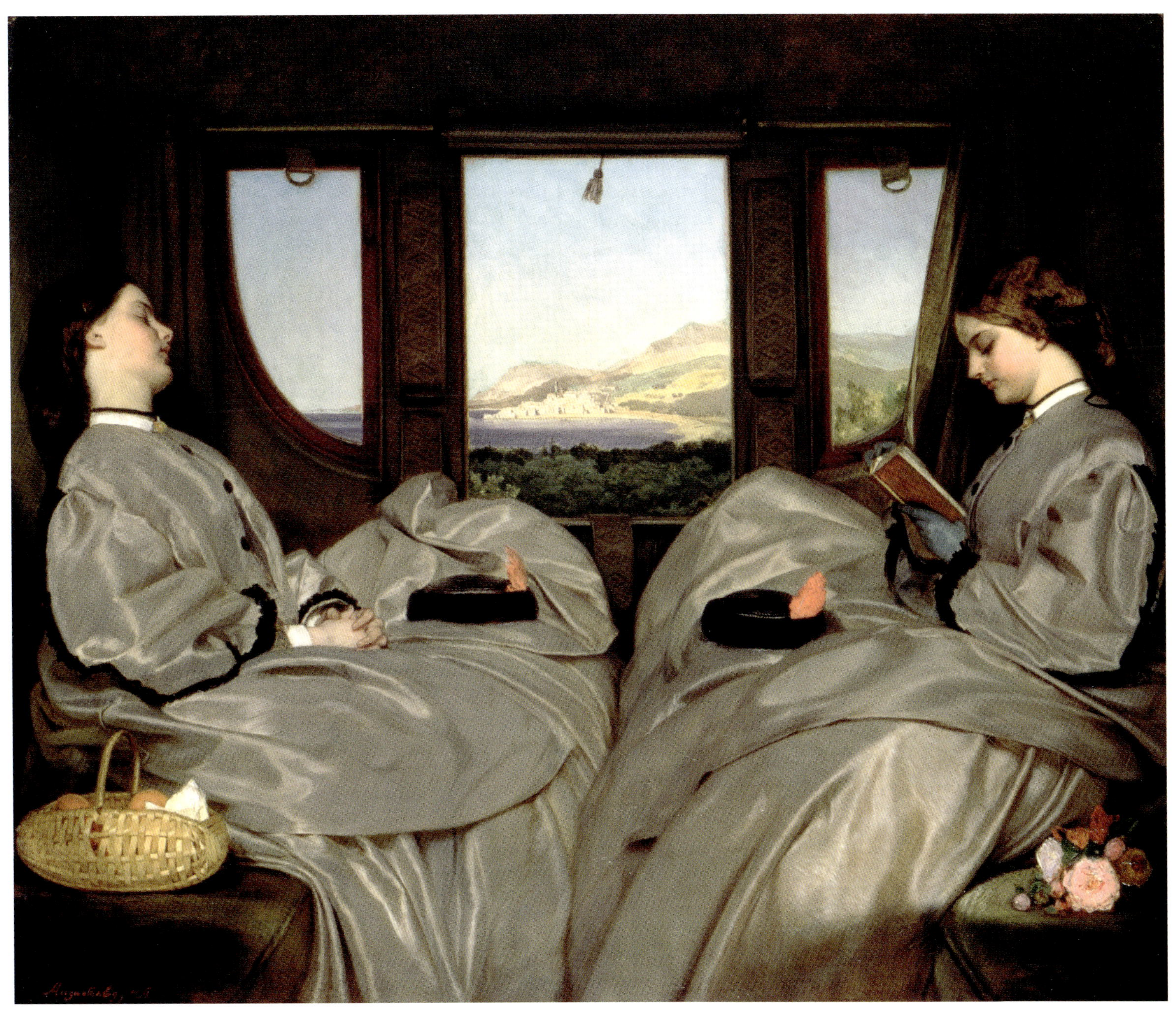

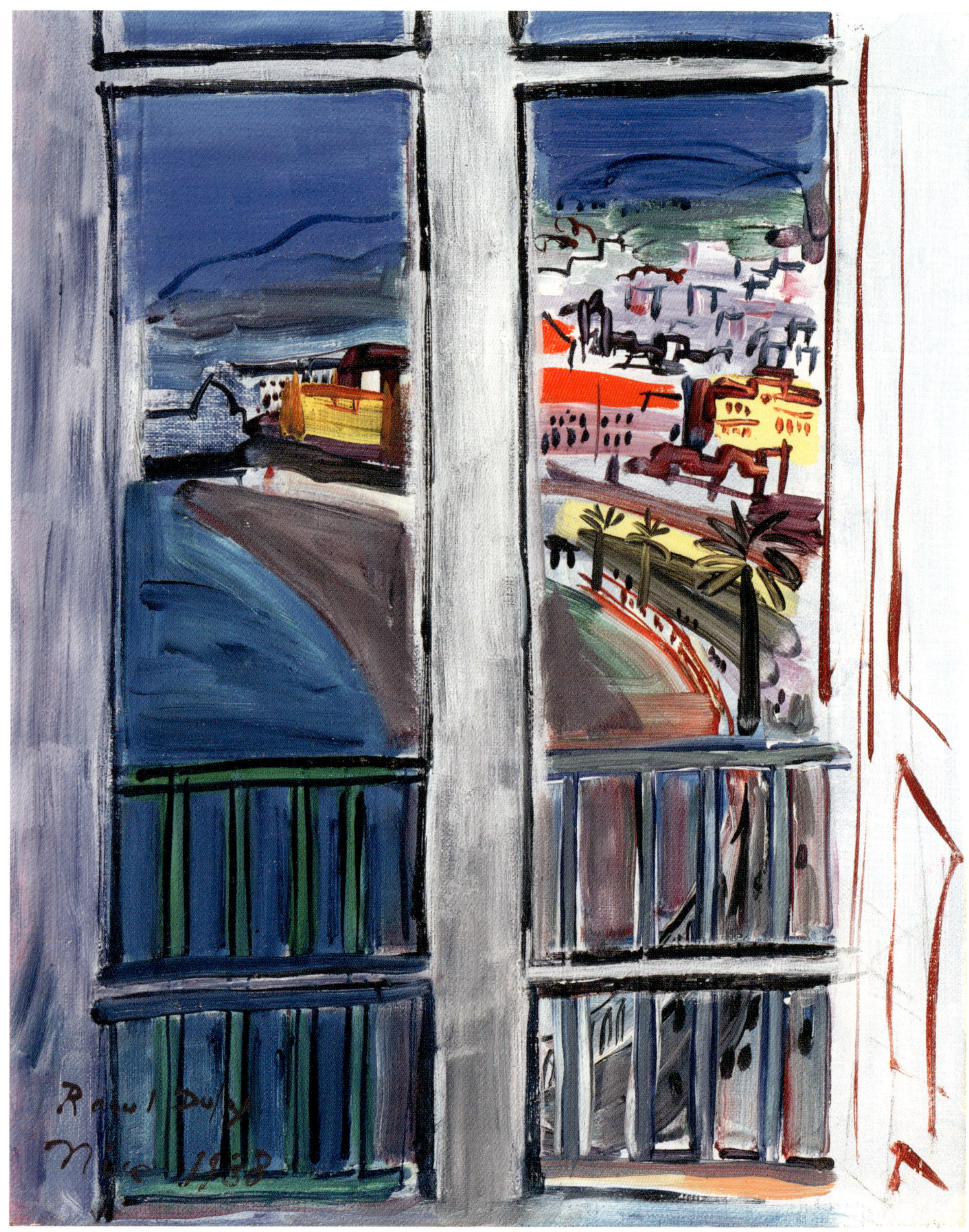

Raoul Dufy

(1877–1953)

Window on the Promenade des Anglais, Nice

1938
Oil on canvas
46 × 38.3 cm (18⅛ × 15⅛ in.)
PHILADELPHIA MUSEUM OF ART

Raoul Dufy's image of this prestigious setting is one of a series of canvases that he made of the same scene. The variety is considerable: sometimes the window is open, while at others the artist steps back to reveal a fashionably informal apartment. Here, however, he has closed the window and banished any hint of the room behind him, so that we see only the city captured by the window frame. As well as developing the old conceit that a picture is a window on the world, the composition, together with the homogeneous handling of paint and lack of perspective, has the effect of seizing the distant promenade and bringing it closer. The palm trees and brilliant light are no longer something remote; instead, they have become an integral part of the window. The painter has taken possession of the view, and, in the process, has expressed both his artistic credentials and his social status.

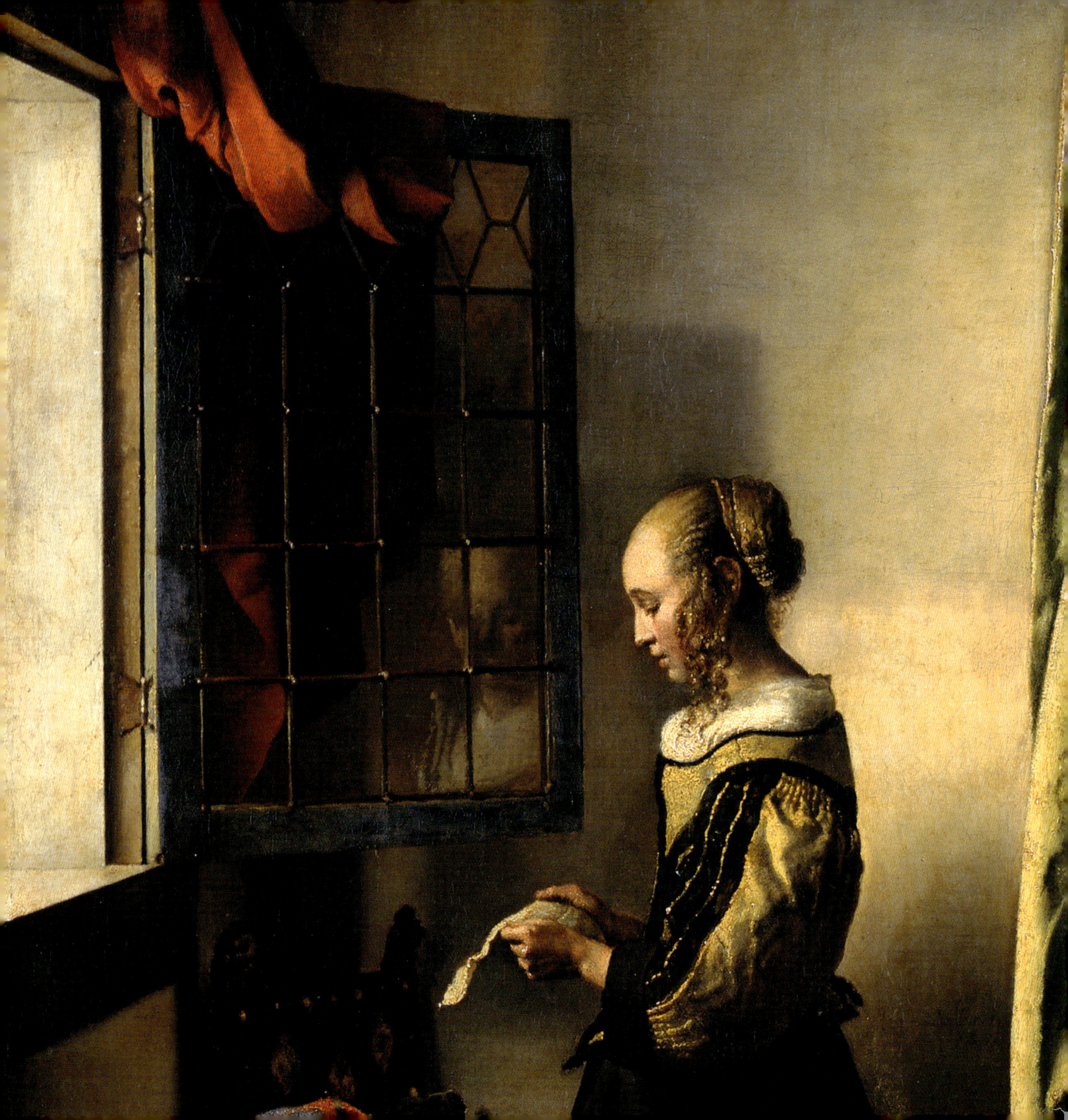

Revelations

The reflection of a window in the background of William Holman Hunt's *Awakening Conscience* (page 48) is a detail that is often overlooked, and yet it plays a vital role in the painting's narrative. By connecting moral or spiritual insight with the entry into a room of natural light, the artist is continuing an iconographical tradition that is fundamental to Western art.

It was Abbot Suger, a twelfth-century prelate, who referred to the journey 'through the true lights / To the True Light where Christ is the True Door' in an inscription over the portal of his abbey church at Saint-Denis in Paris. The belief in the divine significance of light was one of the motivations for the creation of the great stained-glass windows of medieval Europe, such as those in the Sainte-Chapelle in Paris (page 159) and in the cathedral at Chartres (page 51), about 80 kilometres (50 miles) to the south-west. Another rationale was provided by the French theologian Bernard of Clairvaux (1090–1153), who compared the passing of light through glass to the penetration of the Virgin's womb by the Word of God. Windows were also praised for their ability to protect the faithful from storms, both physically and metaphorically.

Although stained glass provides arguably the most perfect symbol of divine light, the window is crucial to many sacred paintings, perhaps most spectacularly in Caravaggio's *Calling of St Matthew* (page 71). While many images represent religious revelations in terms of rays or pools of light, such experiences are sometimes embodied by an angel, as in Giotto's *Annunciation to St Anne* in the Arena Chapel in Padua (page 59). However, the most complex use of windows to convey a multiplicity of meanings can be seen in Leonardo da Vinci's seminal *Last Supper* (pages 54–55).

Religion is not the only source of revelation in Western painting. Jacques-Louis David's *Oath of the Tennis Court* (pages 72–73) adapts the artistic devices exemplified by Caravaggio in order to give a political principle an almost sacred quality. Oblique light falling through a window also dramatizes the scientific discoveries of the subject of *The Astronomer* by Jan Vermeer (page 75), although this image may have a religious dimension too. Most strikingly, the intimate disclosures of a love letter sometimes borrow similar conventions. Vermeer's *Girl Reading a Letter at an Open Window* (page 77) is careful to preserve the subject's enigmatic air through a variety of expressive and compositional devices; a century later, however, Jean-Honoré Fragonard gaily abandons any remaining mystery (page 79). Revelation has been transformed into mundane communication.

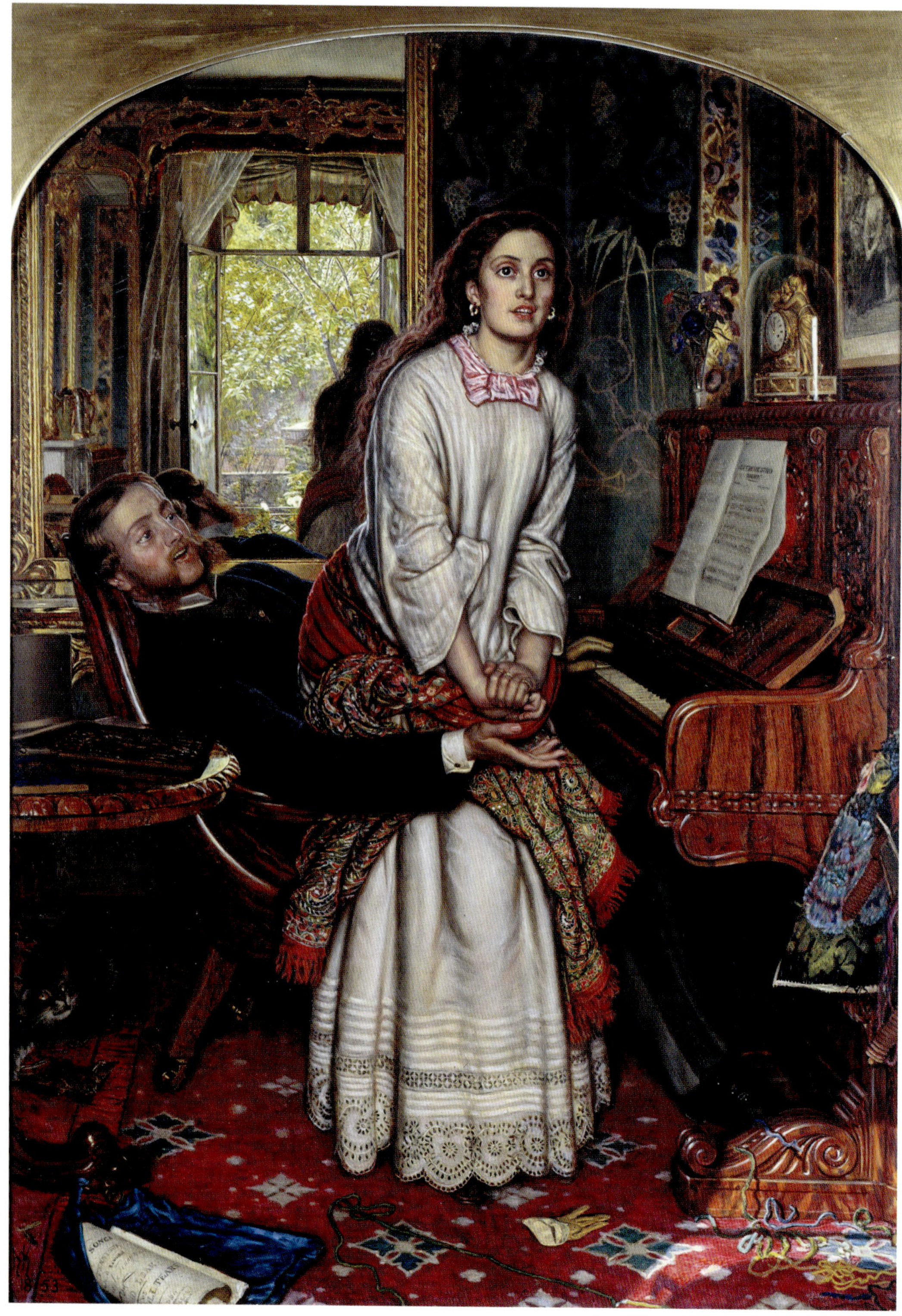

William Holman Hunt

(1827–1910)

The Awakening Conscience

1853
Oil on canvas
76.2 × 55.9 cm (30 × 22 in.)
TATE, LONDON

Woodbine Villa, 7 Alpha Place, St John's Wood, London, seems an unlikely setting for a moment of moral insight. However, this was the address of the room hired by William Holman Hunt as the studio for this celebrated Pre-Raphaelite painting, in which a kept woman rises from her lover's lap, suddenly aware of her sinfulness. As her repentance has only just begun, she is still surrounded by the sordid trappings of her existence, and the modish French window that illuminates her face and body so intensely is seen only as a reflection in the mirror behind. Yet its symbolism, and that of the natural world it reveals, is unmistakable. The woman remains enclosed by half-shadows, but the patch of direct sunlight in the bottom right-hand corner suggests that redemption may not be far away.

Chartres Cathedral
Rose window and lancets, south transept

c. 1217–25

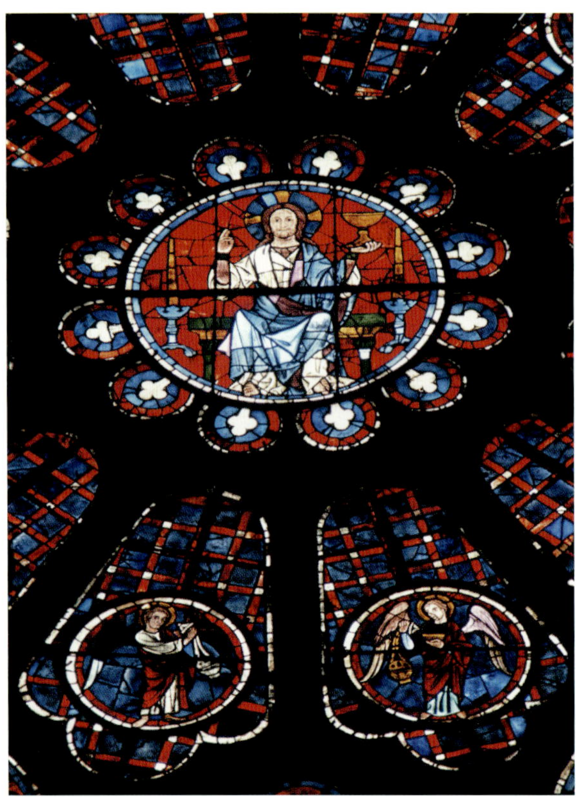

This hieratic, jewel-like image of the glorified Christ is at the heart of Chartres Cathedral's great south rose window. It shows the Saviour seated on an altar-like throne between two candelabra, holding a chalice and raising his right hand in blessing.

Chartres Cathedral's immense south rose window – a composition of luminous glass and delicate stone tracery – takes its imagery from the Apocalypse, as described in the book of Revelation. This subject relates to the depiction of the Last Judgement carved on the exterior of the south transept, and has itself been presented in a highly systematic way. Christ, the 'True Light', is at the centre of the window (see detail, left), immediately surrounded by angels and the symbols of the Evangelists (the writers of the Gospels); the Elders of the Apocalypse, crowned and holding perfume and musical instruments, can be seen nearer the edge. In the tall lancet windows, the Virgin and Child are flanked by the Evangelists, who are literally sitting on the shoulders of Prophets, emphasizing how the New Testament is founded on the Old. Beneath them, images of the window's donors and their arms remind the viewer of the realities of medieval piety and economics. Although much of the window has a visionary quality, it is clearly determined by a rigorous structure that reflects its sophisticated intellectual and social context.

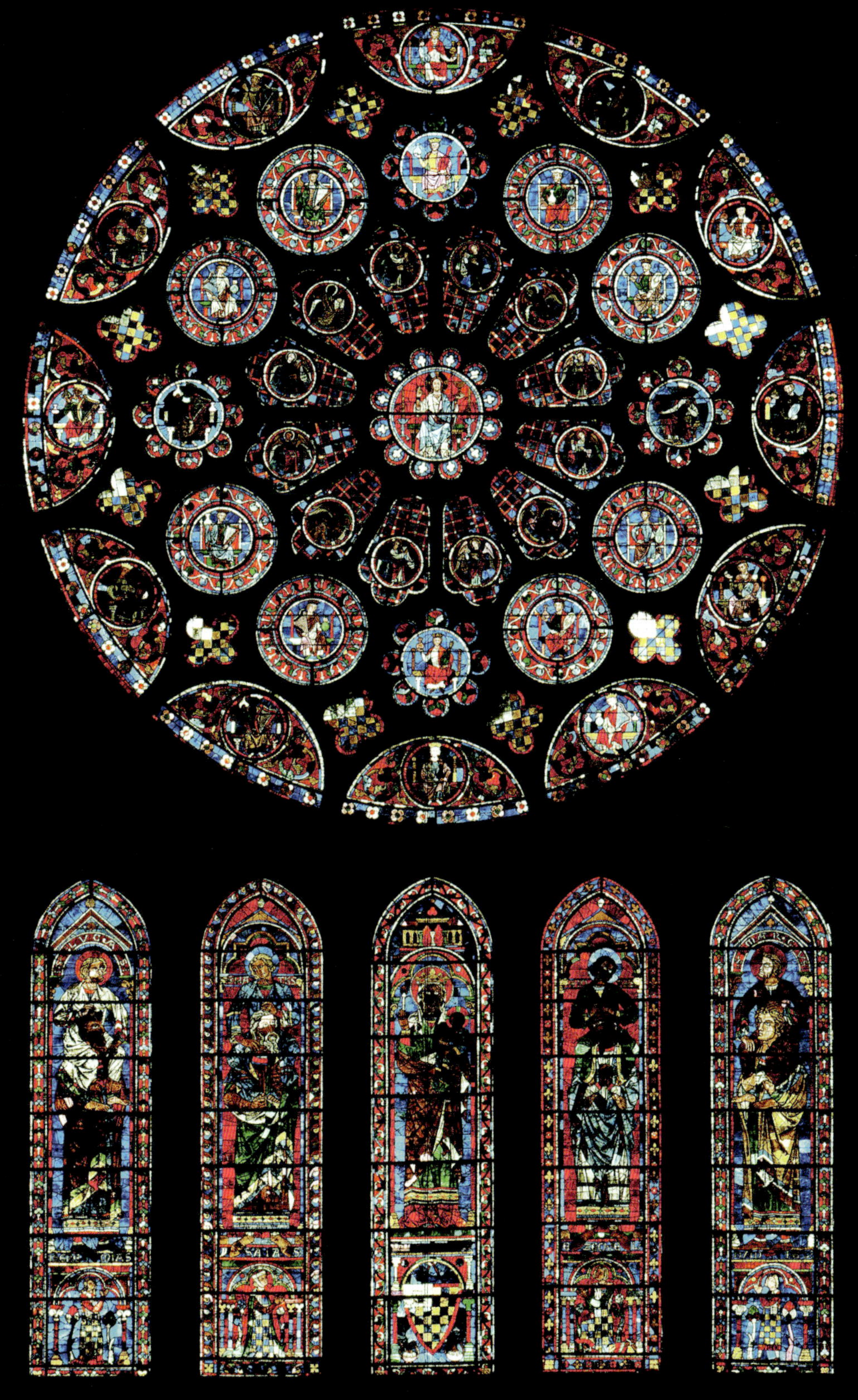

Odilon Redon

(1840–1916)

The Window

c. 1905
Pastel on blue-grey wove paper with fibrous
inclusions faded to greyish tan
81 × 68 cm (31⅛ × 26¾ in.)
COLLECTION OF JACK AND MURIEL WOLGIN, PHILADELPHIA

The intense colours favoured by the French artist Odilon Redon have sometimes been linked to his interest in the teachings of the Theosophical Society, the spiritualist movement co-founded by Helena Blavatsky in 1875 partly under the influence of Buddhism. The artist responded to Blavatsky's description of enlightenment as the attainment of an inner radiance, although he also drew on the Christian theology of light as expressed through stained glass. This image revives the tracery and luminous effects of a medieval window, but without the Christian iconography. It also displays the artist's versatile use of pastel, ranging from the dark pigment in the window surrounds – delicately applied over the textured paper – to the luscious colours biting into the tracery at the heart of the composition.

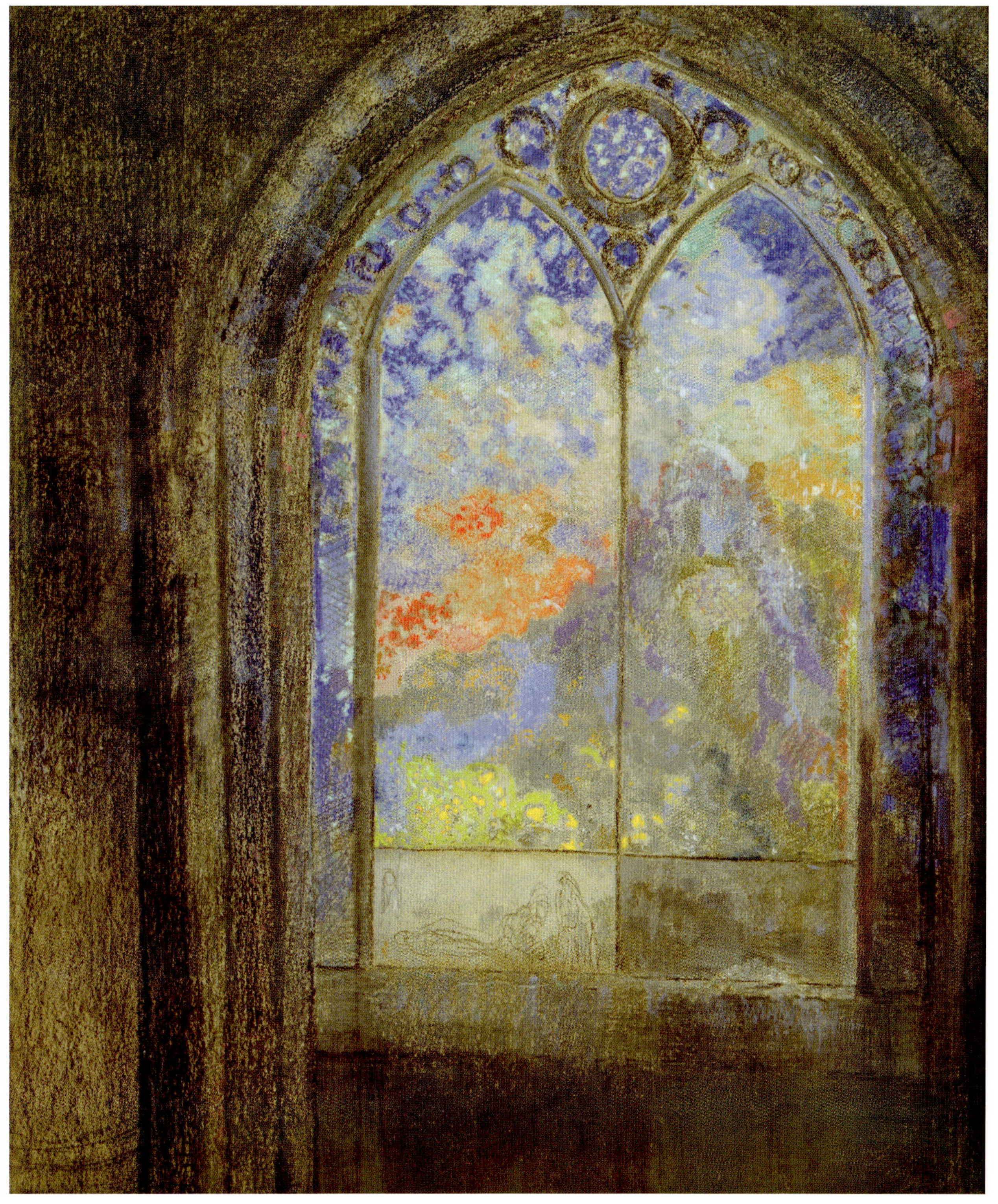

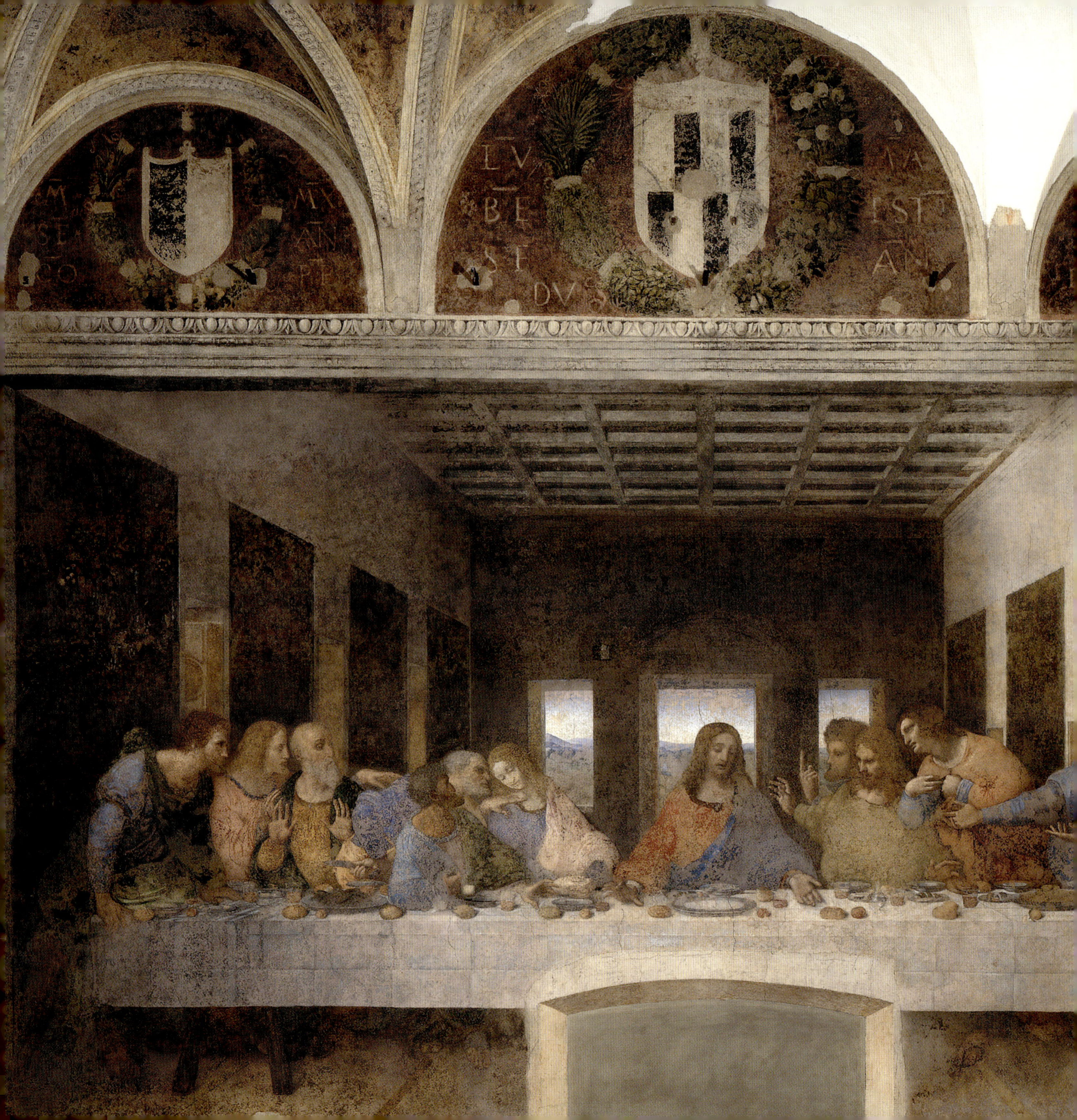

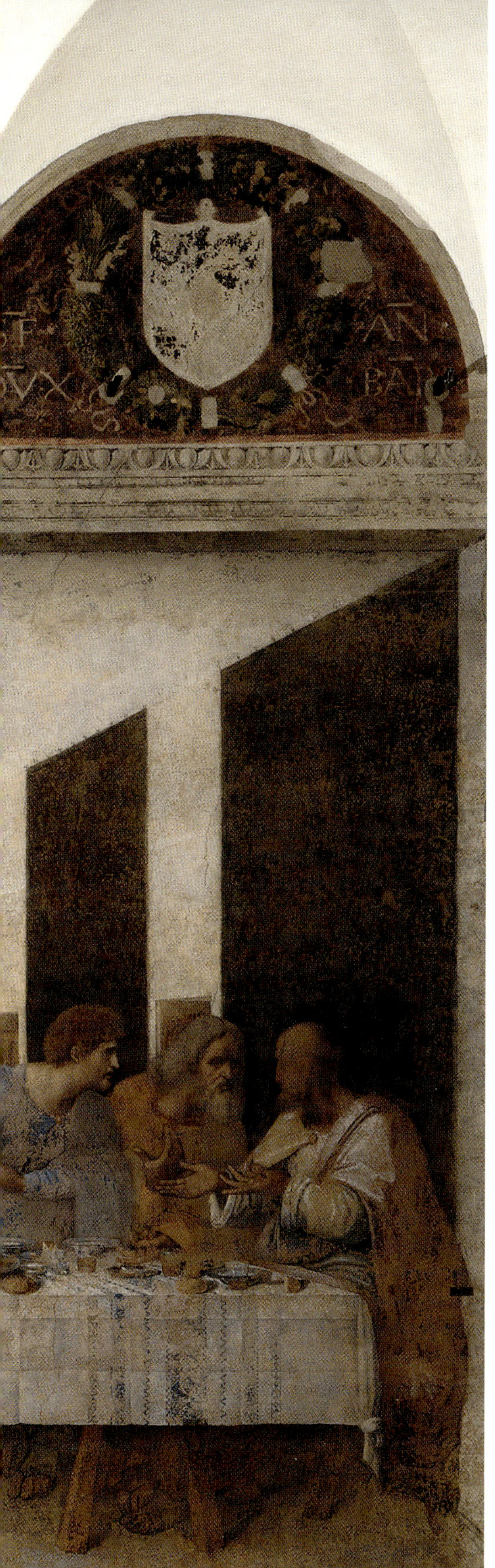

Leonardo da Vinci

(1452–1519)

The Last Supper

1495–97/98
Tempera on plaster
REFECTORY OF SANTA MARIA DELLE GRAZIE, MILAN

Leonardo's celebrated mural, depicting Christ's revelation that he is about to be betrayed, demands to be seen *in situ*. The perspective of the painted room breaks open the north wall of an actual dining hall in a Dominican monastery, and the illusion of space is continued by the three openings at the far end. While the number three relates to the Christian belief in the Holy Trinity, the windows and door have a far wider significance. Leonardo took considerable care to adjust their dimensions so that they would be in harmony with the room's proportions: analysis of the underdrawing has shown that they were originally around 5 centimetres (2 inches) wider.

The windows also reveal a visionary landscape of considerable beauty, so expansive that it perhaps suggests the view from the 'upper room' described in the Gospel of St Mark. Even more striking is the contrast that they provide with the figures in the foreground. The apostle John, for example, inclines away from the window on the left, while Thomas and James the Elder are partly framed by the window on the right. In this way the openings, and the areas of brightness they create, help to emphasize the different poses and gestures of the witnesses to this crucial episode.

Salvador Dalí
(1904–1989)

The Sacrament of the Last Supper

1955
Oil on canvas
166.7 × 267 cm (65⅝ × 105⅛ in.)
NATIONAL GALLERY OF ART, WASHINGTON, D.C.

For his version of the Last Supper Salvador
Dalí clearly took inspiration from Leonardo's
masterpiece (pages 54–55). Significantly,
however, Dalí's painting is almost overwhelmed
by its windows, which reveal a poetic, liquid
landscape, as well as bathing the image in an
ethereal light. The ghostly frames exemplify
the pervading sense of immateriality, which
culminates in both the figure of Christ blessing
the sacrament and the idealized torso with
arms outstretched, as in the Crucifixion.

The windows also define the room's
dodecahedral shape, reflecting Dalí's belief
in 'the paranoiac sublimity of ... twelve', the
number not only of the apostles but also of the
zodiac and the months of the year.[1] He also,
less remarkably, asserted that 'the Communion
must be symmetrical', a principle that
determined the windows' structure as much as
the arrangement of Christ and his disciples.[2]
Despite its passing resemblance to a spaceship,
this image has had its admirers, not least its
patron, the American collector Chester Dale.
He boldly declared that 'I consider Picasso a very
great painter. I have fifteen of his canvases in
my collection, but never will he paint a picture
to equal Dalí's Cena [the Last Supper], for
the very simple reason that he is not capable
of doing so.'[3]

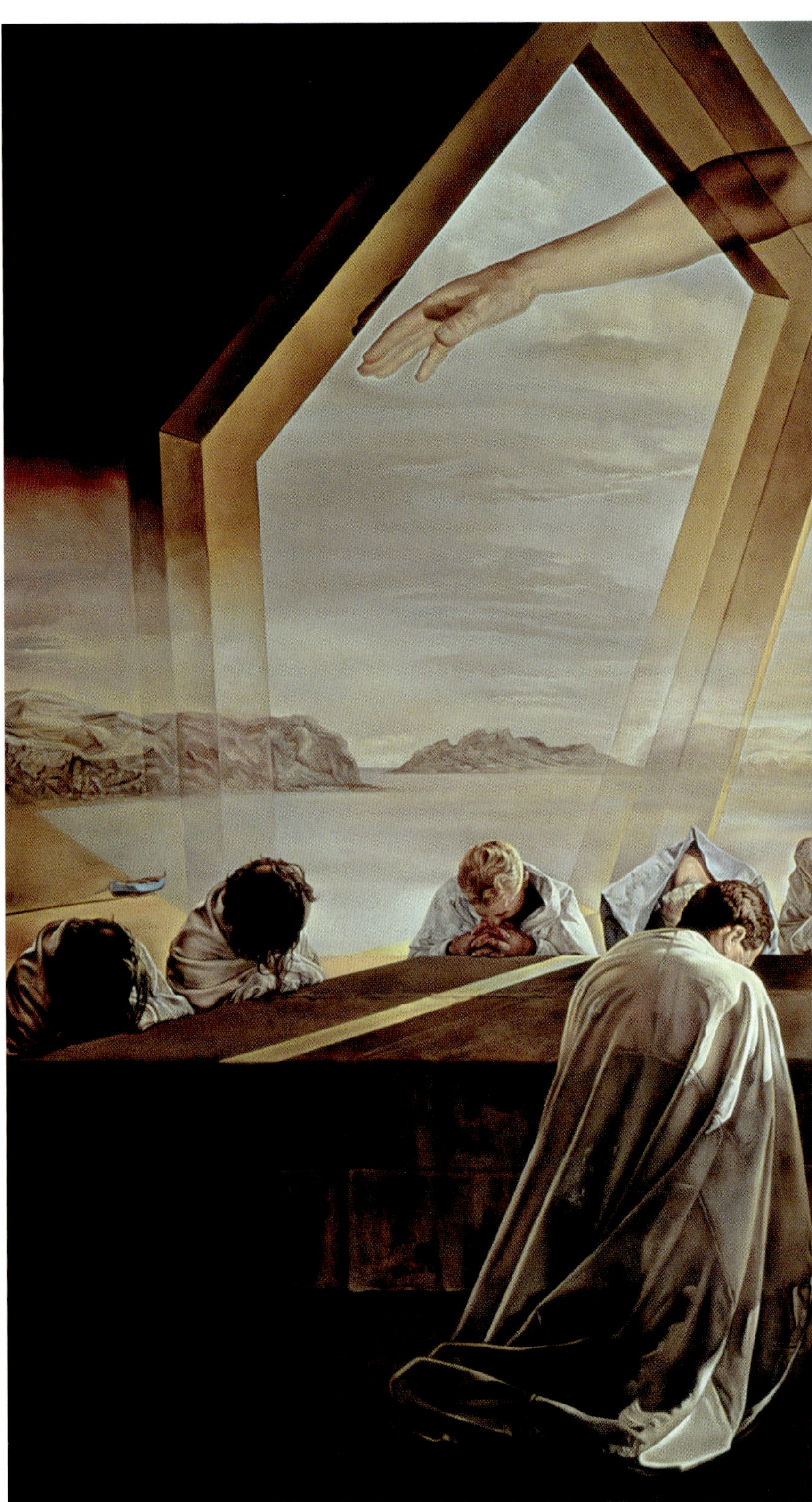

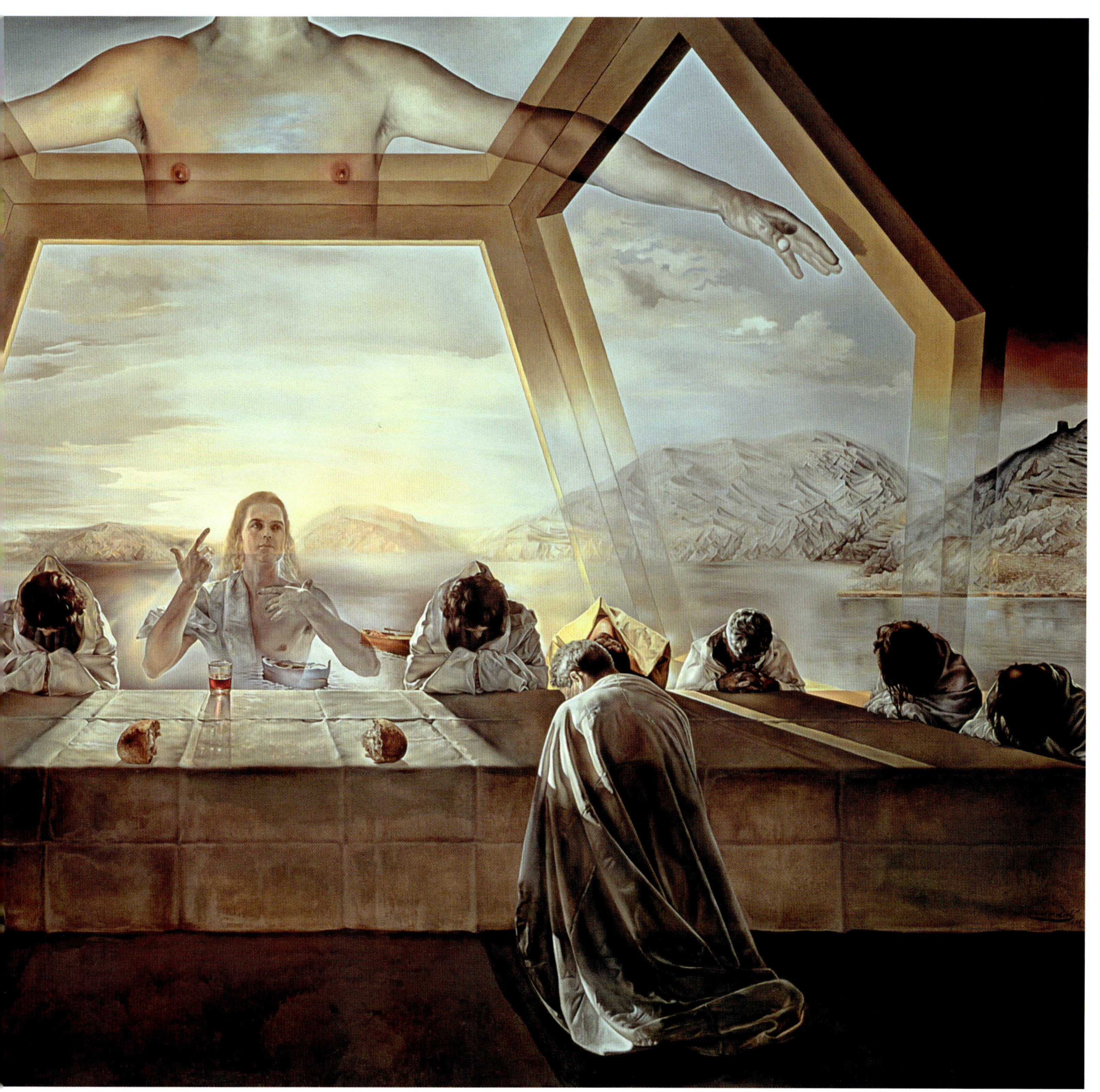

The Annunciation to St Anne

c. 1303
Fresco
ARENA (SCROVEGNI) CHAPEL, PADUA

This fresco is one of six that recount the story of the Virgin Mary's parents high up in the Arena Chapel, a building in Padua, northern Italy, that is also known as the Scrovegni Chapel after its patron, Enrico Scrovegni. The story of the angel telling the elderly Anne that she will give birth to one who 'will be admired for all centuries' is taken from an apocryphal text.[4] However, Giotto borrows conventions that were used to depict the Annunciation to the Virgin Mary, as described in the Gospel of St Luke. One of the most vivid and original details is the positioning of the angel, who is shown squeezing through an opening in the right-hand wall (see detail, right), clearly the medium for a very special type of revelation. Yet Giotto's achievement is to make the whole mural seem like a window, with its azure background surrounded by a simulated marble frame within which the pictorial space opens up convincingly.

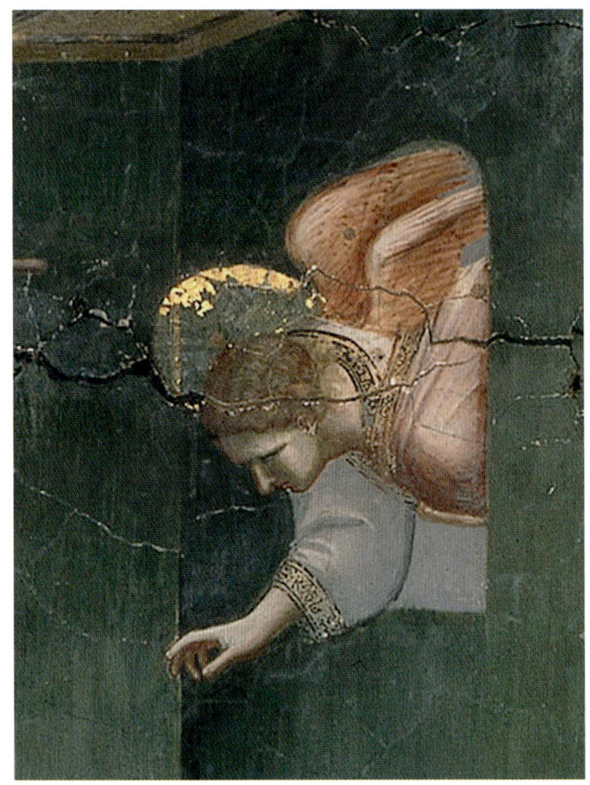

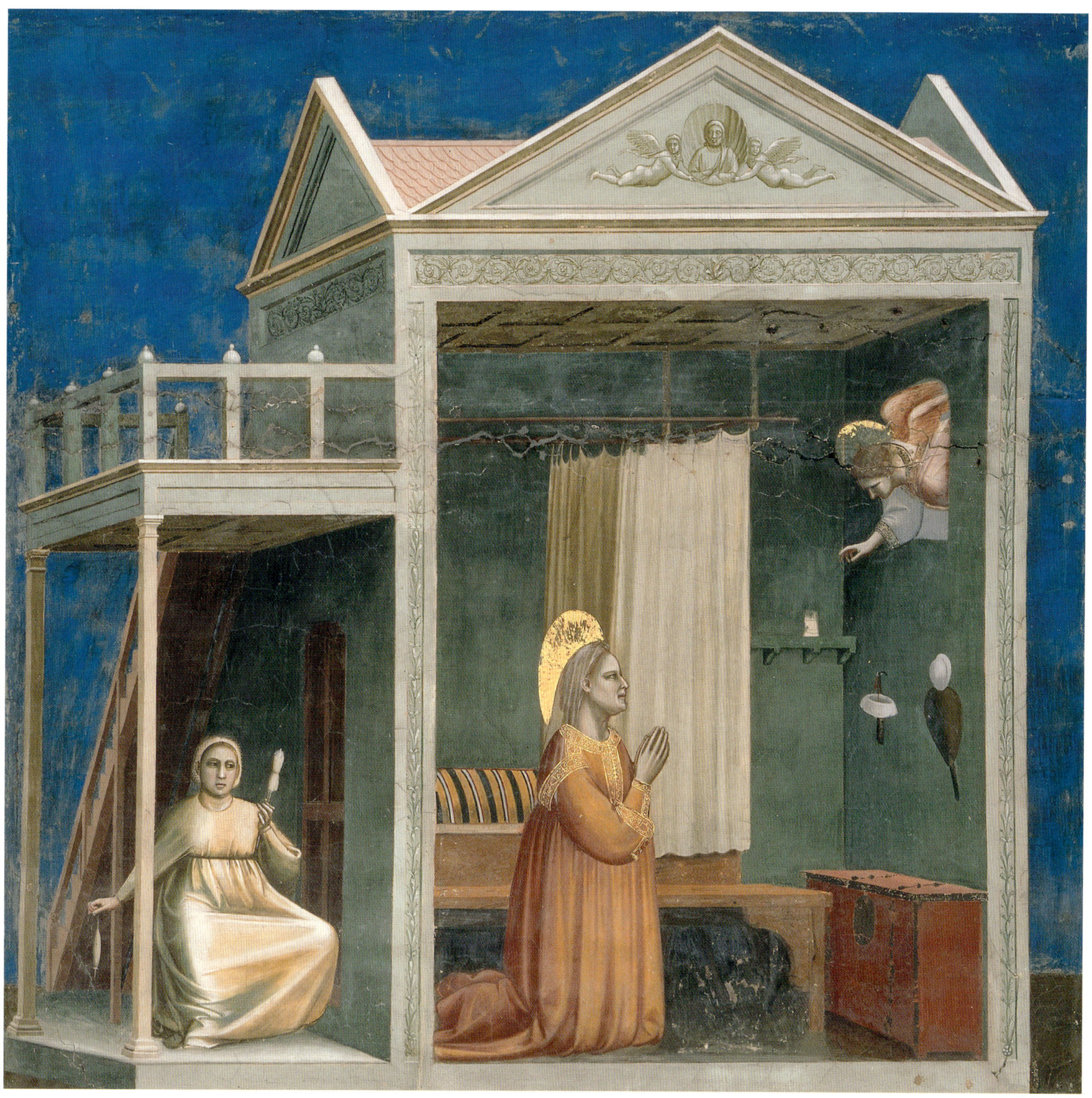

Alberto Savinio

(1891–1952)

Apparition (The Annunciation)

1932
Tempera on canvas
97 × 73 cm (38¼ × 28¾ in.)
CASA-MUSEO BOSCHI DI STEFANO, MILAN

Although 'Apparition' is the title written on the frame of this painting, the work has always been exhibited as an Annunciation. Certainly, it borrows traditional imagery associated with this theme, not least the window through which the angel peers so intently. Yet here the male figure is an immense classical god, while the Virgin Mary has been replaced by a bird-headed woman whose demure posture resembles that of someone sitting for a bourgeois portrait. In common with his brother, the artist Giorgio De Chirico, Alberto Savinio created an ironic personal mythology out of imagery drawn from different historical periods, defying the constraints of time and space. As if to emphasize the point, the canvas – conventionally a window on reality – has been given a strange, irregular shape analogous to that of the painted opening in the centre of the work. In this way Savinio creates a setting in which art becomes a form of mystical revelation, liberated from reason and the laws of the physical world.

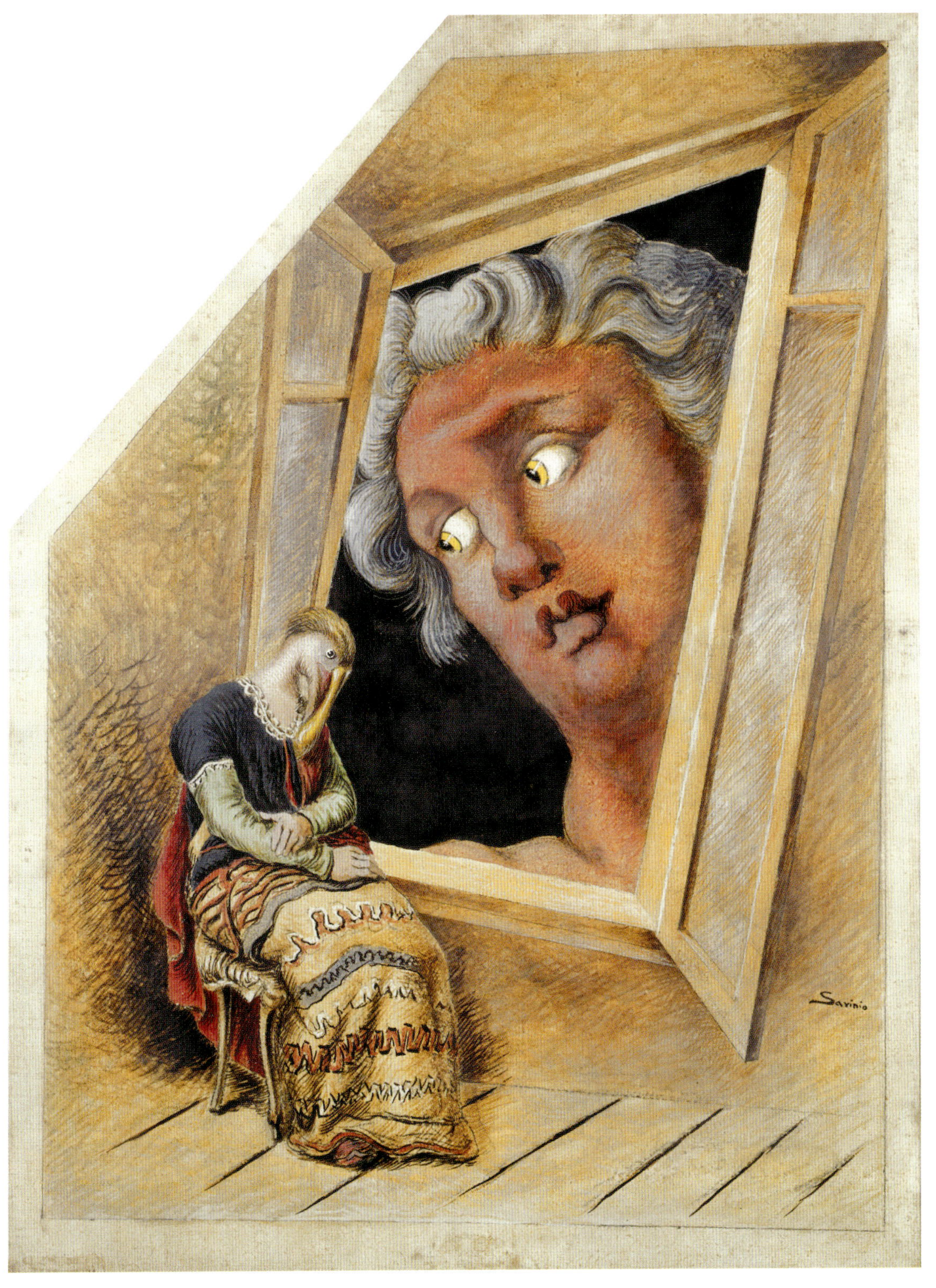

Albrecht Dürer

(1471–1528)

St Jerome in His Study

1514
Engraving
24.7 × 18.8 cm (9¾ × 7⅜ in.)
VARIOUS LOCATIONS

This image, one of Dürer's three *Master Engravings*, shows the fourth- to fifth-century translator of the Hebrew Bible working in the study of a Renaissance scholar, with a low ceiling that cuts into the curved arch of one of the mullioned windows. The unorthodox perspective, with a vanishing point near the right-hand margin, makes the left wall more prominent, allowing the artist to lavish attention on the windows made from bull's-eye, or crown, glass. These circular panes, thickest in the middle, have been made by blowing molten glass into a 'crown', or hollow globe, and then reheating and spinning the glass into a disc (see also page 69). With delightful variation, Dürer has represented the windows themselves with delicate concentric outlines, while the shadows on the embrasures have been created using horizontal hatching.

The light streaming through the glass creates a warm, idyllic atmosphere, in which a dog and a lion, whose paw Jerome is said to have healed, doze in the foreground. Even the skull on the window seat has lost its terror. Above all, the sunshine creates a visual equivalent to the spiritual enlightenment that inspired the labours of this Doctor of the Church.

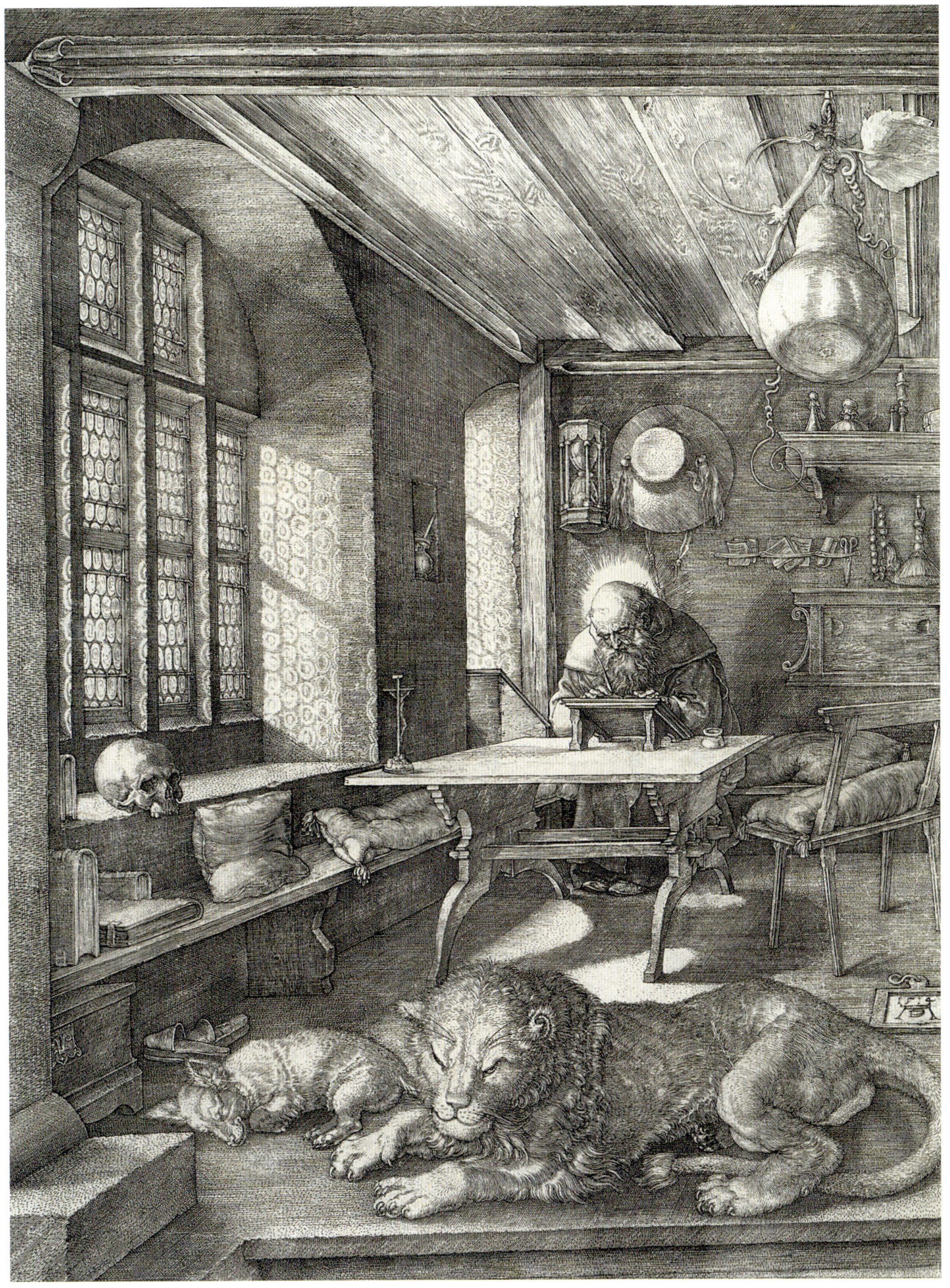

Sulamith and Maria

1811
Oil on panel
Diptych, 34.5 × 32 cm (13⅝ × 12⅝ in.) overall
MUSEUM GEORG SCHÄFER, SCHWEINFURT

Franz Pforr's painting is related to his own text of the same title, a tale of two sisters and their artist-husbands, while also alluding to the biblical figures after whom the women are named. Sulamith, an Old Testament character from the Song of Songs, is shown holding a baby as if in anticipation of the birth of Christ, while Maria, representing the Virgin Mary, distractedly arranges her hair with an expression suggesting that she foresees not only his arrival but also his Passion. Light floods in through a bull's-eye window in a manner that recalls Albrecht Dürer's *St Jerome in His Study* (page 63), in this case illuminating the Bible on the window ledge. As in the Renaissance engraving, the rays symbolize divine enlightenment, reminding us that Mary is the *sedes sapientiae* (seat of wisdom). They also clearly evoke the imagery connected with the Annunciation.

As well as emphasizing the link between the Old and New Testament, Pforr's diptych combines the reference to Dürer with the Italianate style of the Sulamith panel. This desire for artistic synthesis was shared by all the Nazarenes, a group of German artists living in Rome that included Pforr and his close friend Friedrich Overbeck (1789–1869).

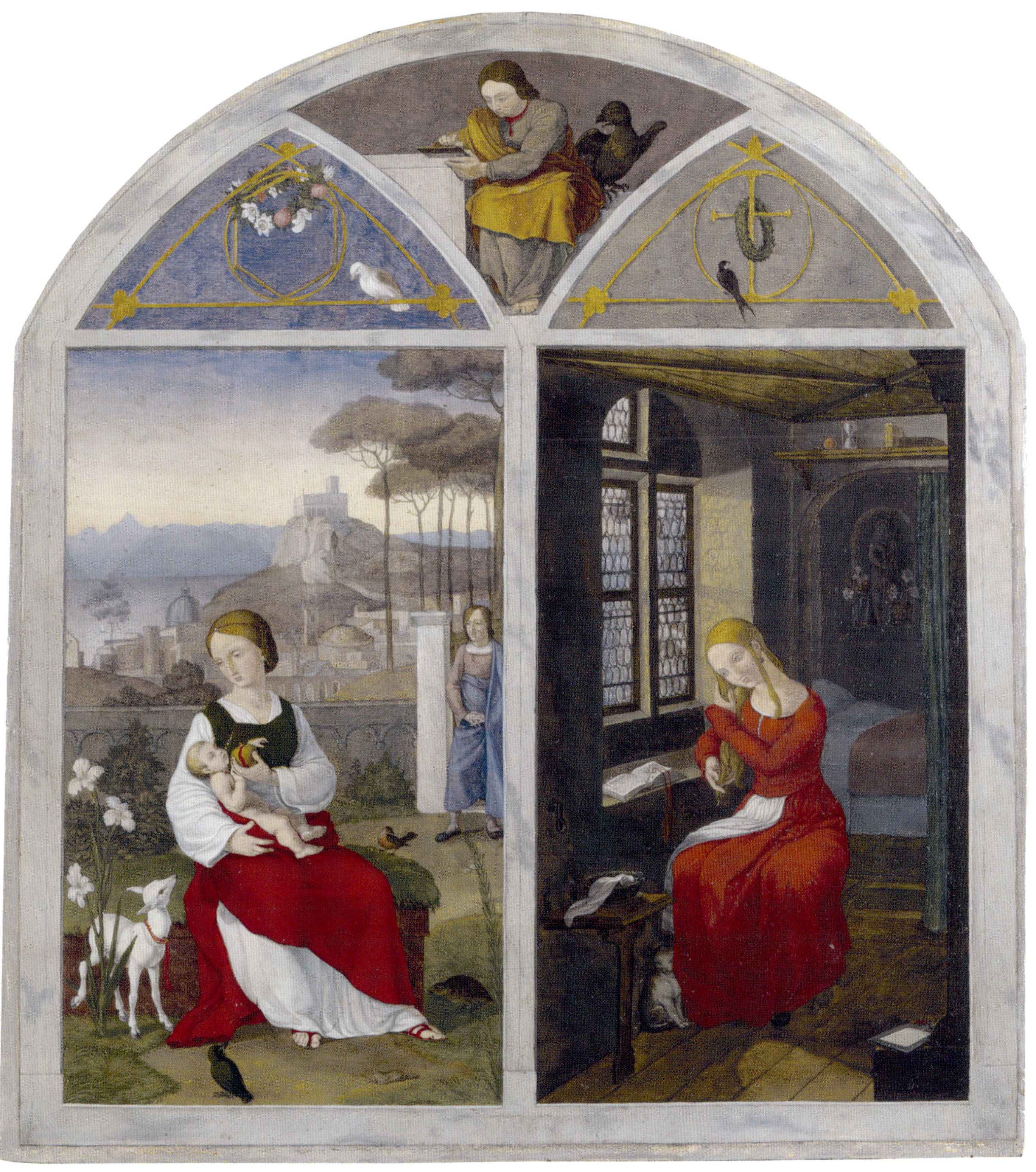

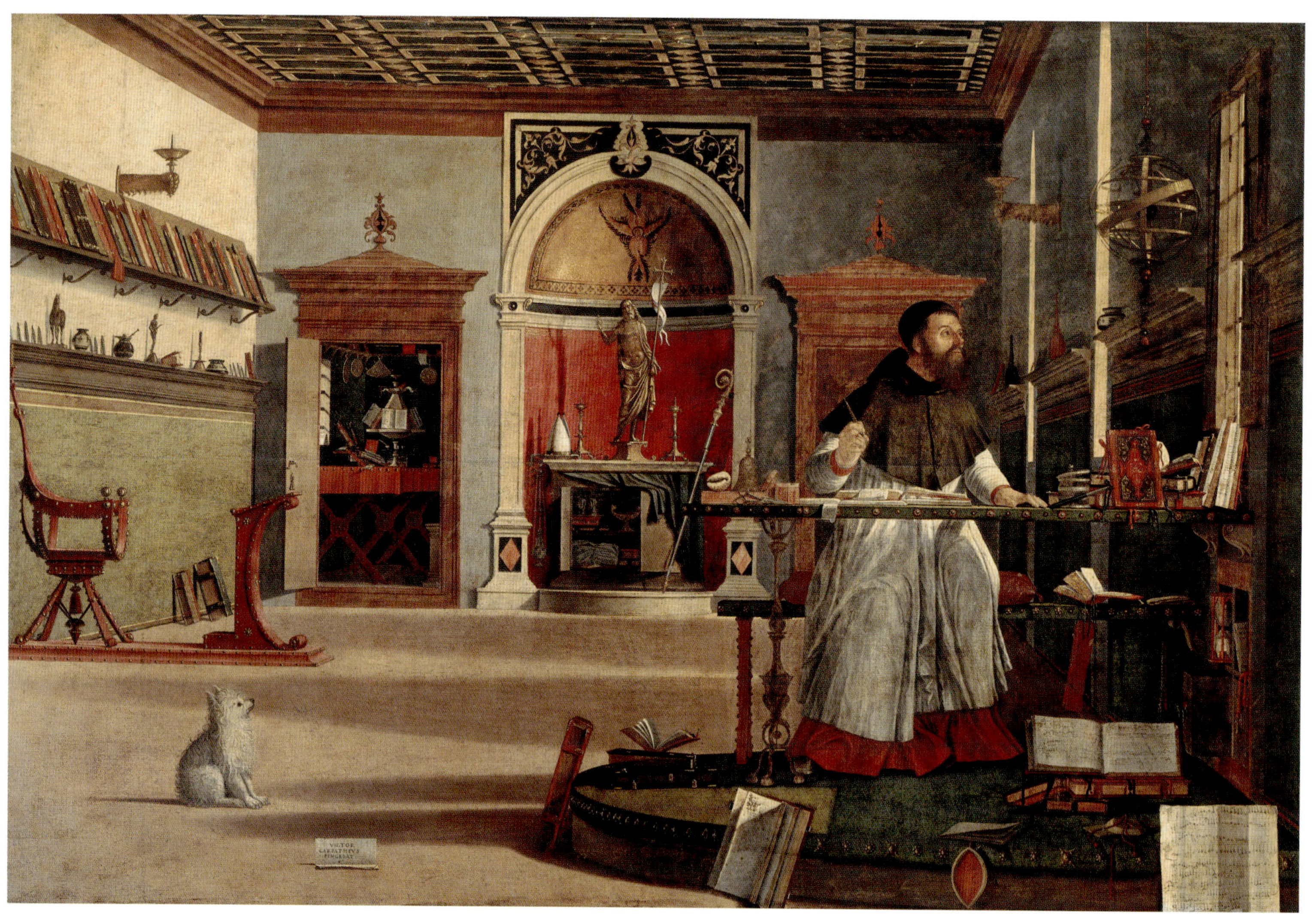

Vittore Carpaccio

(?1460/66–1525/26)

St Augustine in His Study

c. 1502–1507
Oil and tempera on canvas
141 × 211 cm (55½ × 83⅛ in.)
SCUOLA DI SAN GIORGIO DEGLI SCHIAVONI, VENICE

With their embrasures and bars hardly visible
(see detail, right), the windows in this scene are
not at all prominent, and yet they play a vital
role in the event depicted. As the apocryphal
life of St Jerome relates, St Augustine was
preparing to write a letter to Jerome when
'an indescribable light, not seen in our times,
and hardly to be described in our poor language,
entered the cell in which I was, with an
ineffable and unknown fragrance, of all
odours, at the hour of compline'.[5] It was at
this moment that Augustine realized that his
friend had just died – a miraculous revelation
of which the light is not merely a symbol but
also an actual messenger.

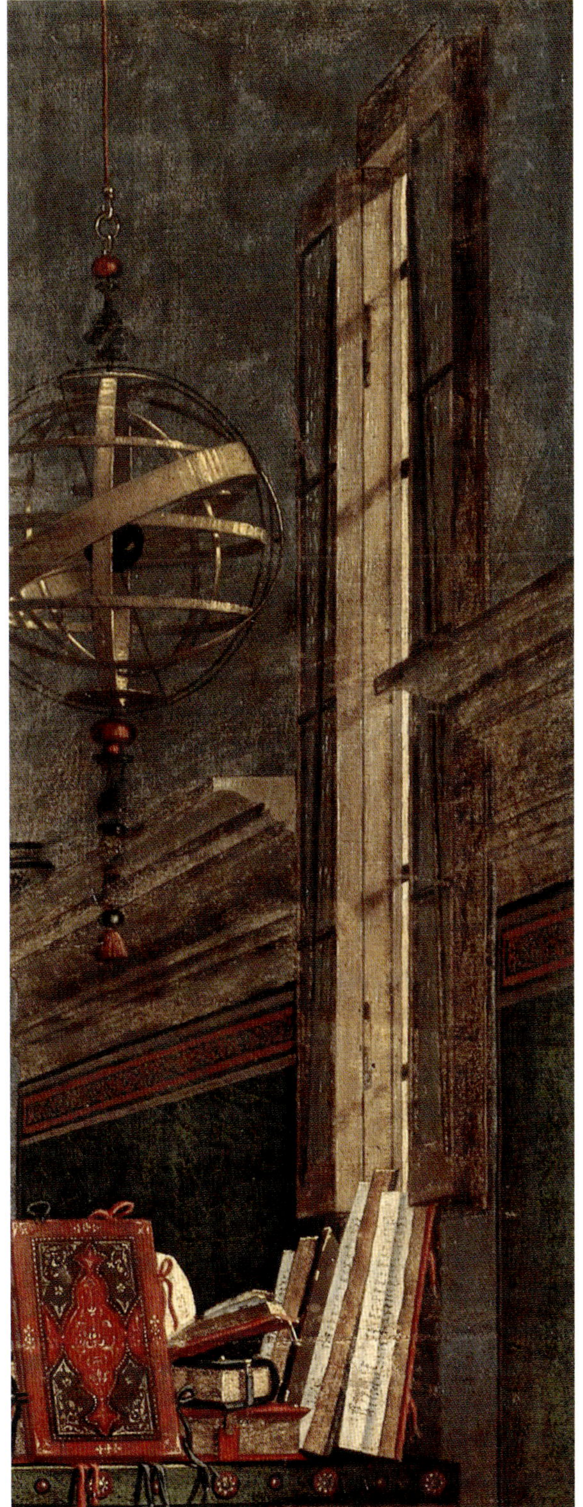

Matthias Grünewald
(*c.* 1475/80–1528)

St Anthony and a Devil
Panel from the Isenheim Altarpiece

1512–16
Oil on panel
232 × 75 cm (91⅜ × 29½ in.)
MUSÉE D'UNTERLINDEN, COLMAR

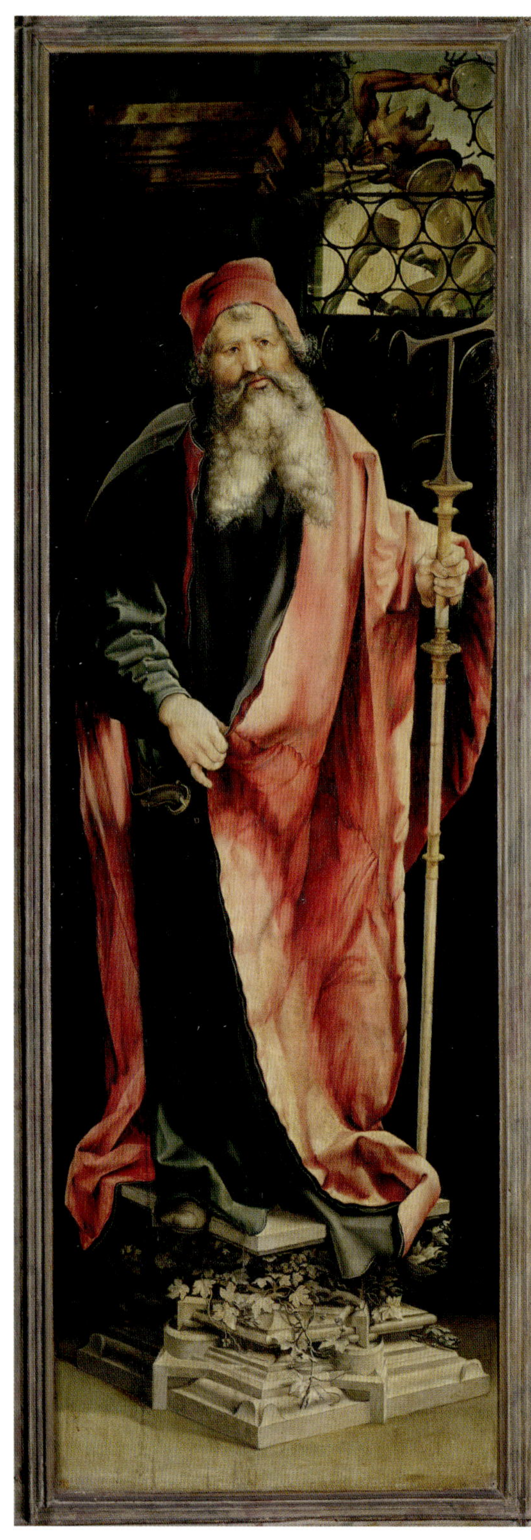

While other depictions of St Anthony show him surrounded by torments and temptations, Matthias Grünewald creates a simpler image in which a bull's-eye window (see page 62), battered as it is, helps to shield the saint from a demon raving above his left shoulder (see detail, opposite). The glass here is not a medium of spiritual illumination but a form of protection: the everyday physical function of the window has been given a sacred significance.

This panel forms part of an extremely complex altarpiece originally located in the chapel of the monastery hospital at Issenheim, a small town in north-eastern France. Flanking a particularly stark image of the Crucifixion, the figure of Anthony resisting the devil provided a moral example. It also represented a saint who was a patron and intercessor for the patients, many of whom suffered from ergotism, a disease also known as St Anthony's fire.

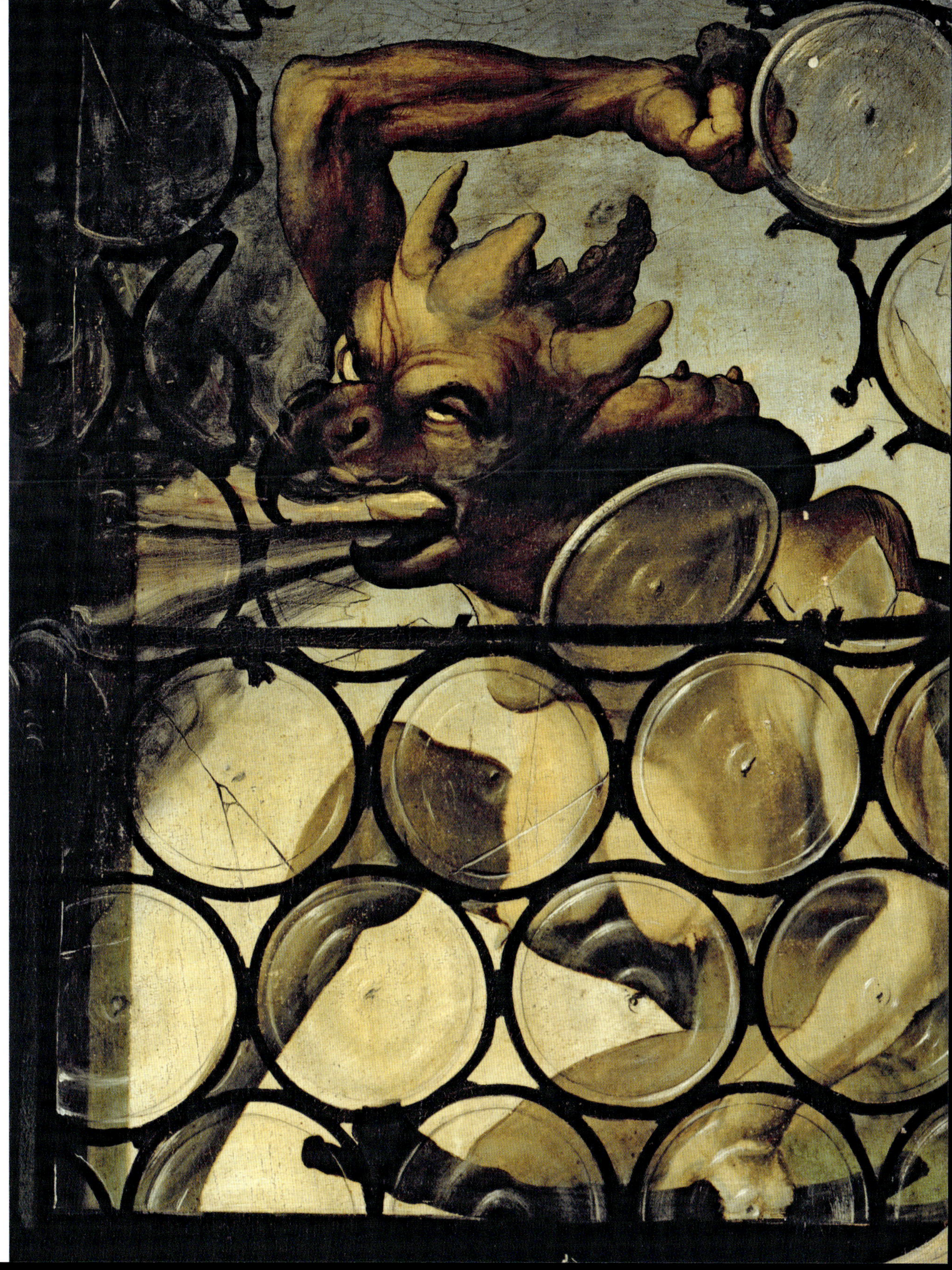

Michelangelo Merisi da Caravaggio

(1571–1610)

The Calling of St Matthew

1598–1600
Oil on canvas
322 × 340 cm (126¼ × 133⅜ in.)
CONTARELLI CHAPEL, SAN LUIGI DEI FRANCESI, ROME

'Jesus … saw a man called Matthew sitting at the tax office; and he said to him, "Follow me." And he rose and followed him' (Matthew 9:9). An intense ray of light follows Christ's pointing hand, illuminating the face of the tax collector, who gestures in astonishment while his friends continue their game. Although Christ and his companion, St Peter, must have entered the house in conventional fashion, through a door, the beam falls obliquely, as if modelled on the effects of sunlight shining through a high opening in Caravaggio's studio. This unseen window can be usefully compared to its equivalent at the top of the composition – partly shuttered, opaque and symbolic of the darkness enveloping humanity, which Christ has come to save.

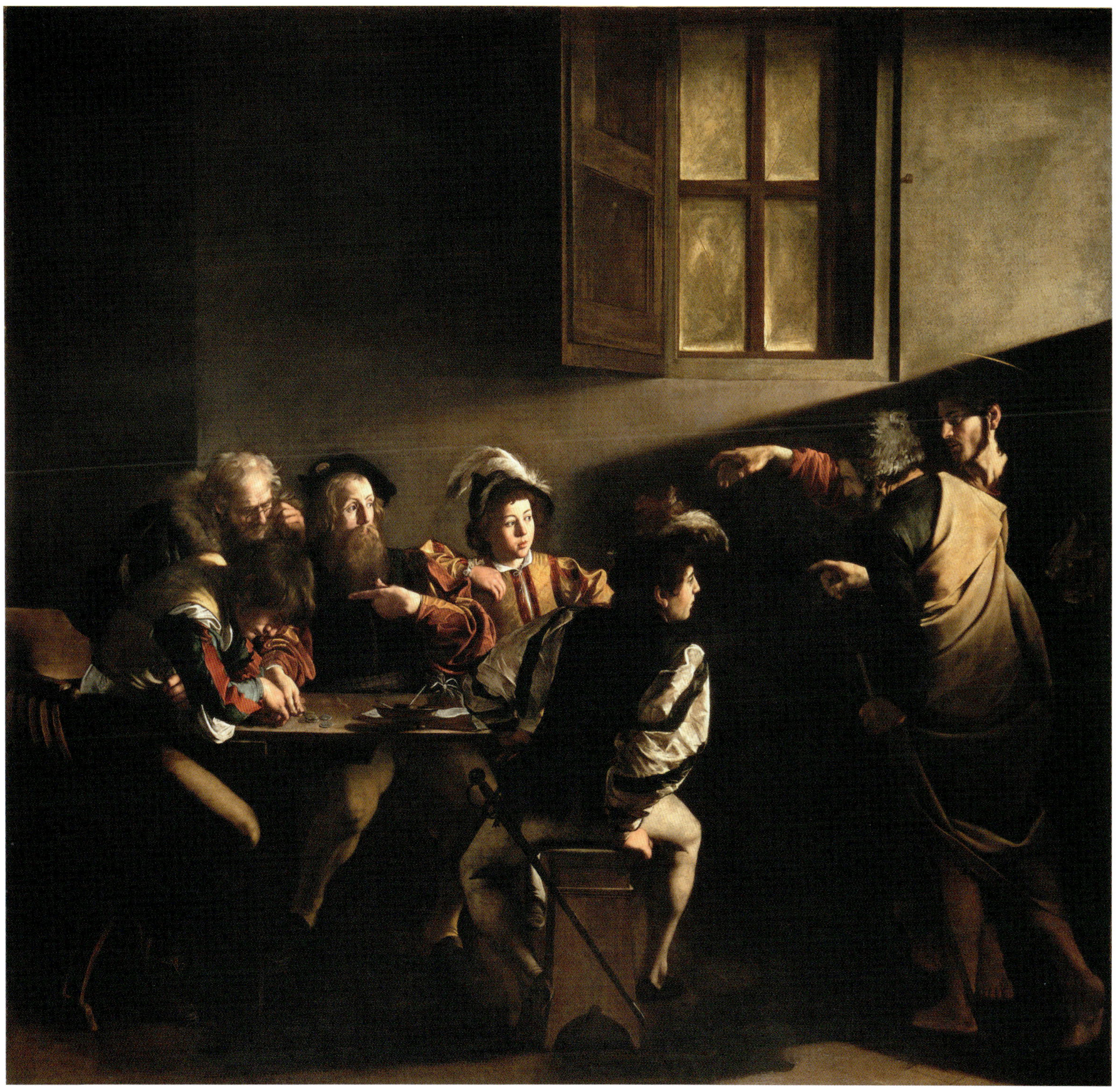

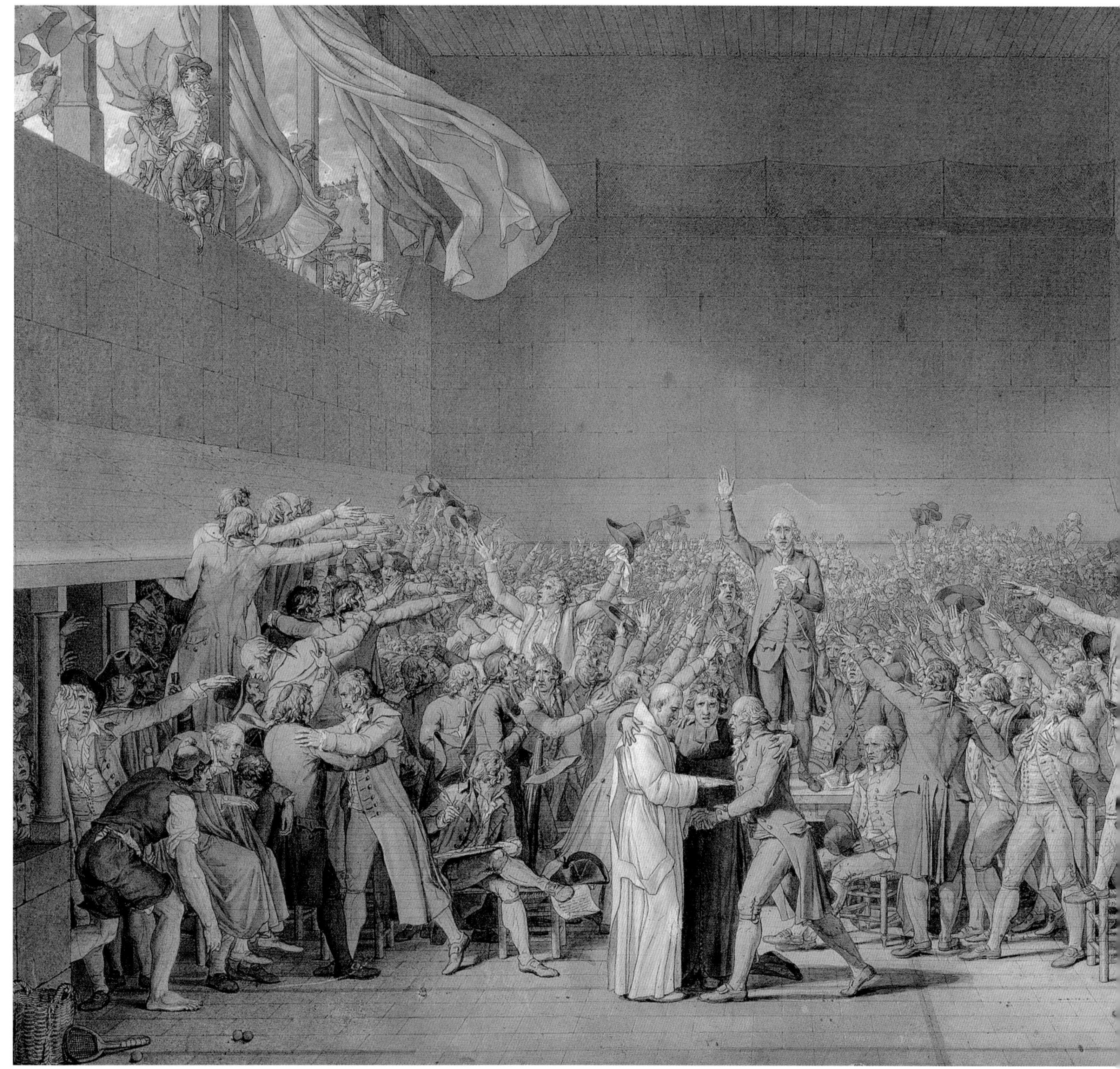

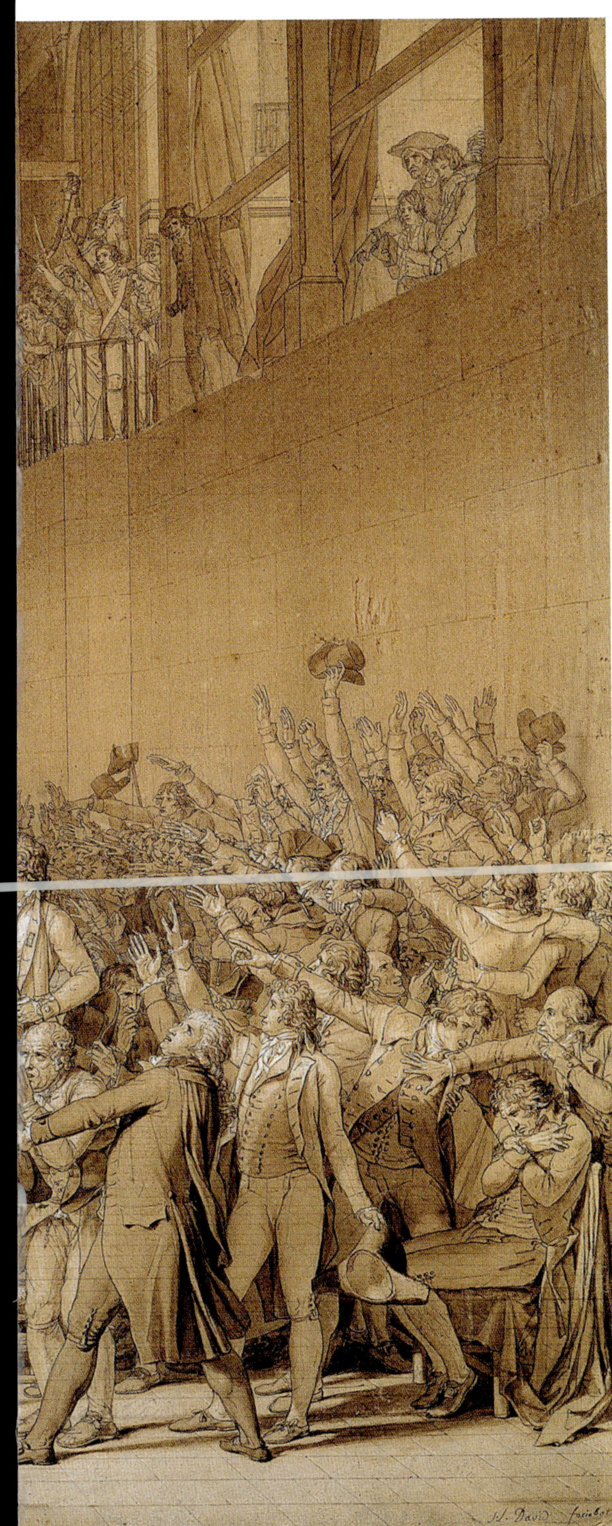

Jacques-Louis David

(1748–1825)

Oath of the Tennis Court

1791
Pen, bistre wash and white highlights on paper
66 × 105 cm (26 × 41⅜ in.)
MUSÉE NATIONAL DU CHÂTEAU DE VERSAILLES

In this celebrated scene from the French Revolution, the members of the newly established National Assembly gather in June 1789 inside a real tennis court at Versailles. As they swear 'to God and the Patrie [fatherland] never to be separated until we have formed a solid and equitable Constitution', daylight floods in from windows high up in the wall, and the drama is heightened by the spectacular billowing curtains.[6] The light effects, and even the pointing gestures, recall moments of divine revelation in earlier paintings (see, for example, page 71), giving this secular event an almost religious significance.

The political reality was, unfortunately, somewhat different, as the Revolution's early idealism gave way to dissension and violence. Jacques-Louis David's drawing was the study for a more ambitious project, a canvas with life-size figures intended for the National Assembly. Although various versions of the composition exist, the full-scale painting was abandoned in 1792, as France descended towards the horrors of the Terror.

Jan Vermeer

(1632–1675)

The Astronomer

1668
Oil on canvas
50 × 45 cm (19⅝ × 17¾ in.)
MUSÉE DU LOUVRE, PARIS

While much of Vermeer's painting remains in shadow, a bold light shines on the face of the astronomer, as well as on the instruments and book spread before him. The window is itself a significant feature in the composition, with a circular stained-glass panel that corresponds to the shapes of the astrolabe and celestial globe on the table.

At first glance the revelations in this scene might seem of a purely scientific nature, and yet this impression is contradicted by the painting of the finding of the infant Moses that hangs on the far wall. Moses's appearance may be linked to his reputed knowledge of the stars. Most importantly, however, he is a biblical character who prefigured Christ, and so his presence indicates a spiritual insight, which is also represented by the astronomer's scrutiny of the heavens. It is significant that this canvas has a pendant, *The Geographer* (1669; Städel Museum, Frankfurt am Main), concerned with a complementary, terrestrial form of understanding.

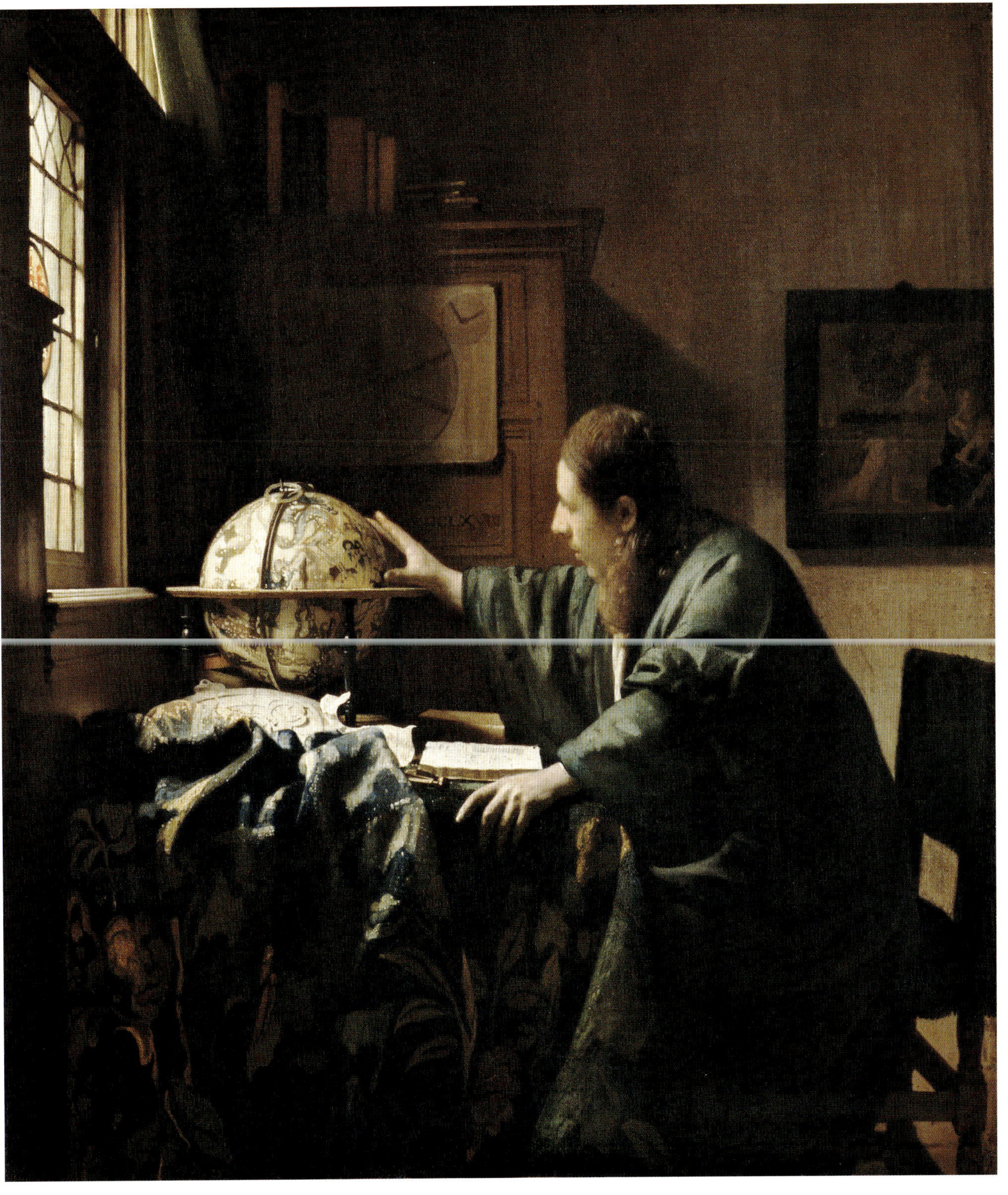

Jan Vermeer

(1632–1675)

Girl Reading a Letter at an Open Window

c. 1658–61
Oil on canvas
83 × 64.5 cm (32⅝ × 25⅜ in.)
GEMÄLDEGALERIE ALTE MEISTER, STAATLICHE KUNSTSAMMLUNGEN, DRESDEN

The precise nature of the communication, subtly lit by daylight coming through the open window, seems unclear. The young woman remains impassive, her face partly averted from the viewer, although it was initially turned even further away. The original position accounts for the angle of the head in the reflection, a feature that also emphasizes the introspective mood. Despite this sense of reserve, a dramatic quality is created by the presence of the curtains, particularly the length of crimson draped behind the window. The green hanging on the right, a late addition to the composition, helps to increase the girl's physical and emotional distance, while also hinting at the artifice of the canvas. In this period, paintings – fictive windows on reality – were often exhibited with actual curtains, which would be drawn to reveal the illusion underneath.

Only one detail gives us a strong hint as to the content of the correspondence, and that has come to light only with the help of X-rays. These have revealed that, originally, Vermeer included on the back wall a large picture of a standing Cupid, which was derived from an emblem of fidelity. The image still appears in two of Vermeer's other works, but its survival here was unnecessary. Ultimately, the theme of this canvas is something that we can perhaps guess.

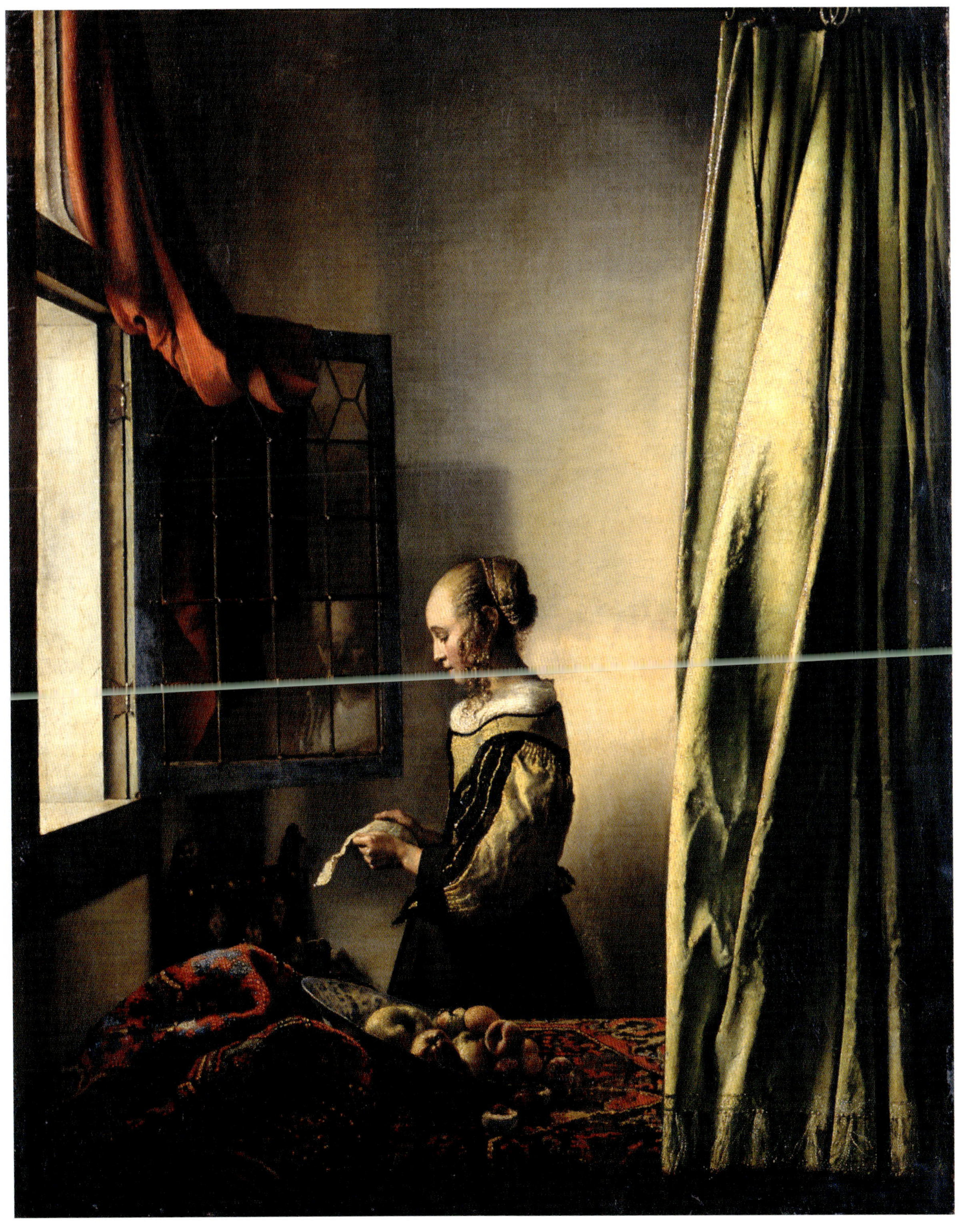

Jean-Honoré Fragonard

(1732–1806)

The Love Letter

c. 1770
Oil on canvas
83.2 × 67 cm (32¾ × 26⅜ in.)
THE METROPOLITAN MUSEUM OF ART, NEW YORK

In contrast to the reserved mood of Vermeer's *Girl Reading a Letter at an Open Window* (page 77), Jean-Honoré Fragonard's painting introduces a sense of complicity. The woman gazes directly at us, and holds her correspondence in such a way that we can at least attempt to read its contents. Despite its playfulness and air of the unexpected, the painting probably represents an amour that is quite proper. The writing seems to spell the name of Charles-Étienne-Gabriel Cuvillier, who was married to Marie-Emilie Boucher, the daughter of the artist François Boucher, Fragonard's teacher. It is assumed that she is the subject of this painting.

The window not only illuminates the couple's communication but also reveals the suitably sensuous, warm colours: the translucent golds and browns, the jade of the dress reflecting the yellow curtains, and the brilliant highlights applied with the tip of the brush. Although natural light often has a narrative or even symbolic function, it can also be a source of aesthetic pleasure in its own right.

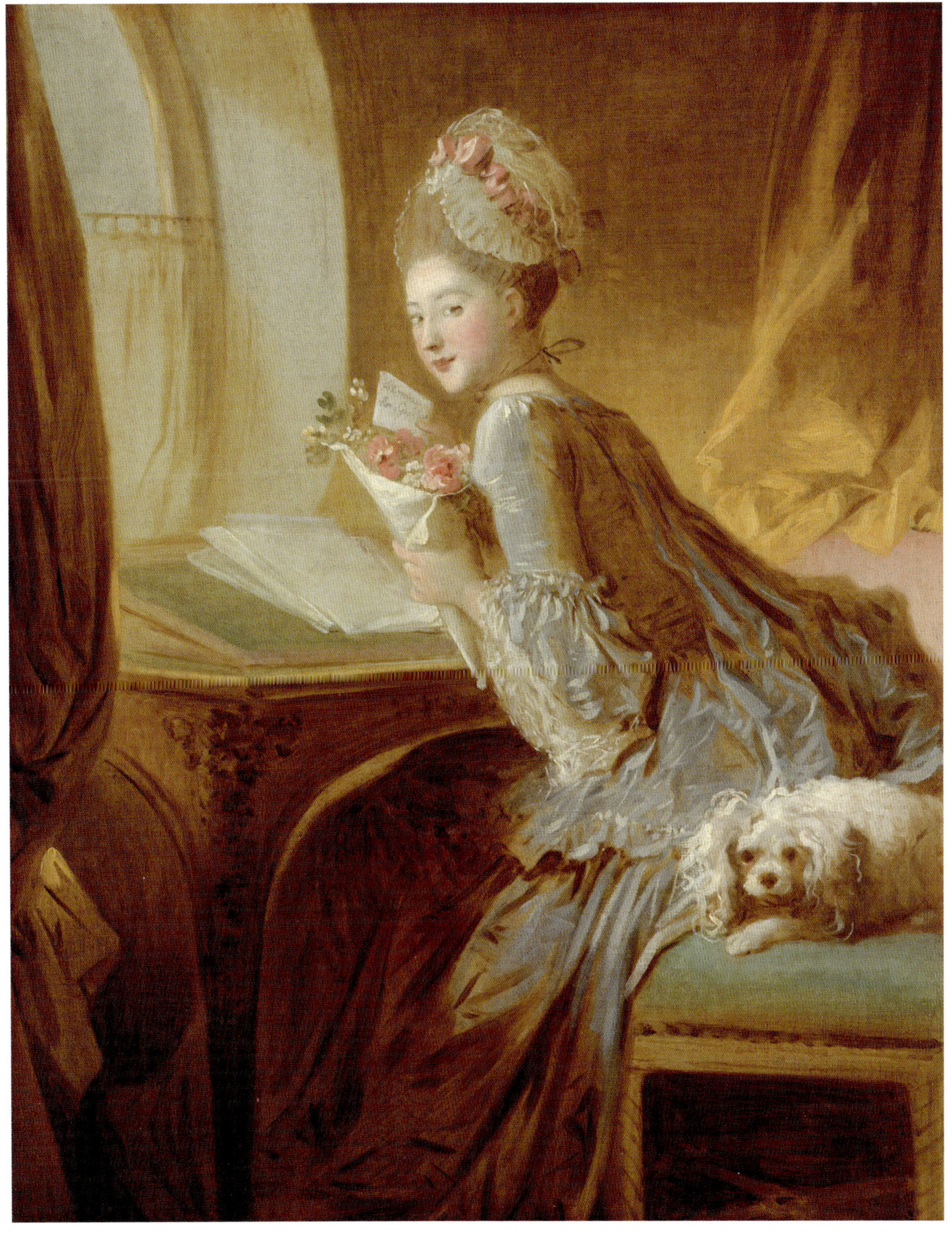

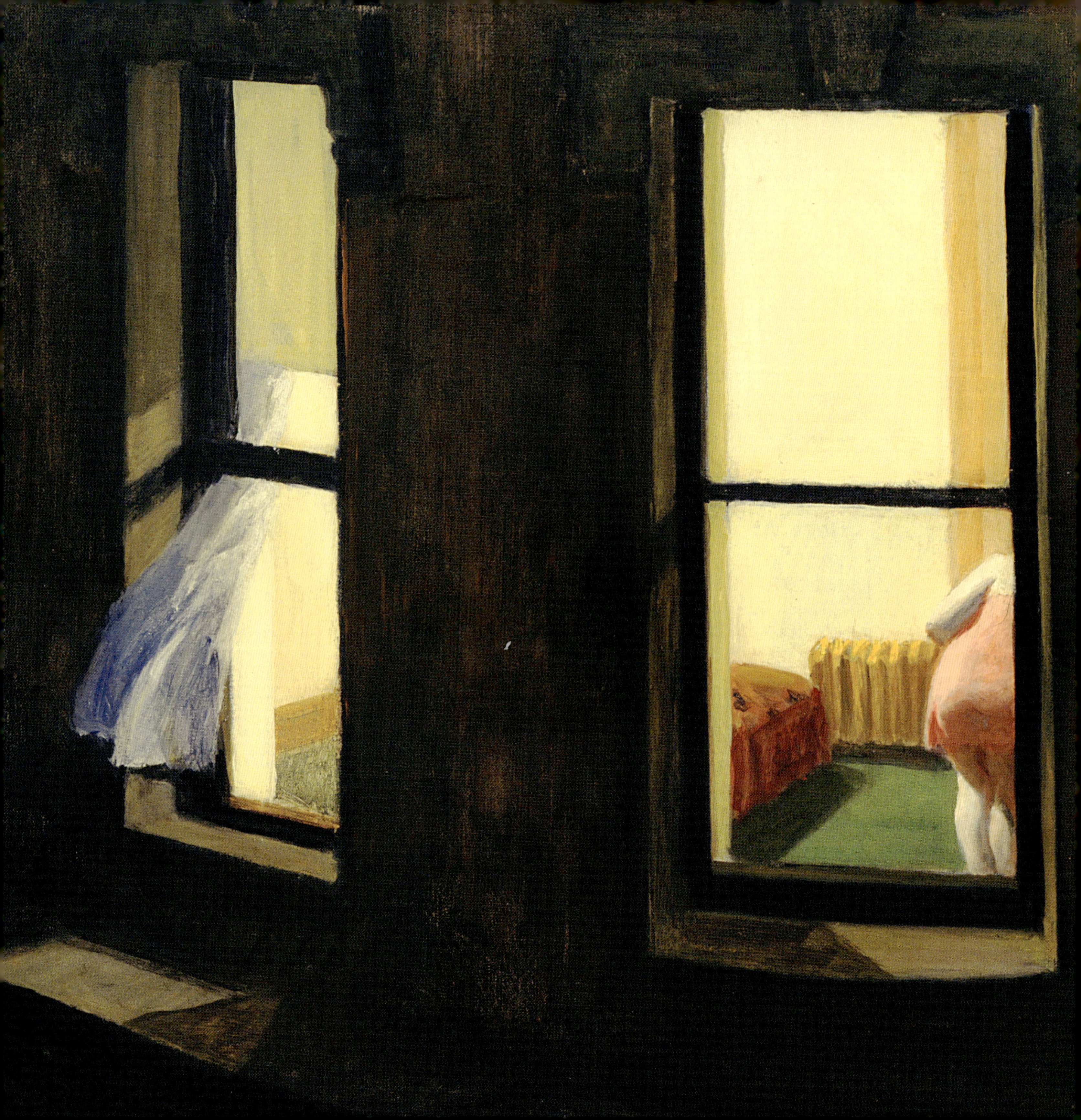

Windows on the World

The idea that a painting is a window on the world is given a clever twist in *The Marriage Settlement* by William Hogarth (pages 82–83). The window in the painting is linked visually to the pictures hanging near by, and, like them, helps to explain the narrative, in which a marriage pays for the construction of a mansion – at a terrible cost.

Windows often complement a picture's main theme even when they do not provide such specific information. Two early Netherlandish panels (pages 84 and 87) offer a glimpse of external reality that offsets the sense of enclosure around the Virgin Mary, while her death is made more solemn by the grand setting in Andrea Mantegna's painting (page 89). The portrait by Mstislav Dobuzhinsky (pages 90–91) could hardly be more different in theme, but, once again, the backdrop helps the viewer to interpret the subject. Thus, even a bespectacled writer can be turned into a contemporary man of action.

Voyeurs observe the world while using the window frame to exhibit themselves, often in ways that do not follow expectations of history or gender. The medieval women of Ambrogio Lorenzetti's fresco (page 93) and Jacques Cœur's house (page 94) may not be as dramatic as the characters in Banksy's graffiti (page 99), but they are less retiring than Berthe Morisot's husband on holiday in the Isle of Wight (page 100).

Conventional images of male and female gazes are offered by Gustave Caillebotte (pages 102 and 103). His man on a balcony is observing the metropolis, although he may not be relishing his experience quite as much as the spectator (and artist) in Edward Hopper's *Night Windows* (pages 104–105), in which a well-lit apartment provides a thrilling opportunity for seeing and being seen.

Freedom, a sense of imminent possibility, is a common theme of window paintings, and yet is often linked to a corresponding feeling of captivity, symbolized by both Childe Hassam and Martinus Rørbye (pages 108–109 and 110, respectively). Caspar David Friedrich, Rørbye's mentor, also creates an effect of confinement in *Window with a View of a Park* (page 111), where the flat landscape is enmeshed by the grid of the window. This emphasis on two-dimensionality became a characteristic of modernism, but without negating the autobiographical element of such masterpieces as Pierre Bonnard's *Open Window* (page 113).

People – viewing and being viewed, seen and unseen – are the principal subject of this chapter, and yet the plate glass lining our high streets presents another spectacle: the consumerism evoked by Christo's wrapped shopfronts (page 121). Most fetishistic of all is Don Eddy's photorealist canvas (page 123), which also refers to the concept of the painting as a window while obscuring the image with layers of contradictory reflections.

William Hogarth

(1697–1764)

The Marriage Settlement
From the series *Marriage à la Mode*

c. 1743
Oil on canvas
69.9 × 90.8 cm (27½ × 37¾ in.)
THE NATIONAL GALLERY, LONDON

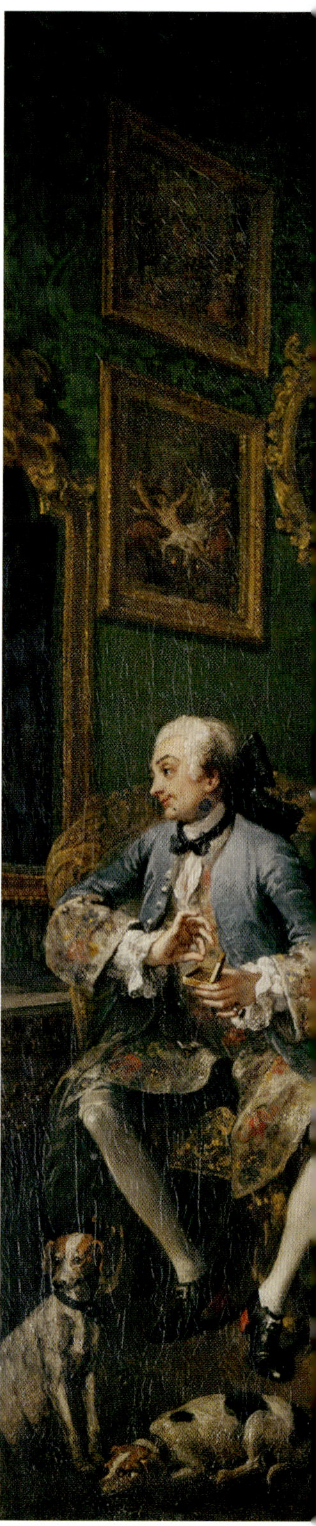

This famous image is the first of a series of six
by William Hogarth depicting the mercenary
marriage between an aristocrat's son and the
daughter of a City alderman, who is shown in
the centre of the painting inspecting the legal
settlement. The earl's lawyer, plan in hand, is
looking through a sash window at the mansion
that the dowry will help to complete. It is a top-
heavy monstrosity that shows scant regard for
the rules of classical architecture, with four
columns supported by three, and the Ionic order
resting on the Corinthian. Hogarth also derided
the Renaissance style in his treatise *The Analysis
of Beauty*, claiming that 'were a modern architect
to build a palace in Lapland or the West-Indies,
Palladio must be his guide, nor would he stir
a step without his book'.[1] The impracticality of
some Palladian buildings manifests itself here
in the tiny, dark coach house, while the liveried
staff lolling around near by complete this image
of idleness and futility.

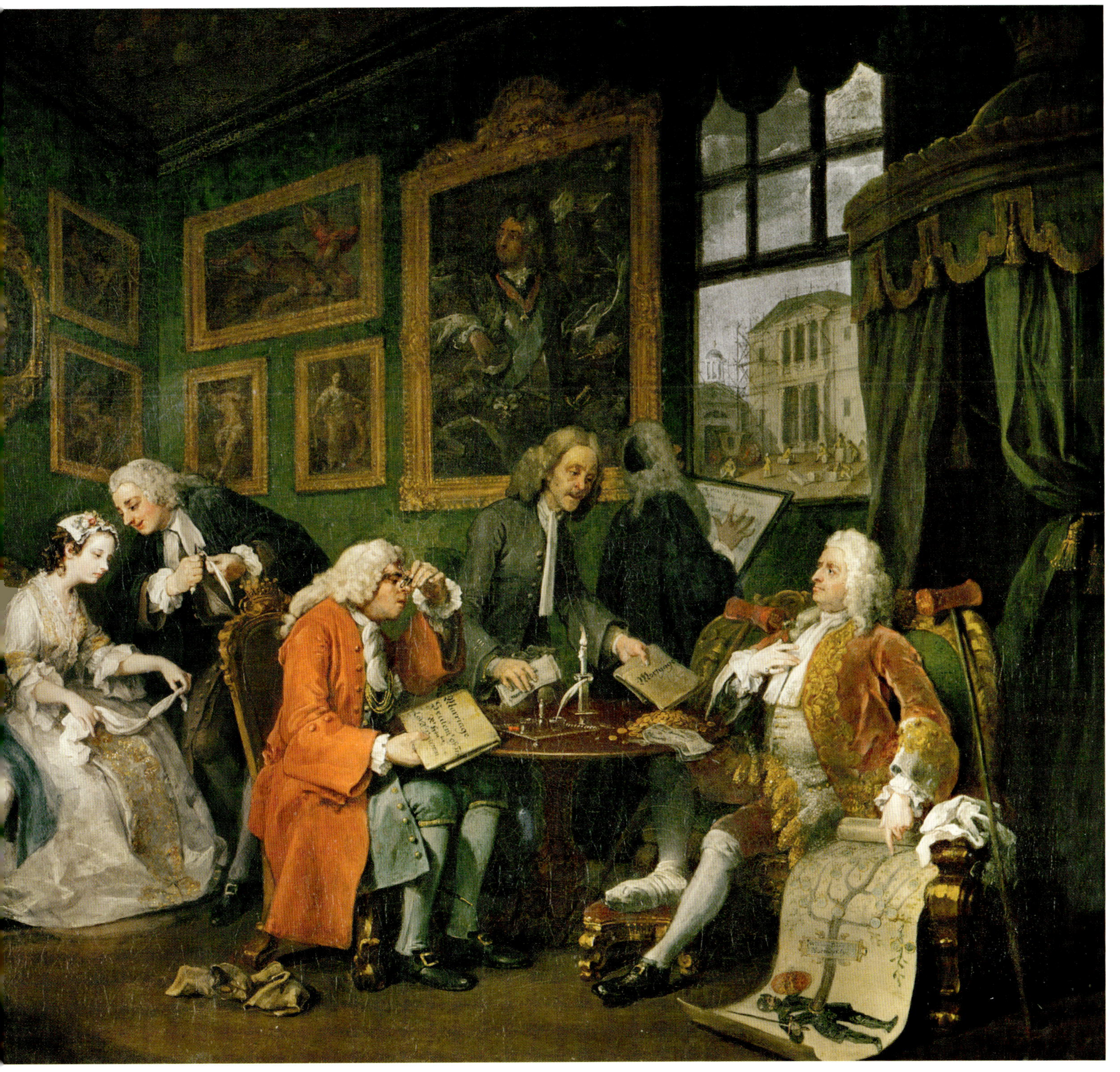

Follower of Robert Campin

(*c.* 1375/79–1444)

The Virgin and Child before a Firescreen

c. 1440
Oil with egg tempera on oak with walnut additions
63.4 × 48.5 cm (25 × 19⅛ in.)
THE NATIONAL GALLERY, LONDON

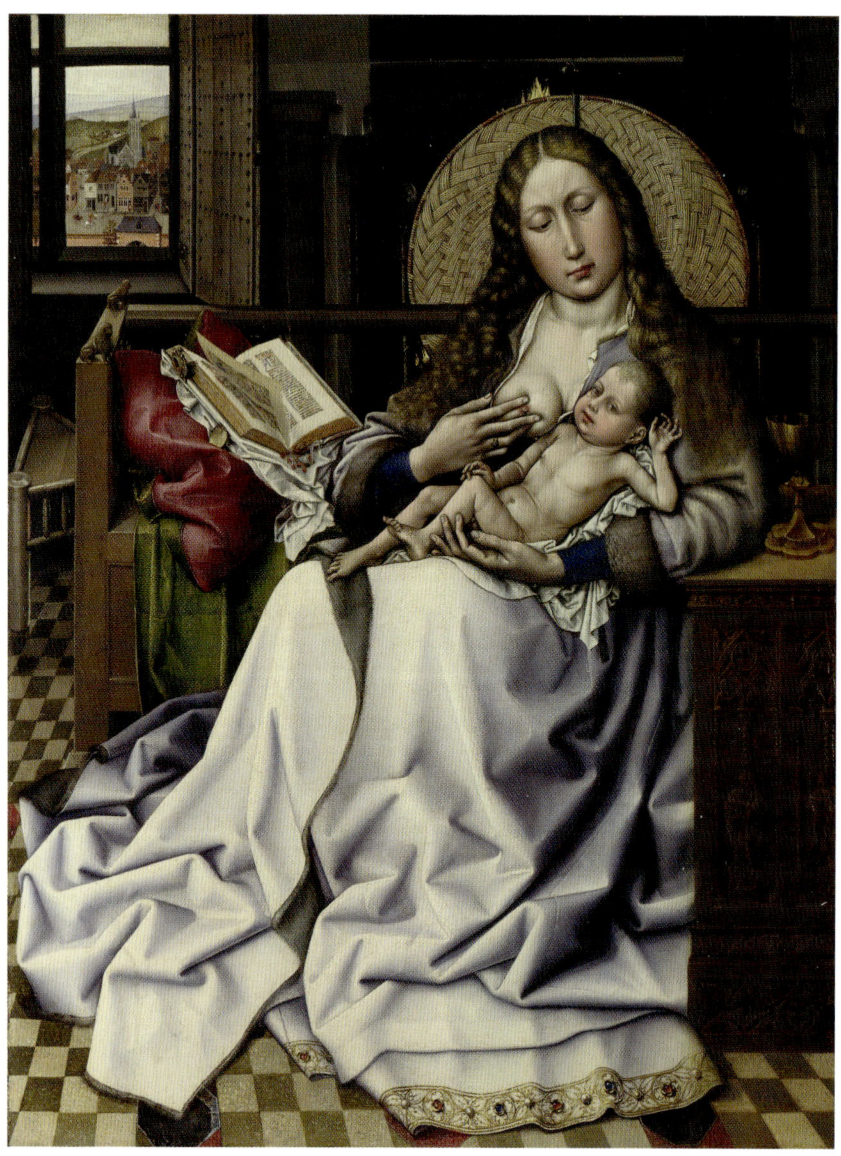

The worldly reality visible through the window in this panel (see detail, opposite) has two functions: it creates a contrast with the enclosed space around the Virgin and Child, while also establishing a connection between the subject and the patron's everyday life. The elaborate walled cityscape depicted by the artist includes a church with Gothic tracery and prosperous brick and half-timbered houses, themselves expensively glazed. The scene is animated by tiny figures riding, walking, talking through windows and even climbing a ladder.

The inclusion of the window also allowed the artist to indulge his skill with oil paint, with which he created atmospheric effects in the far distance as well as delicate variations of tone and convincing representations of different materials. This is especially remarkable in the representation of the shutters and their metal hinges and nails; even the stains on the wood are conveyed with astonishing realism.

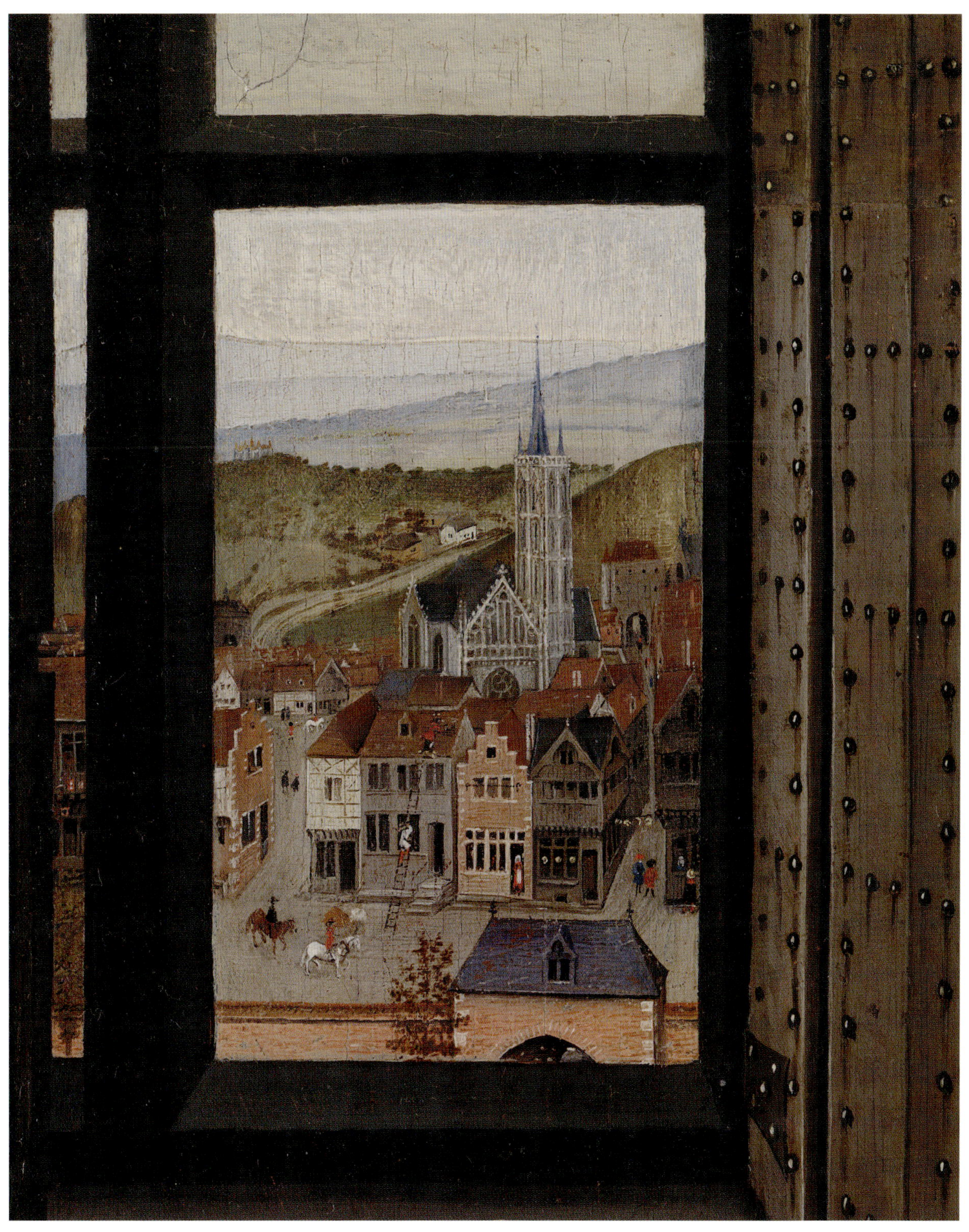

Hubert van Eyck

(c. 1385/90–1426)

Jan van Eyck

(c. 1395–1441)

The Ghent Altarpiece, with wings closed

c. 1423–32
Oil on panel
351 × 229 cm (138¼ × 90⅛ in.)
ST BAVO, GHENT

When its wings are closed, the celebrated Ghent Altarpiece displays in its middle register an image of the Annunciation set inside a contemporary room. Certain interior details, such as the lavabo (a basin used for ritual washing) in the third panel from the left, symbolize the Virgin's purity, in contrast to the worldly view framed by the central window (see detail, right). In this cityscape, half-timbered gabled houses with projecting upper storeys are balanced by an embattled stone structure, adorned with blind tracery, on the right. In the distance, a spire with a weathervane and a circular tower complete the architectural ensemble, while wheeling and roosting birds make the scene even more vivid.

Hubert van Eyck originally decorated the Annunciation panels with traceried stone arches similar to those that appear in the lowest section of the closed altarpiece. These were then painted over by Hubert's brother Jan, who covered them with the brilliant naturalistic composition visible today.

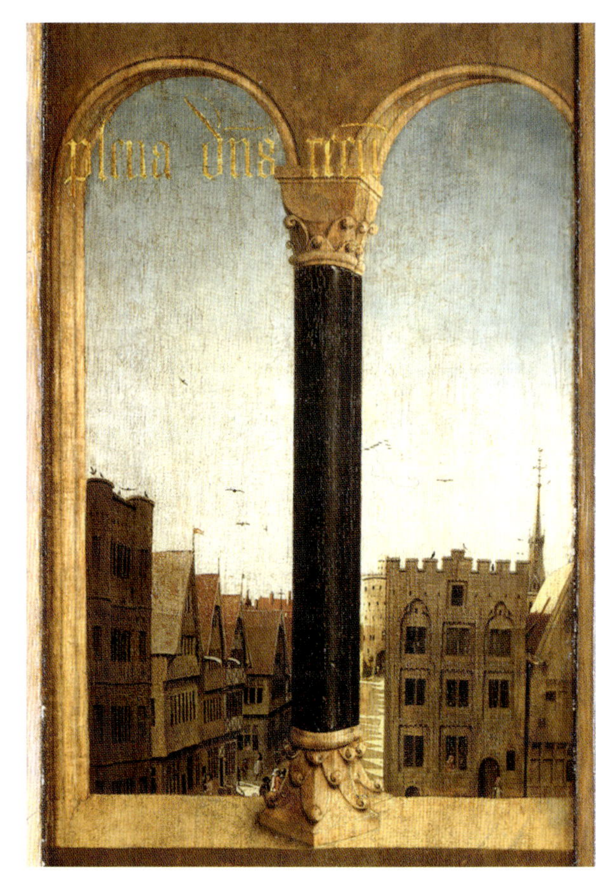

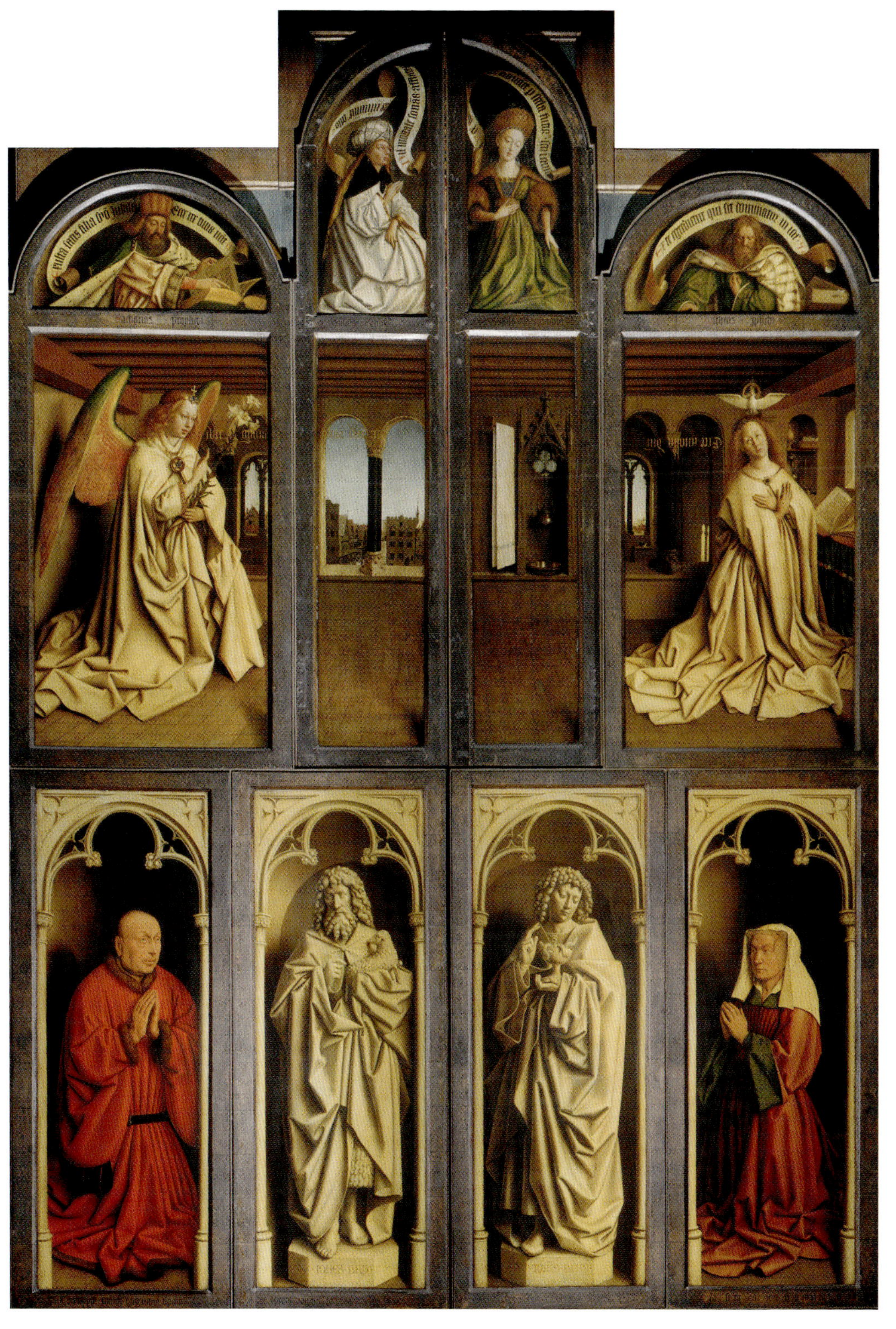

Andrea Mantegna

(1430/31–1506)

The Death of the Virgin

c. 1462
Tempera and gold on wood
54.5 × 42 cm (21½ × 16½ in.)
MUSEO NACIONAL DEL PRADO, MADRID

The Virgin Mary's funeral rites, led by St Peter while another apostle censes her body, are conducted in a classical chamber (the vault of which appears in a fragment held by the Pinacoteca Nazionale in Ferrara). The view is equally magnificent, representing the lake around Mantua and the bridge of San Giorgio, as seen from the castle of the work's patron, Ludovico II Gonzaga, Marquis of Mantua. Early seventeenth-century paintings also show the bridge with the roof and tower, before they were damaged in 1630.

The importance of the landscape, set beneath an impressive cloudy sky, is emphasized not only by its heroic scale but also by the orthogonals in the foreground, which lead towards a high vanishing point at the far end of the bridge. By such means the high solemnities of the Virgin's death are grounded in the contemporary reality of the painting's maker and patron, and their city.

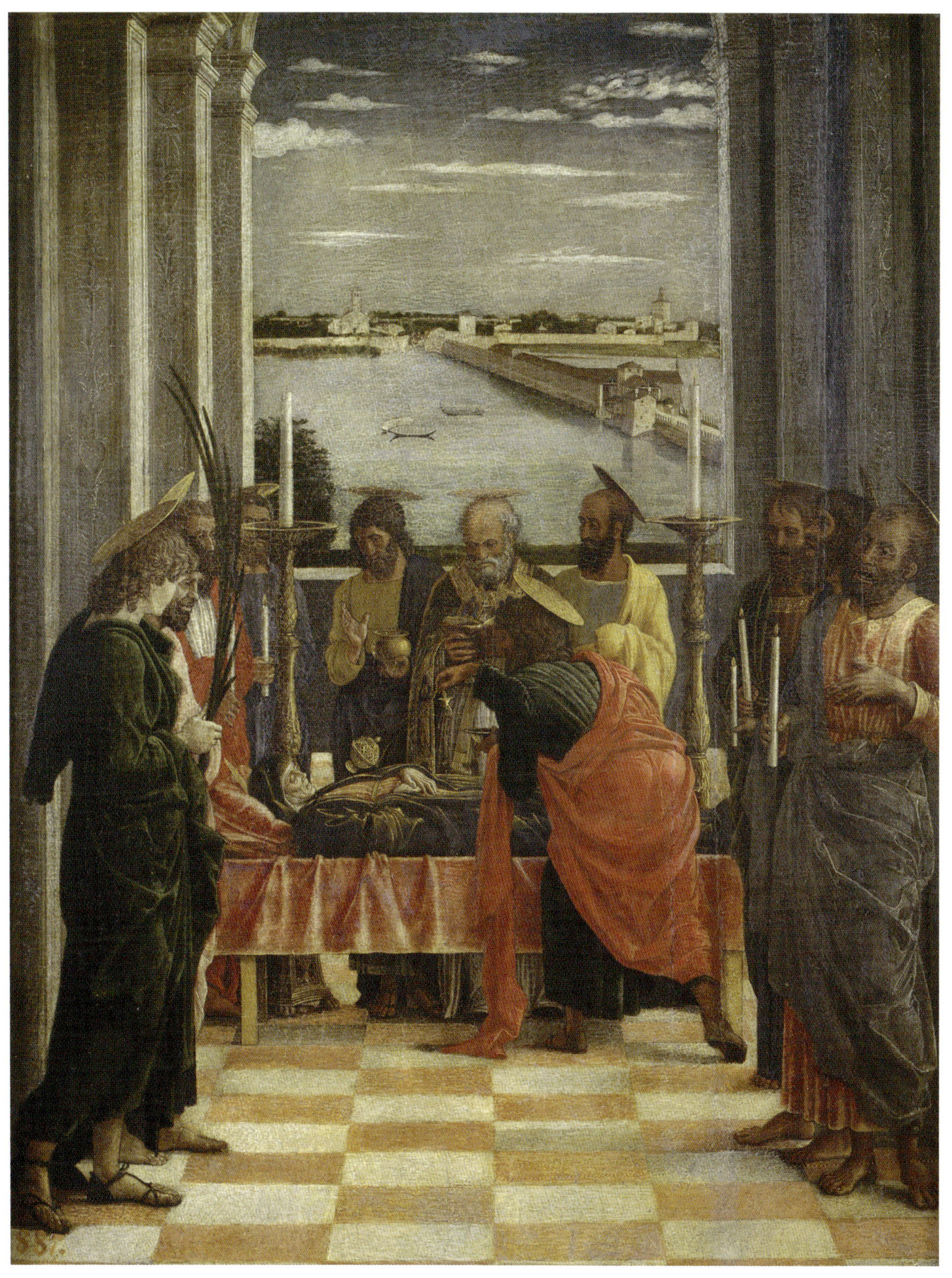

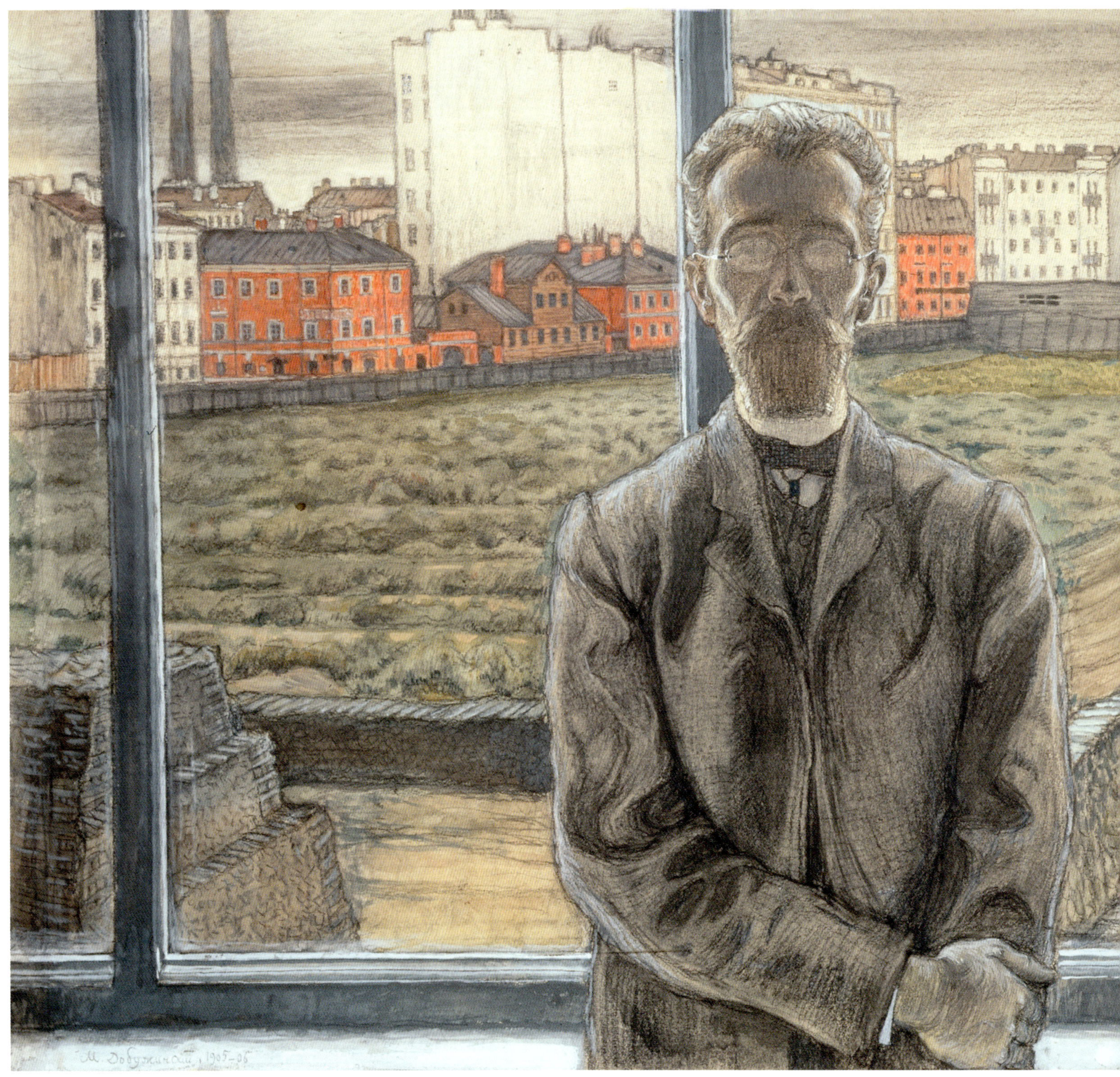

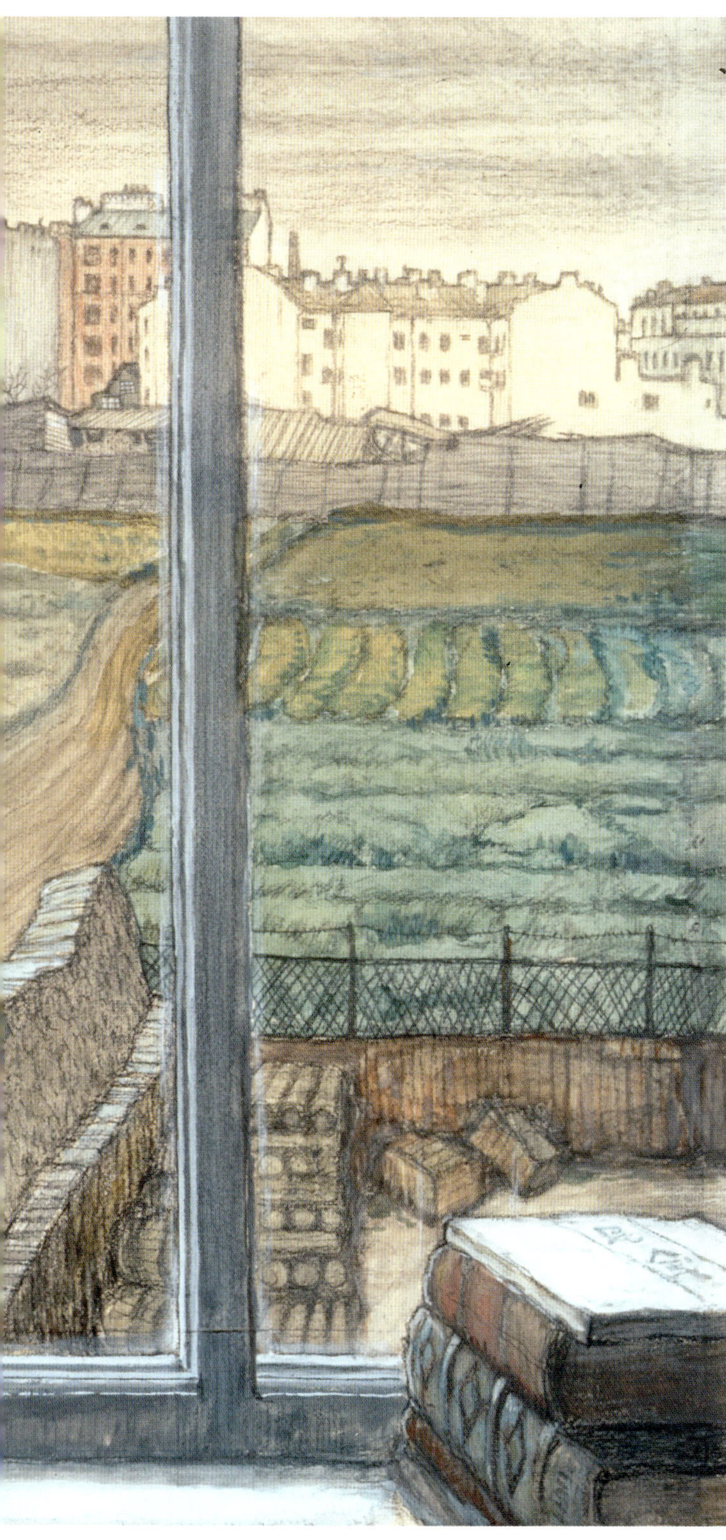

Mstislav Dobuzhinsky

(1875–1957)

Man in Glasses

1905–1906
Charcoal and watercolour on paper mounted on cardboard
63.3 × 99.6 cm (24⅞ × 39¼ in.)
THE STATE TRETYAKOV GALLERY, MOSCOW

In this portrait of the Russian art critic and poet Constantin Sunnerberg (1871–1942), Mstislav Dobuzhinsky places his compatriot in front of a large, modernist window overlooking an industrialized suburb. Sunnerberg has his back to the scene, and his books and scholarly appearance could be regarded as contrasting with the proletarian landscape behind him. Nonetheless, foreground and background are tied together by their colours and composition. The verticals of the window frame correspond with the lines of the chimneys and other buildings, while cool hues interspersed with flashes of brightness recur throughout the picture. Sunnerberg's study is in harmony with its surroundings, and the life of the mind and the world of labour are shown to be complementary rather than mutually exclusive.

Ambrogio Lorenzetti

(*fl. c.* 1317–1348)

The Effects of Good Government on Town and Country (detail)

1338–39
Fresco
EAST WALL, SALA DELLA PACE, PALAZZO PUBBLICO, SIENA

A fresco illustrating the effects of good government – accompanied on adjacent walls by allegories of government, both good and bad – is a fitting decoration for the room occupied by the Noveschi, or the Nine, Siena's ruling body from 1287 to 1355. This detail shows a blonde woman looking down from an arched opening at the city's thriving street life, which includes a group of dancers as well as a plethora of commercial activity. In peacetime windows provide rooms with views rather than defensive positions, while elsewhere in the fresco they are places for growing flowers or hanging a birdcage. The vigorous execution of both the arch and the figure reflects the skill with which Ambrogio Lorenzetti practised *buon fresco*, a fresco-painting technique in which the pigments are applied to the plaster while it is still wet, thereby increasing their durability.

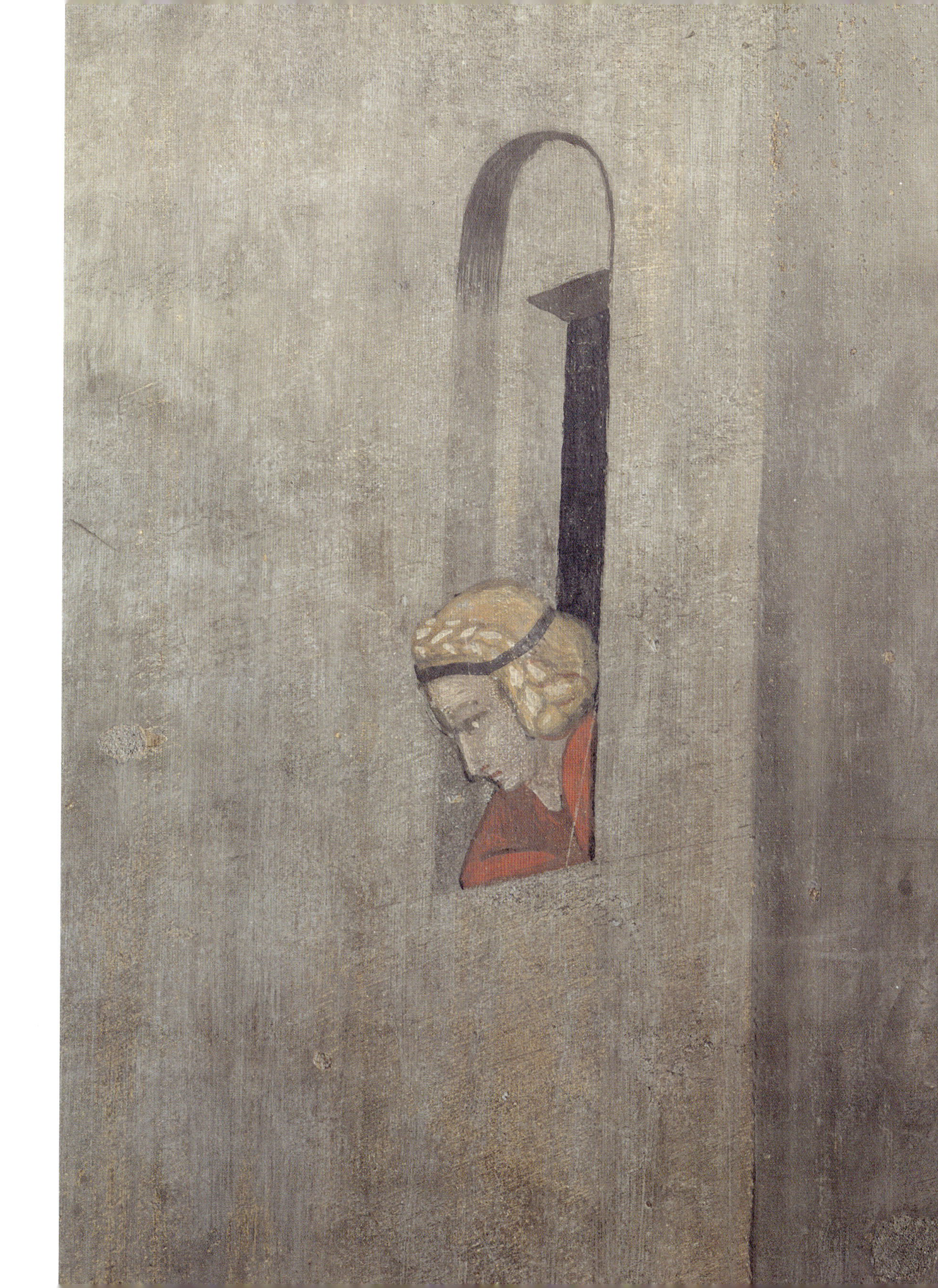

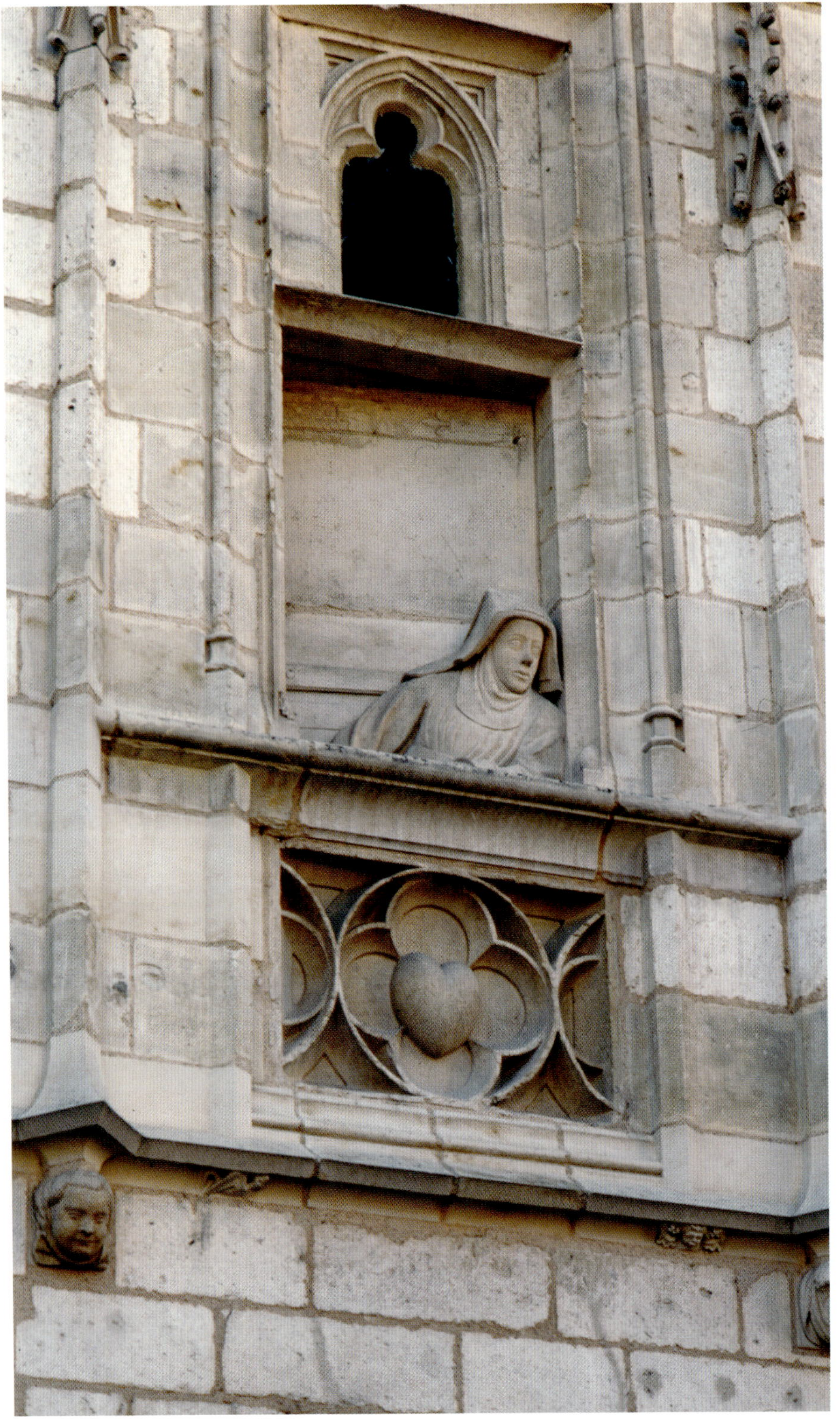

A Woman Looking out of a Window

1443–51
Relief from the entrance pavilion of the
Palais Jacques Cœur, Bourges

The French merchant Jacques Cœur
(*c.* 1395–1456) created a palace in Bourges,
central France, that reflected his ambivalent
status as a powerful man of common birth.
Its inner, west range resembles a feudal castle,
but its east-facing street façade is more austere,
with a square entrance pavilion surmounted by
a chapel. As well as bearing Cœur's emblems,
this structure is adorned, on its first floor, with
sculpted figures of a man and a woman leaning
out of false windows. As this image shows, the
effect, when seen from the street, is highly
engaging and illusionistic.

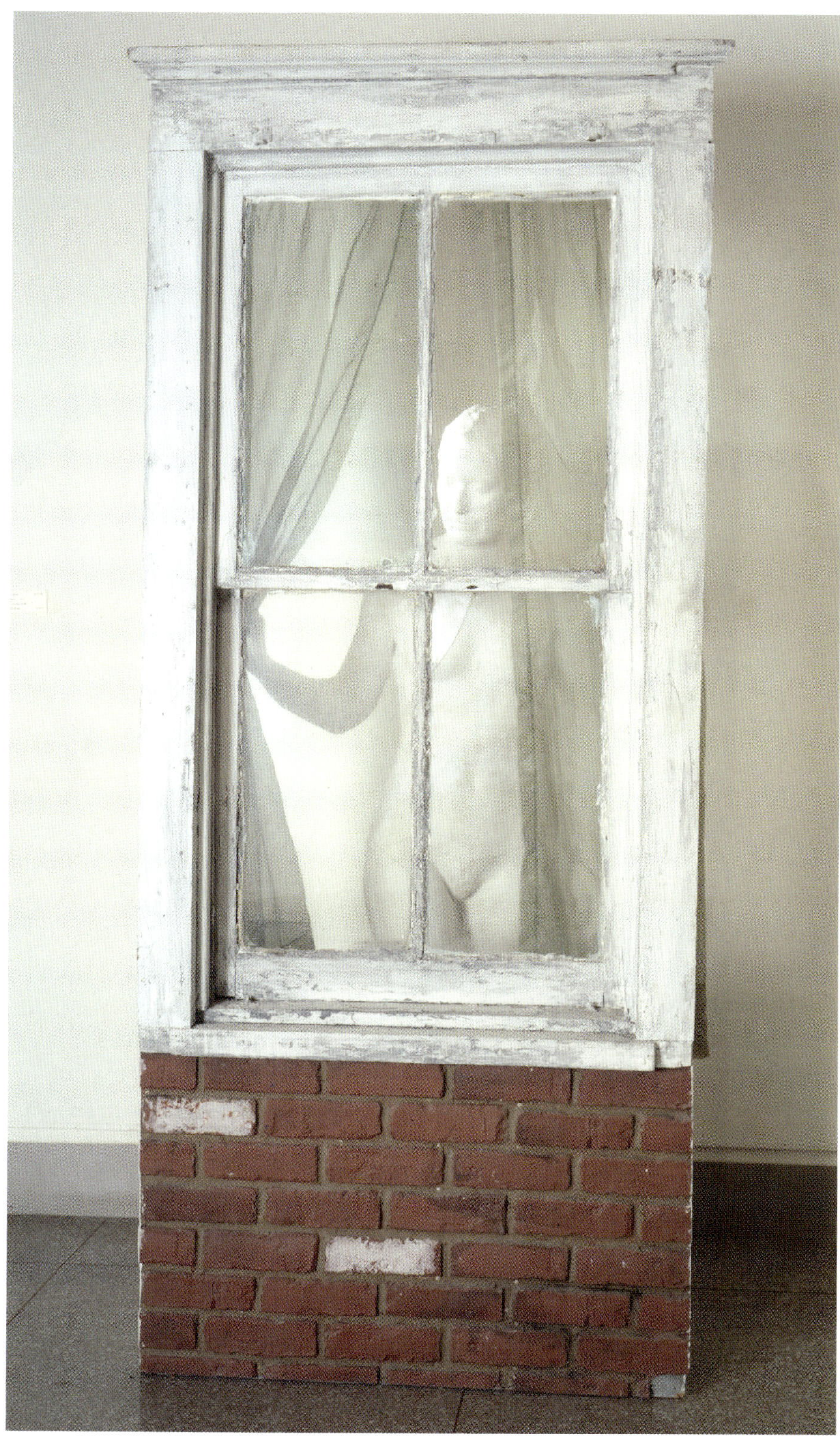

George Segal

(1924–2000)

The Curtain

1974
Plaster, glass and painted wood
214.6 × 99.7 × 90.2 cm (84½ × 39¼ × 35½ in.)
SMITHSONIAN AMERICAN ART MUSEUM, WASHINGTON, D.C.

The American artist and chicken farmer George Segal created this eerie, provocative sculpture from a plaster cast of the human body. The window emphasizes the voyeuristic element of the work, as well as defining the space around the woman. As in other instances of illusionism (see, for example, opposite), the figure has an ambivalent position, to some extent sharing the viewer's reality while also remaining distinct from it. In this case, the effect is made more piquant by the work's immediacy, its potential to be perused closely from numerous angles.

Gerrit Dou

(1613–1675)

Old Woman with Jug at a Window

c. 1660–65
Oil on panel
28.3 × 22.8 cm (11⅛ × 9 in.)
KUNSTHISTORISCHES MUSEUM, VIENNA

In this much-copied painting, the figure of the woman, who glances to her right as she bends forward to water her flowers, seems to be entering the viewer's space. The effect is enhanced by the presence of the arch, one of the favourite motifs of the Dutch artist Gerrit Dou; indeed, the same feature appears in another picture of an elderly woman by Dou, *Old Woman at a Half-Door* (*c*. 1660–65; Museo Civico d'Arte Antica, Milan), which may have been created as a pendant to this panel.

Tending a plant is an activity that seems appropriate to a virtuous old age, although it has also been suggested that the white flowers and empty birdcage are references to lost innocence. Whatever the intended significance, the search for meaning reminds us that, in art, the voyeur is actually the object of scrutiny.

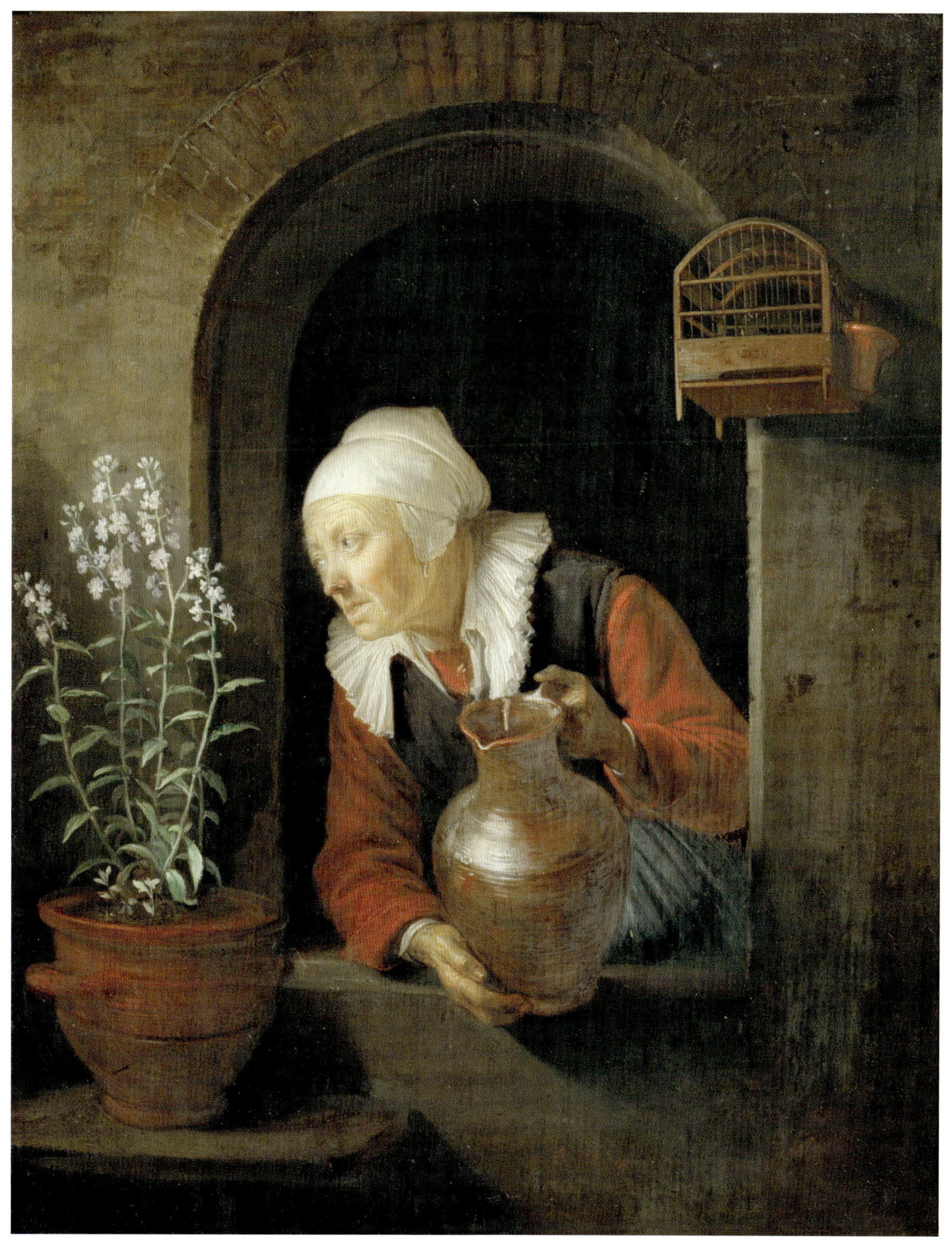

Banksy
(born ?1974)

Graffiti in Park Street, Bristol

2006
Stencil on wall

Banksy's provocative image – once again, who
exactly is the voyeur here? – can be found high
up on an otherwise featureless wall in one of
Bristol's most attractive streets. (It is not an
accident that the window is an elegant sash.)
This bold, stencilled scene cannot really be said
to be illusionistic, as it is so obviously a bit of
a joke; nor is it a typical piece of graffiti, since
it is clearly the work of a professional. In fact,
it has quickly become an accepted part of the
city's landscape. As Banksy has put it, 'People
look at an oil painting and admire the use
of brushstrokes … People look at a graffiti
painting and admire the use of a drainpipe.'[2]
The mystery of how the artist was able to gain
access, and get away with it, is undoubtedly
part of the appeal.

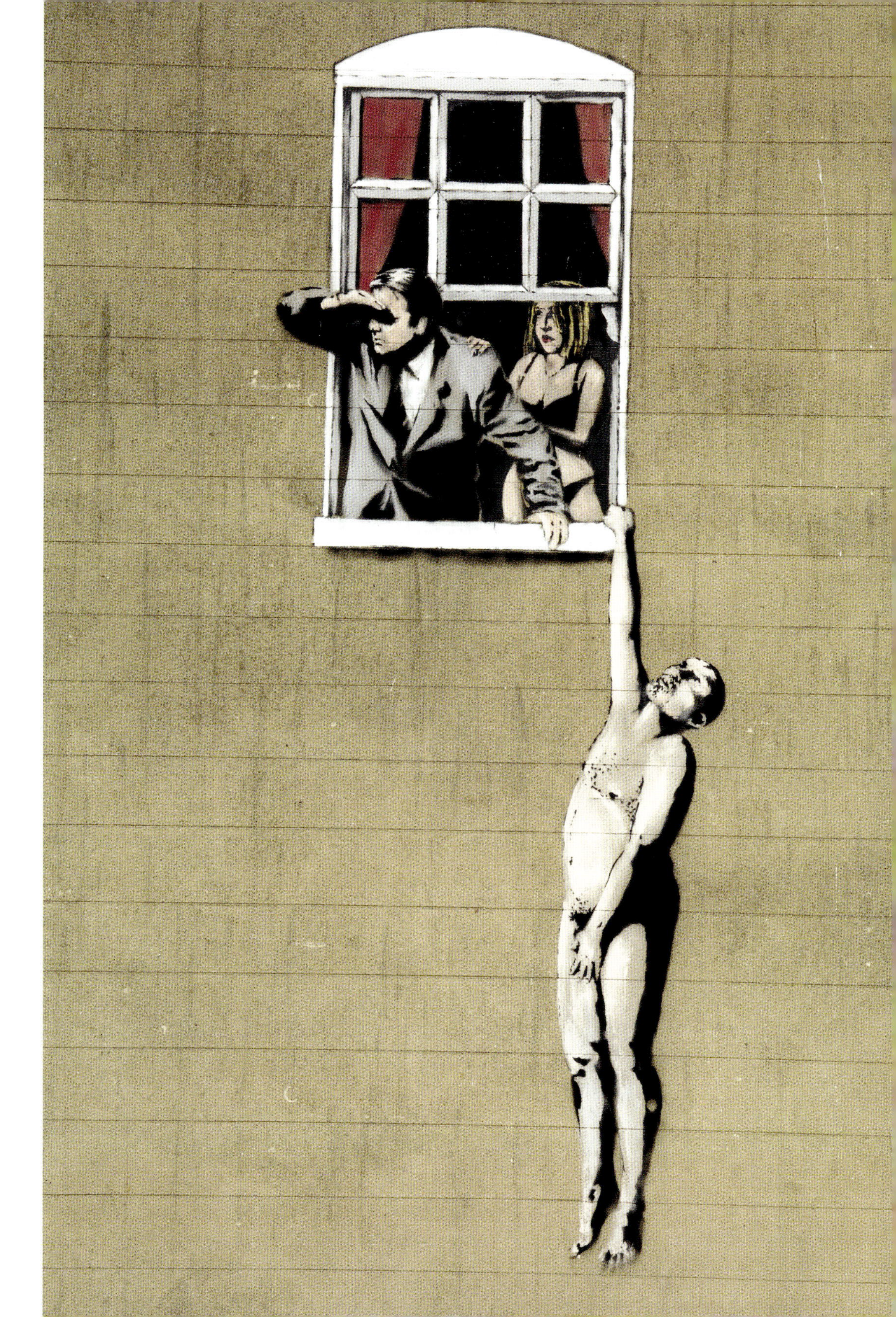

Berthe Morisot
(1841–1895)

Interior, Isle of Wight

1875
Oil on canvas
38 × 46 cm (15 × 18⅛ in.)
MUSÉE MARMOTTAN MONET, PARIS

When the Impressionist Berthe Morisot and her family stayed on the Isle of Wight in 1875, she wrote a letter to her sister Edma in which she explained that the view from her window was 'pretty to look at, but not to paint'.[3] Consequently, she has reduced the yachts in the far distance to mere patches of colour, emphasizing instead the domestic aspects of the scene. In the foreground Morisot's husband, Eugène Manet, the brother of the artist Edouard Manet, sits in an informal pose as he peers around the semi-transparent curtains. He seems happy to be protected from too much public exposure, while we are given only a glimpse of the activity outside.

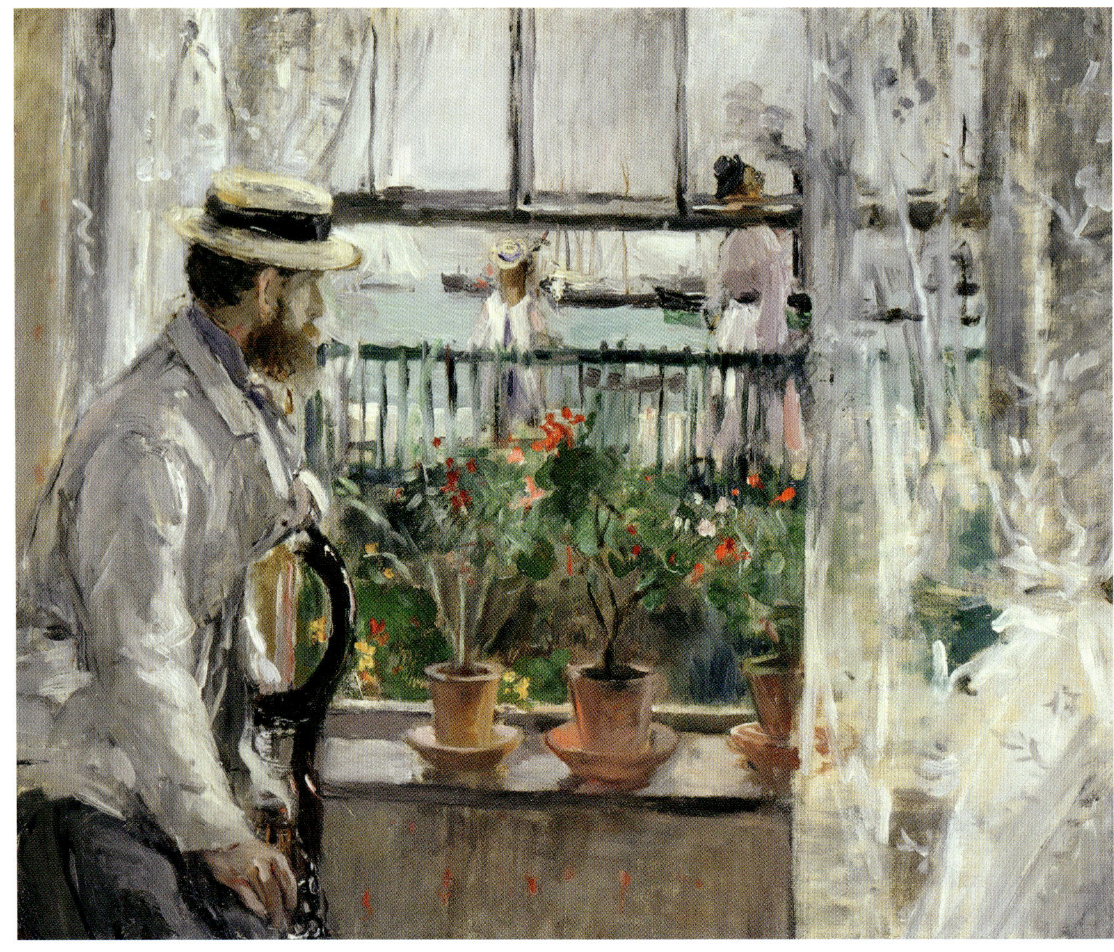

Carl Bloch
(1834–1890)

After the Bath: A Young Girl Knocking at the Fisherman's Window

1884
Oil on panel
45.5 × 32.5 cm (17⅞ × 12¾ in.)
STATENS MUSEUM FOR KUNST, COPENHAGEN

Here, the Danish painter Carl Bloch has transformed the viewer into the inhabitant of a fisherman's cottage and the object of attention of a young girl, who was probably the artist's daughter. The relationship between subject and viewer is made reciprocal, and domestic privacy is shattered. A window has become something to be looked into rather than out of, to be tapped as well as peered through, and the medium for the most direct form of communication between people of different social classes: it is remarkable how revolutionary a slightly saccharine genre picture can be. It is also striking how Bloch uses an extreme range of tones and colours, contrasting the dark interior with the still life and the seascape.

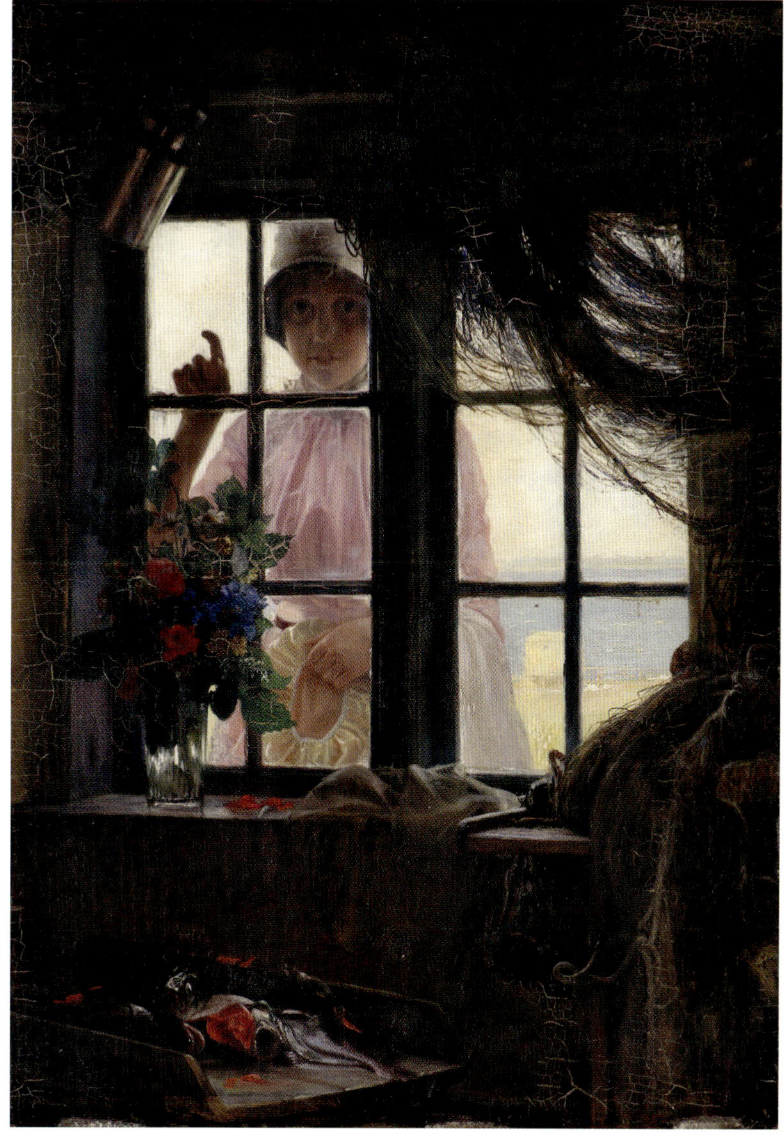

Gustave Caillebotte

(1848–1894)

Interior, Woman at the Window

1880
Oil on canvas
116 × 89 cm (45⅝ × 35 in.)
PRIVATE COLLECTION

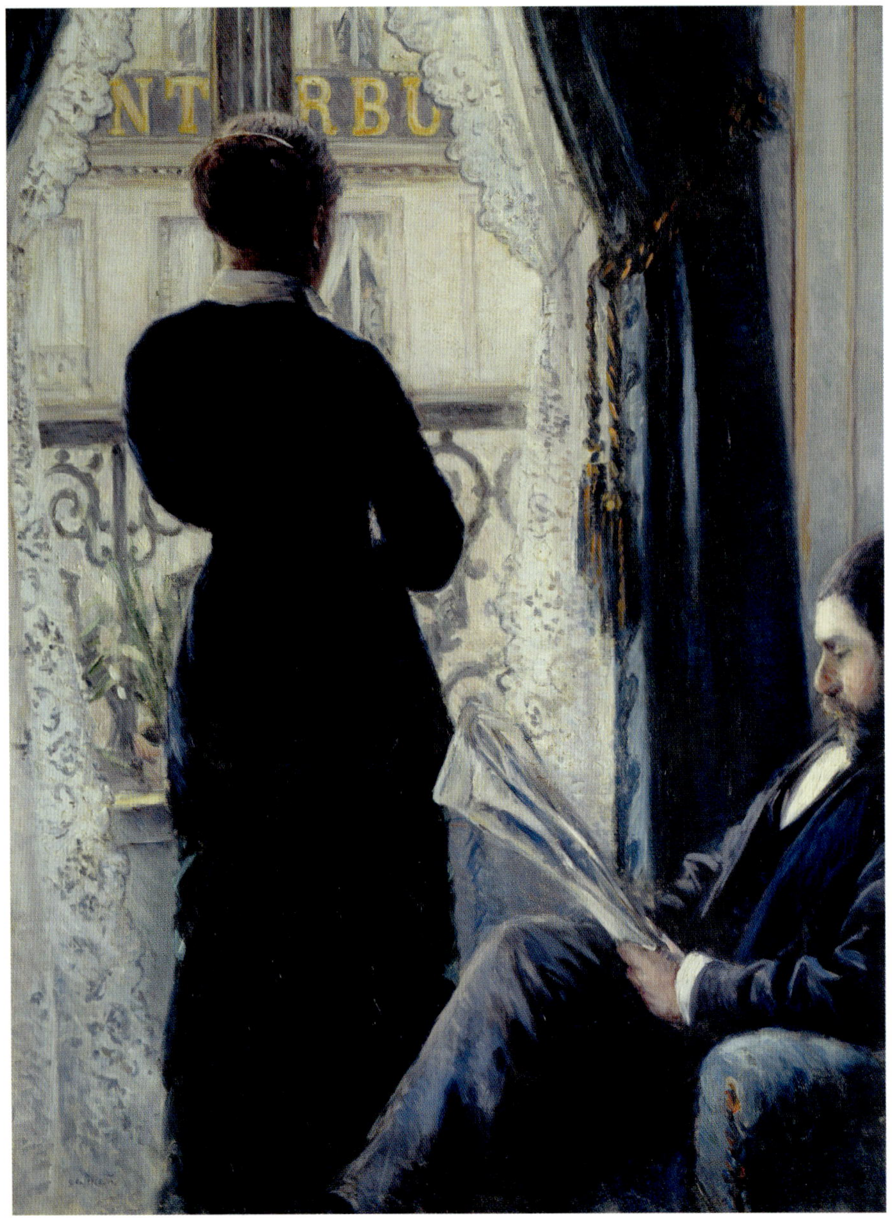

The Impressionist Gustave Caillebotte has
created a remarkable sense of constraint in
a painting exploring stereotypes of gender.
A street sign on the building opposite is reduced
to a few letters, and the façade to fragments of
windows. The net curtain and even the balcony
act as visual barriers, and, while the woman
shows discreet interest in the scene outside,
her husband has retired completely into his
newspaper. The paper can be interpreted as a
masculine form of window on the world, while
the curtain-twitching female has an opposite
number, just visible at a window on the other
side of the street.

Man on a Balcony, Boulevard Haussmann

1880
Oil on canvas
116.5 × 89.5 cm (45⅞ × 35¼ in.)
PRIVATE COLLECTION

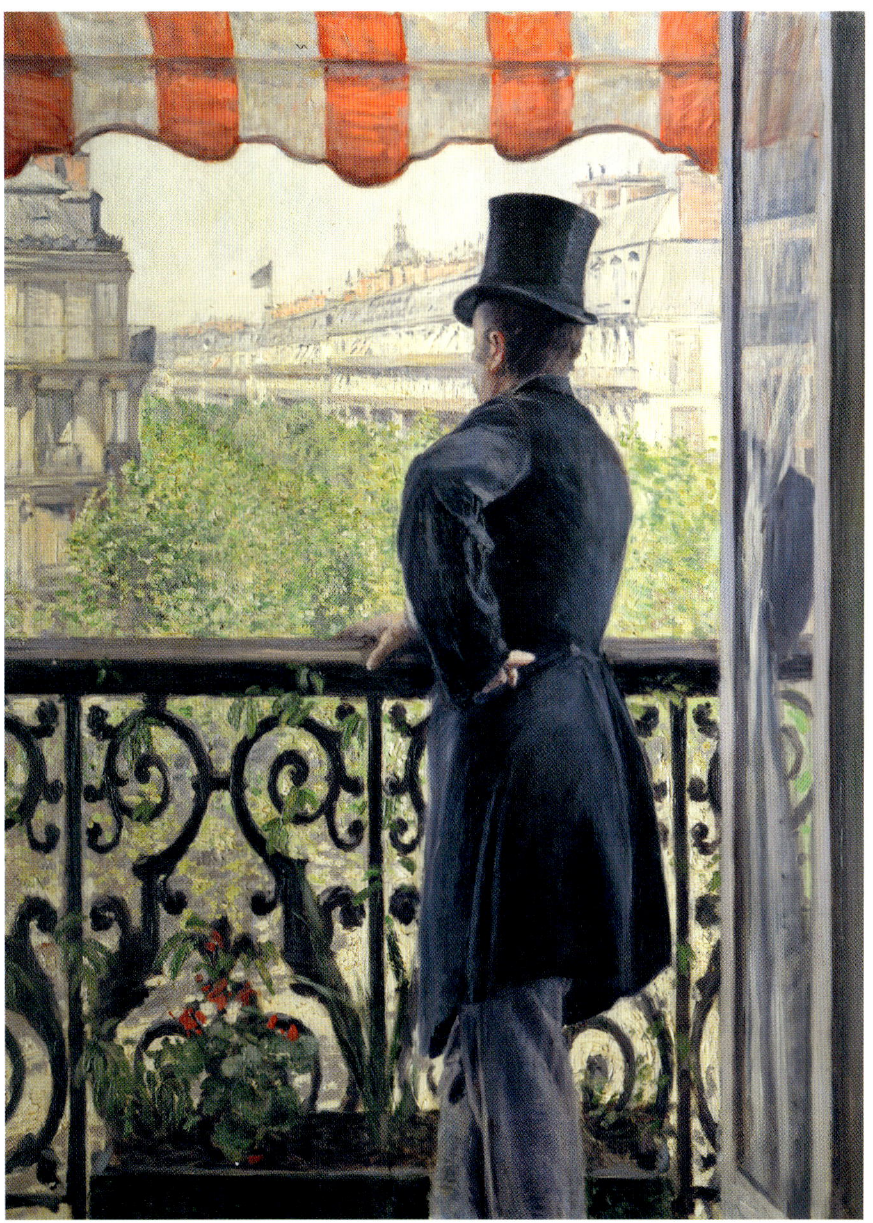

Here, the balcony, with its cheerful awning, is both a vantage point and a place of display. The elegant gentleman, whose figure is partly reflected in the French window, enjoys the spectacle of a Parisian boulevard, even though our view is slightly frustrated by the man's turned head, the railing and its vegetation, and the foliage of the trees. This merely whets our curiosity. The dynamic, slightly twisted pose, not to mention the frock coat and top hat, suggest that we will soon be on the move. This is, after all, a painting of a *flâneur* – the 'stroller', or 'loafer', whose detached observation of the modern city was so memorably described by the poet and critic Charles Baudelaire.

Edward Hopper

(1882–1967)

Night Windows

1928
Oil on canvas
73.7 × 86.4 cm (29 × 34 in.)
THE MUSEUM OF MODERN ART, NEW YORK

Edward Hopper's painting illustrates vividly
how a window, especially at night, is for
looking into as well as out of. Although
something is left to the imagination, the curves
of the woman's body – probably based on those
of Jo Hopper, Edward's wife and principal
model – are emphasized quasi-cinematically by
the billowing curtain. The image reminds us
how windows on the world let in not only
light and prying eyes but also soft breezes and
other harbingers of carnality.

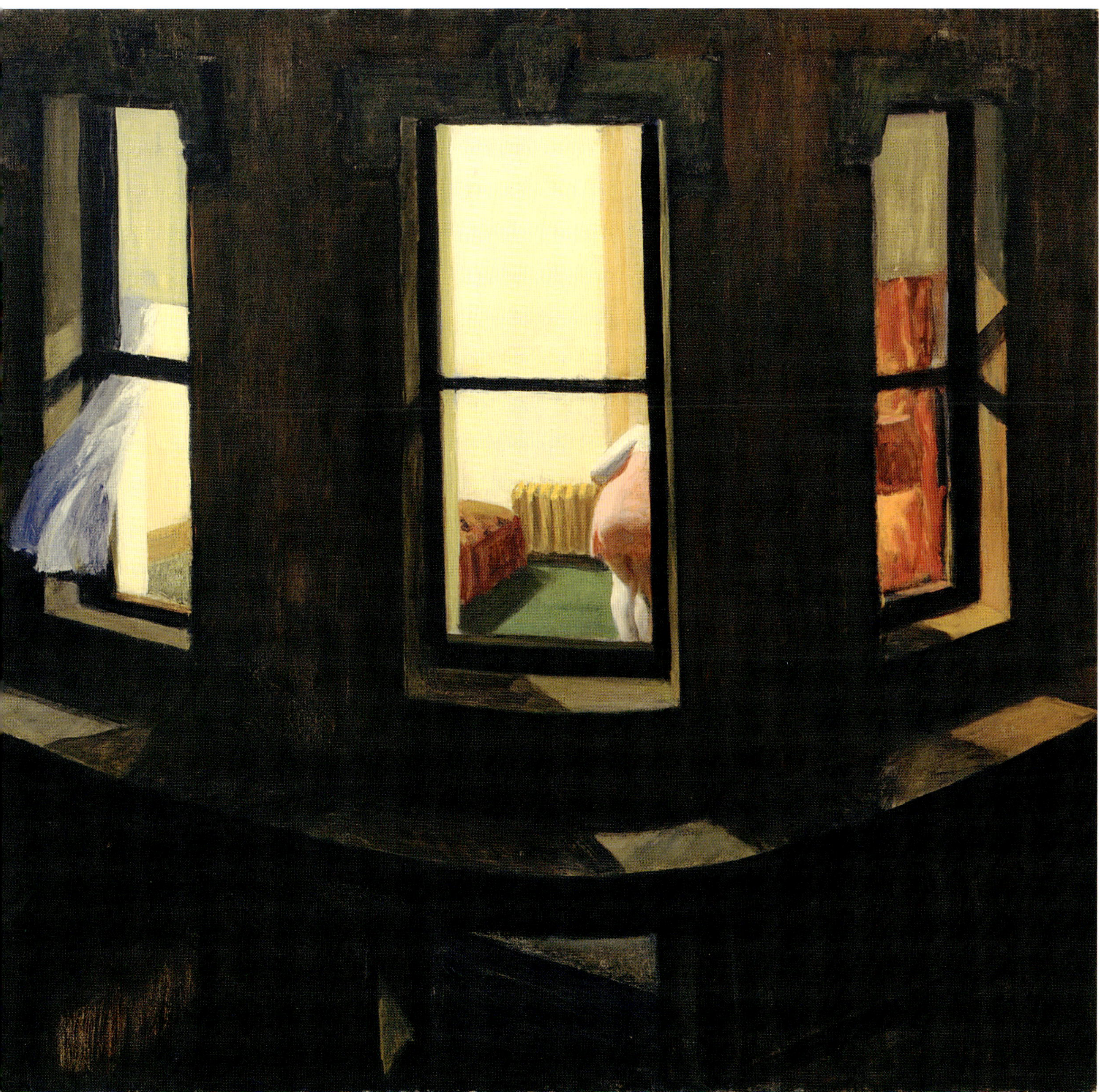

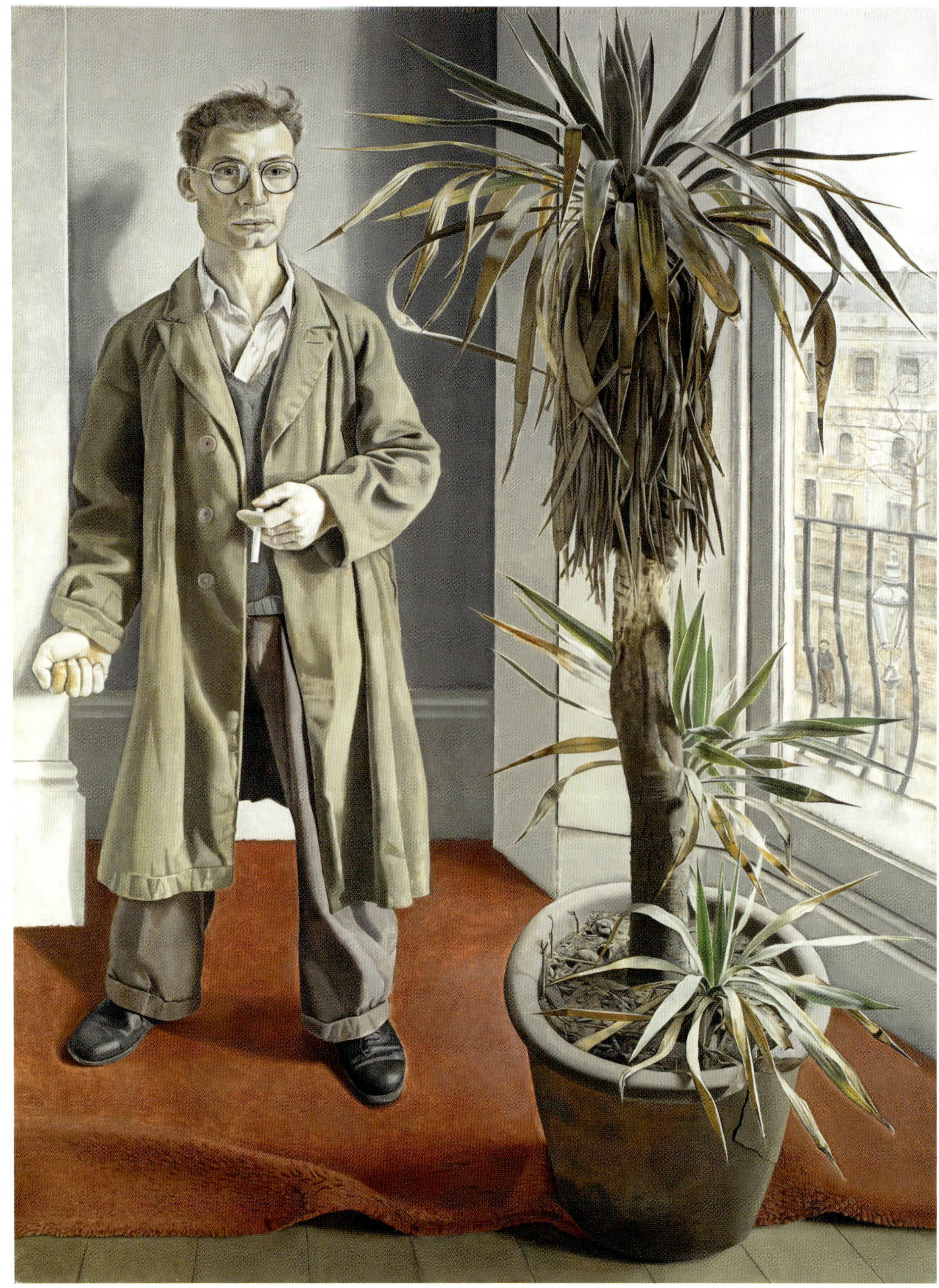

Lucian Freud

(1922–2011)

Interior at Paddington

1951
Oil on canvas
152.4 × 114.3 cm (60 × 45 in.)
WALKER ART GALLERY, LIVERPOOL

This image of a room overlooking the Grand Union Canal in the Paddington area of London was partly inspired by Henri Matisse's paintings of the quai Saint-Michel in Paris. Freud's picture is profoundly disconcerting, despite the fact that its principal subject, the photographer Harry Diamond, was a friend of the artist. A sense of malaise is created by the bristling yucca plant, the man's clenched fist and even his legs, which are clearly far too short for his body. The raincoat introduces an almost tangible chill, while interior and exterior share a prevailing greyness. As if to emphasize that the window provides a view but no protection from the outside world, a boy leaning against a wall is shown staring up at us. The voyeurism perfects the air of menace.

Childe Hassam

(1859–1935)

The Goldfish Window

1916
Oil on canvas
87.3 × 128.6 cm (34⅜ × 50⅝ in.)
CURRIER MUSEUM OF ART, MANCHESTER, NEW HAMPSHIRE

The American Impressionist Childe Hassam was a frequent visitor to the artists' colony at Holley House in Cos Cob, Connecticut, where he began this luminous scene. As if to demonstrate his skill with different genres, the artist has combined a figure, a landscape, an interior and a (nearly) still life.

At first sight, the woman seems at one with her surroundings: her fashionable kimono has the same blueness as the room's reflected light, while the radiance around her head almost resembles a halo. There is, however, a pervasive sense of confinement. The excessive order and balance; the character's sideways gaze and air of withdrawal; the bowl of fish, which seems to have gathered up the colours outside and concentrated them in a tiny sphere, like a microcosm – all these features appear to suggest that although a window may open on to the world, it does not provide a means of easy access or escape.

This image, completed in Hassam's studio after he returned to New York, is part of a sequence in which the artist explored the compositional and expressive opportunities offered by windows, both in the countryside and in Manhattan.

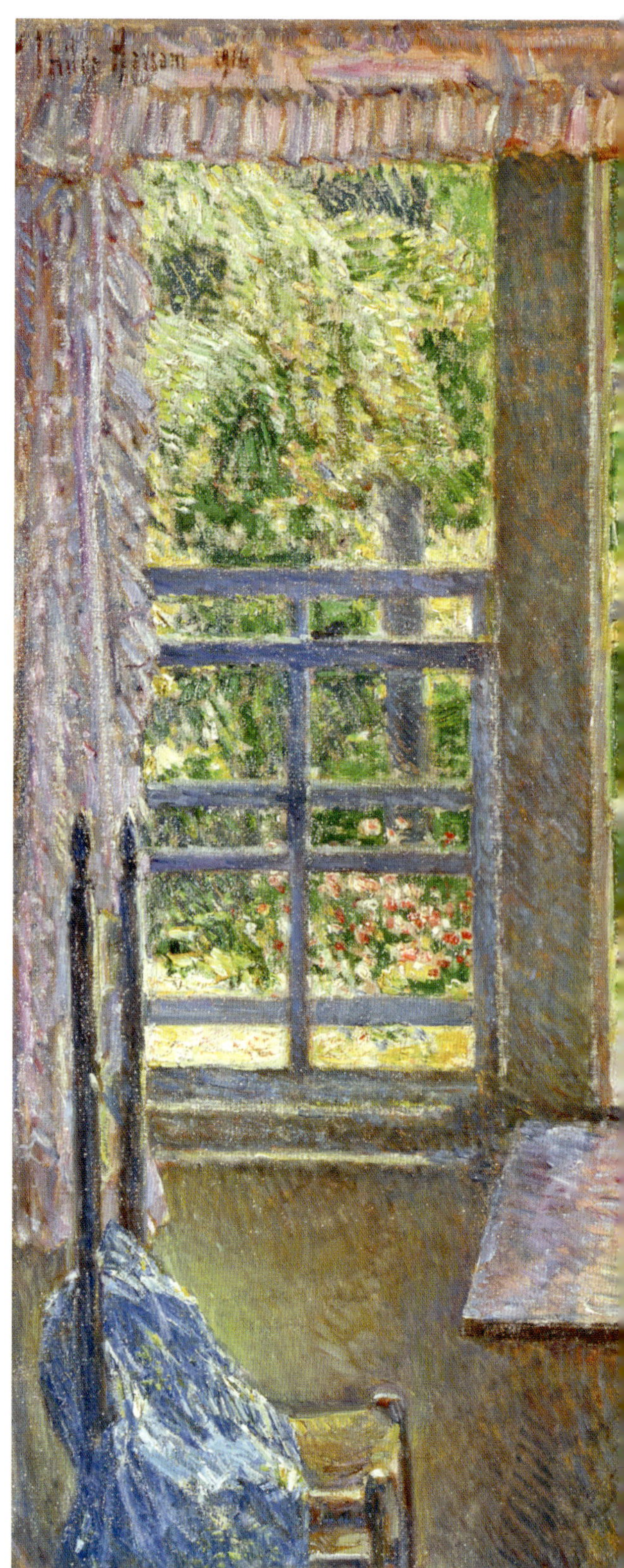

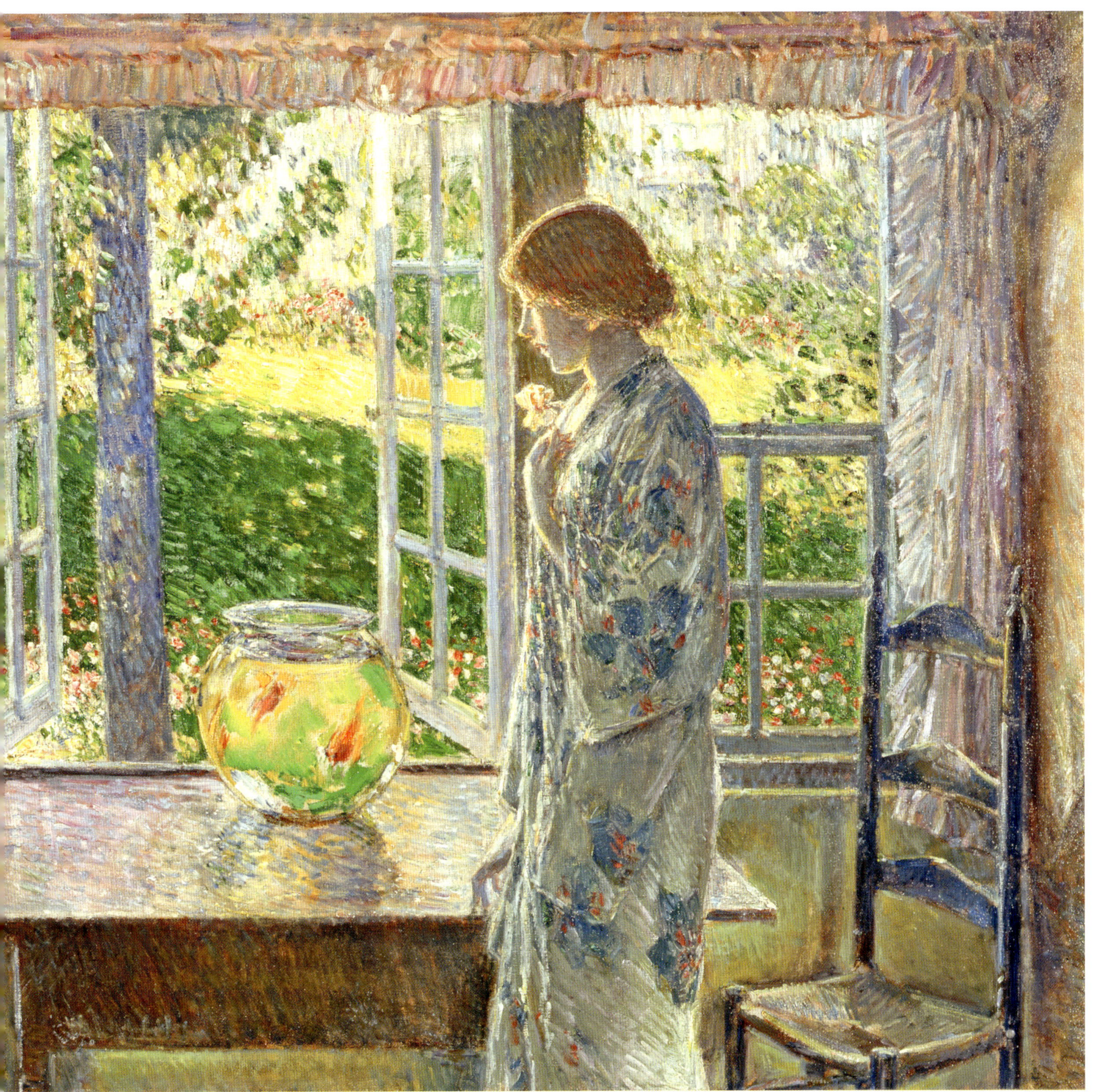

Martinus Rørbye

(1803–1848)

View from the Artist's Window

c. 1825
Oil on canvas
38 × 29 cm (15 × 11⅜ in.)
STATENS MUSEUM FOR KUNST, COPENHAGEN

Martinus Rørbye's view through a casement
window in his parents' house, looking towards
the port of Copenhagen, presents a programme
of his past and future life. The phases of his
personal development are symbolized by the
plants in front of the window, which range
from a seed and a cutting to a flourishing
hydrangea, as well as by the distant naval
ships, shown in various stages of construction.
The restrictions of domesticity are evoked by
the birdcage and the mirror reflecting the
curtain, which stand in contrast to the enticing
prospect of the sea.

The artist was only twenty-two when he
made this picture. Within a few years he had
begun his travels, which took him as far afield
as Greece and Turkey and inspired much of
his painting.

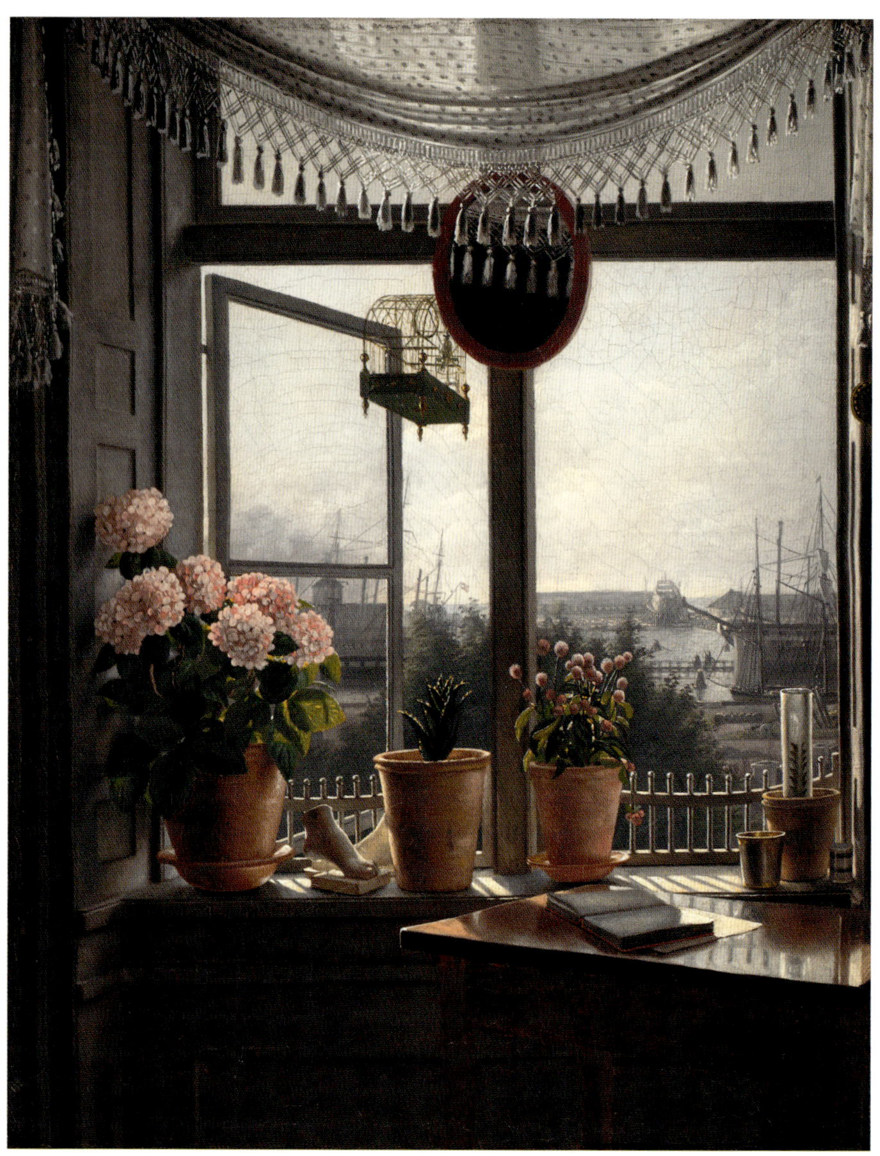

Caspar David Friedrich

(1774–1840)

Window with a View of a Park

1836–37
Graphite and sepia on paper
39.8 × 30.5 cm (15⅝ × 12 in.)
THE STATE HERMITAGE MUSEUM, ST PETERSBURG

This sepia drawing by the German Romantic painter Caspar David Friedrich, whom Martinus Rørbye (opposite) greatly admired, certainly does not present the landscape as a place of release. Not only is the window partly shuttered and firmly closed, but also the grid formed by the bars encloses and flattens the park outside. The two-dimensionality is also emphasized by the correspondence between the vertical lines of the poplar and the larger of the two plants on the ledge. Instead of contrasting the inner and outer worlds, the artist has used the window to impose a distinctive image of nature: austere, drained of colour and abstracted from everyday reality. This is perhaps unsurprising, since the picture was made when Friedrich was an invalid, staying in the spa town of Teplitz (now Teplice in the Czech Republic) and able to work only with physically undemanding media.

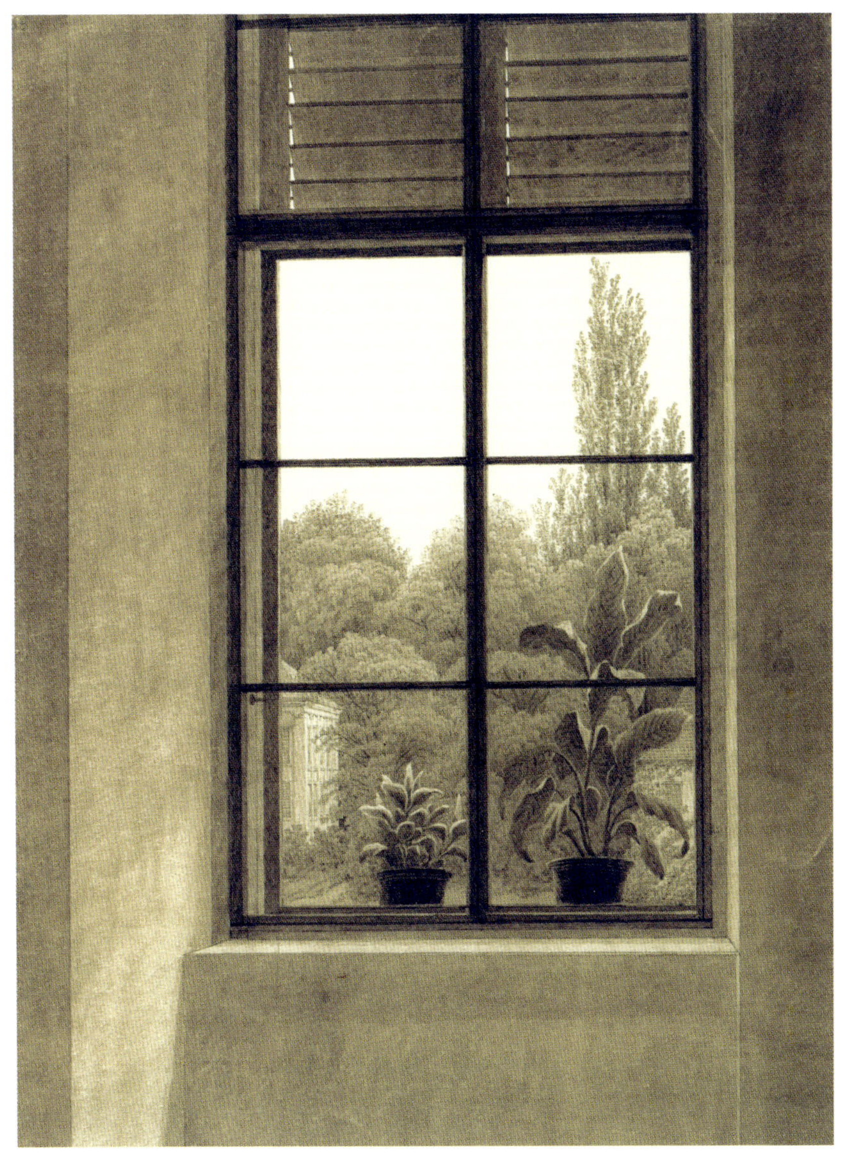

Pierre Bonnard

(1867–1947)

The Open Window

1921
Oil on canvas
118.1 × 95.9 cm (46½ × 37¾ in.)
THE PHILLIPS COLLECTION, WASHINGTON, D.C.

Painted in Vernon, a town in northern France on the banks of the River Seine, this celebrated image has a clear spatial structure defined by crisp lines and the contrast between warm hues and cool, recessive ones. Pierre Bonnard has made striking use of such complementary colours as orange and blue or violet, which enhance the hedonistic mood suggested by the reclining figure in the foreground. The heat is almost tangible as the model, Renée Monchaty, plays lazily with a cat.

Although the inky blind provides a patch of darkness, it is only when we look at the preparatory drawings that we detect an element of tension: Bonnard depicts Maria ('Marthe') Boursin, his long-term mistress, standing over Renée as if she is not entirely welcome. Within five years of the painting's completion Renée was dead, having killed herself less than a month after Bonnard's marriage to Marthe in August 1925. While this knowledge inevitably affects our reaction to the picture, *The Open Window* is primarily a study in light, space and atmosphere, and a brilliant example of Bonnard's mature style.

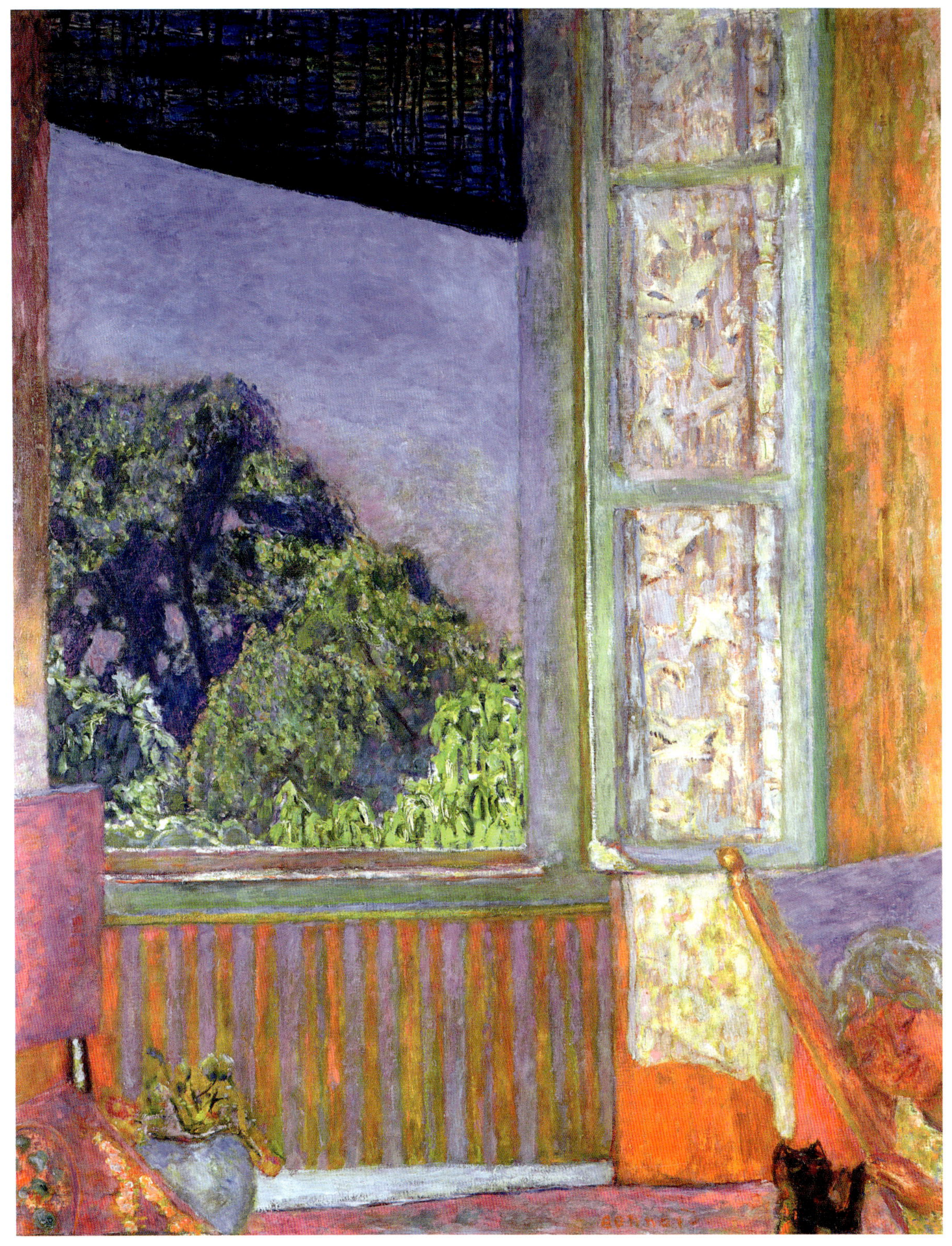

Henri Matisse

(1869–1954)

Open Window, Collioure

1905
Oil on canvas
55.3 × 46 cm (21¼ × 18⅛ in.)
COLLECTION OF MR AND MRS JOHN HAY WHITNEY

This view through a French window at
Collioure, a small town on the Mediterranean
coast of France, is an extravagant assembly of
colours. Matisse has applied luscious spots and
squiggles in such pigments as turquoise and
magenta over a white priming, which remains
visible in places. The patches of thick, impasto
paint represent archetypes of Mediterranean
good living – boats on the water, a balcony with
vines and geraniums – but also emphasize the
material qualities of the picture. This is not
a window in any conventional, illusionistic
sense; rather, it ferociously expresses the
artist's reaction to the sights and experiences
of the South of France. The painting was one
of the works shown at the Salon d'Automne of
1905, an exhibition that famously prompted the
art critic Louis Vauxcelles to describe Matisse
and his fellow artists as *fauves*, or 'wild beasts'.

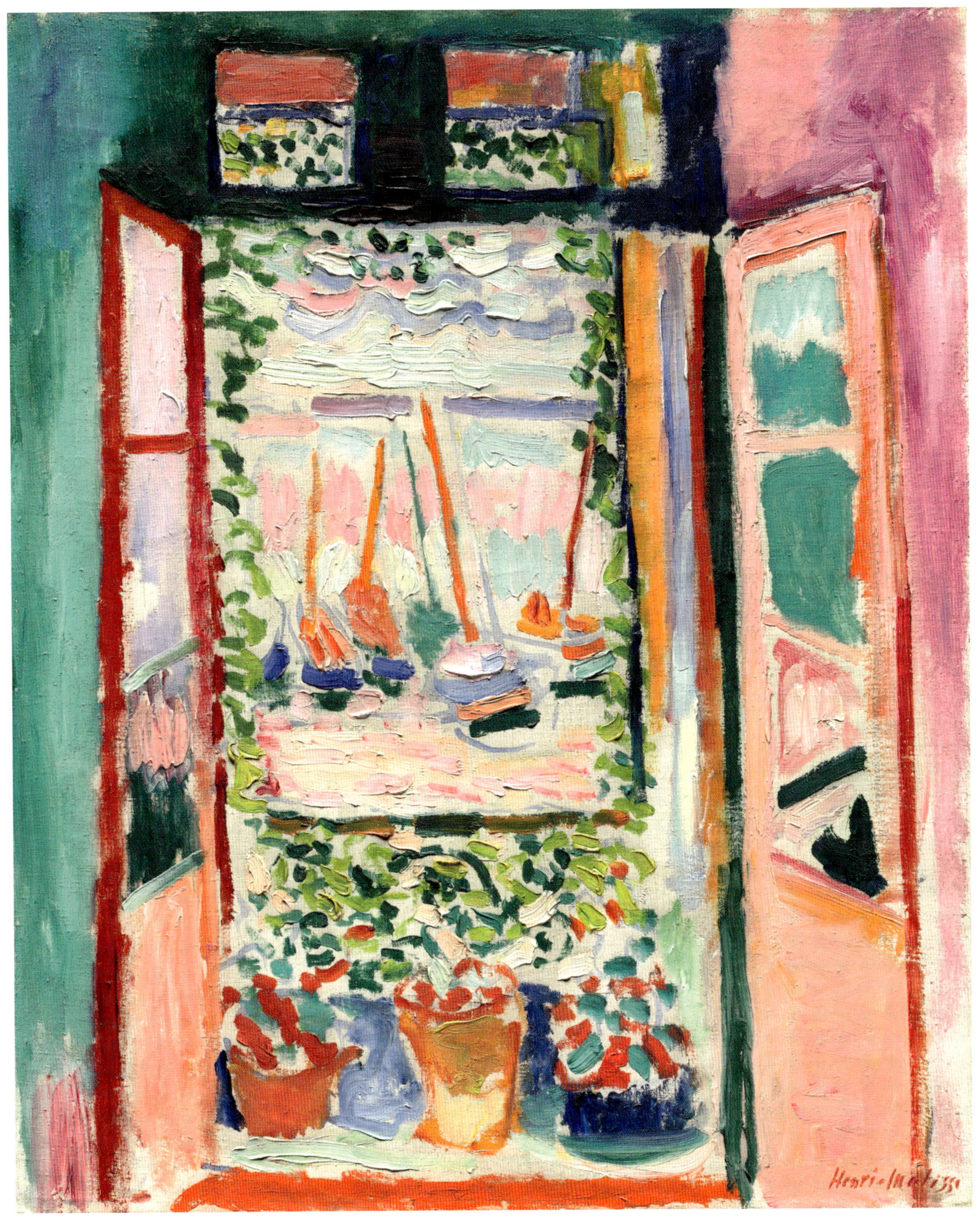

Juan Gris
(1887–1927)

Still Life before an Open Window, Place Ravignan

1915
Oil on canvas
115.9 × 88.9 cm (45⅝ × 35 in.)

Juan Gris's nocturnal **painting** of a window in Montmartre, Paris, is a profoundly ambivalent composition. It is geometric and architectural, but also open and dynamic. It deliberately confuses the distinction between interior and exterior space, between artificial light and darkness, and between positive and negative. It moves from highly abstracted, overlapping planes to easily recognizable features: trees and shutters; an open window with a checked curtain; a wrought-iron balcony; and the familiar components of a still life, a newspaper, a fruit bowl, a bottle and a glass. For all its cubist order and reinvention of pictorial space, it is also a vivid response to a summer's night in Paris, its stillness, warmth and degrees of darkness.

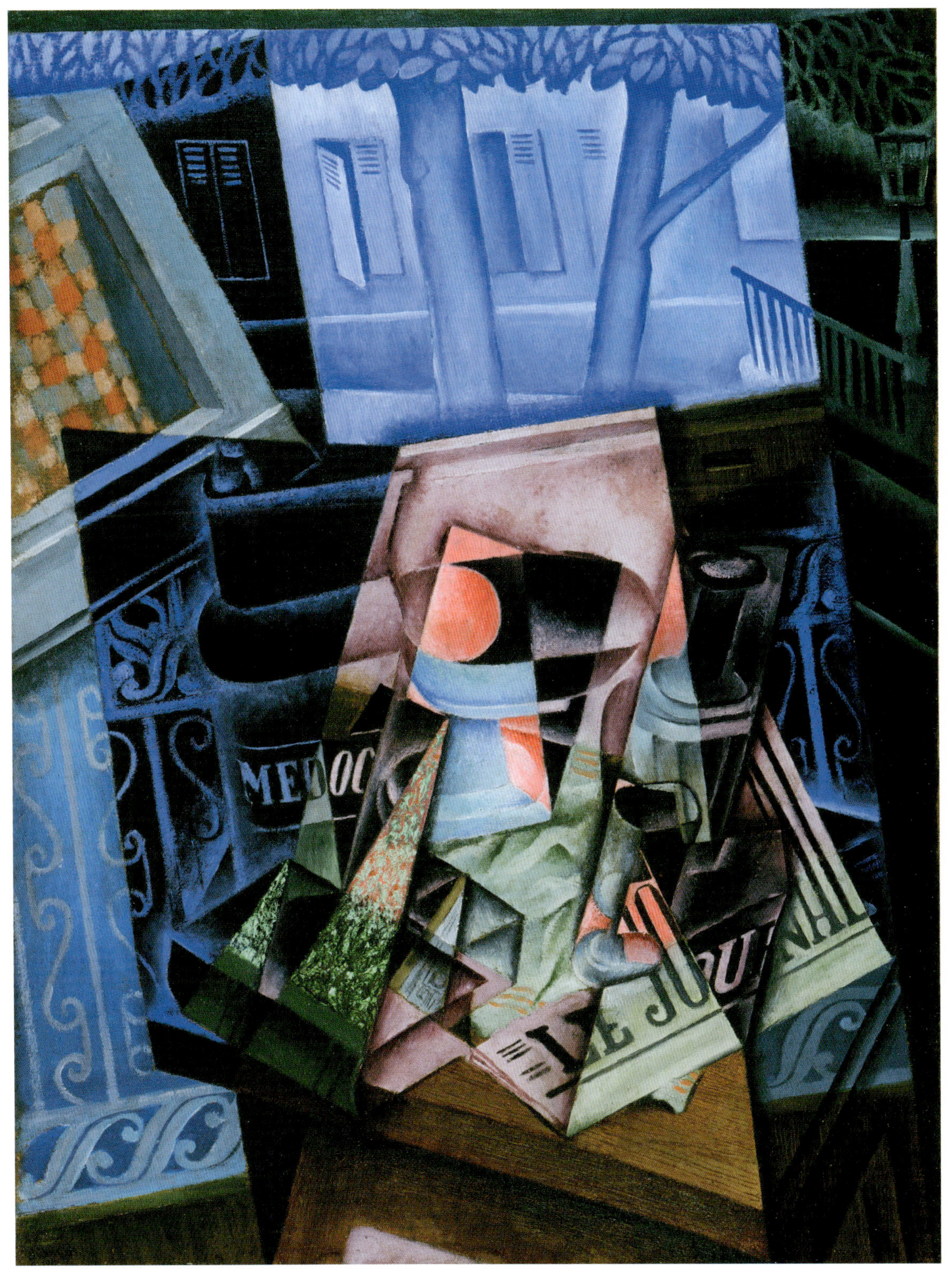

MÉDOC
LE JOURNAL

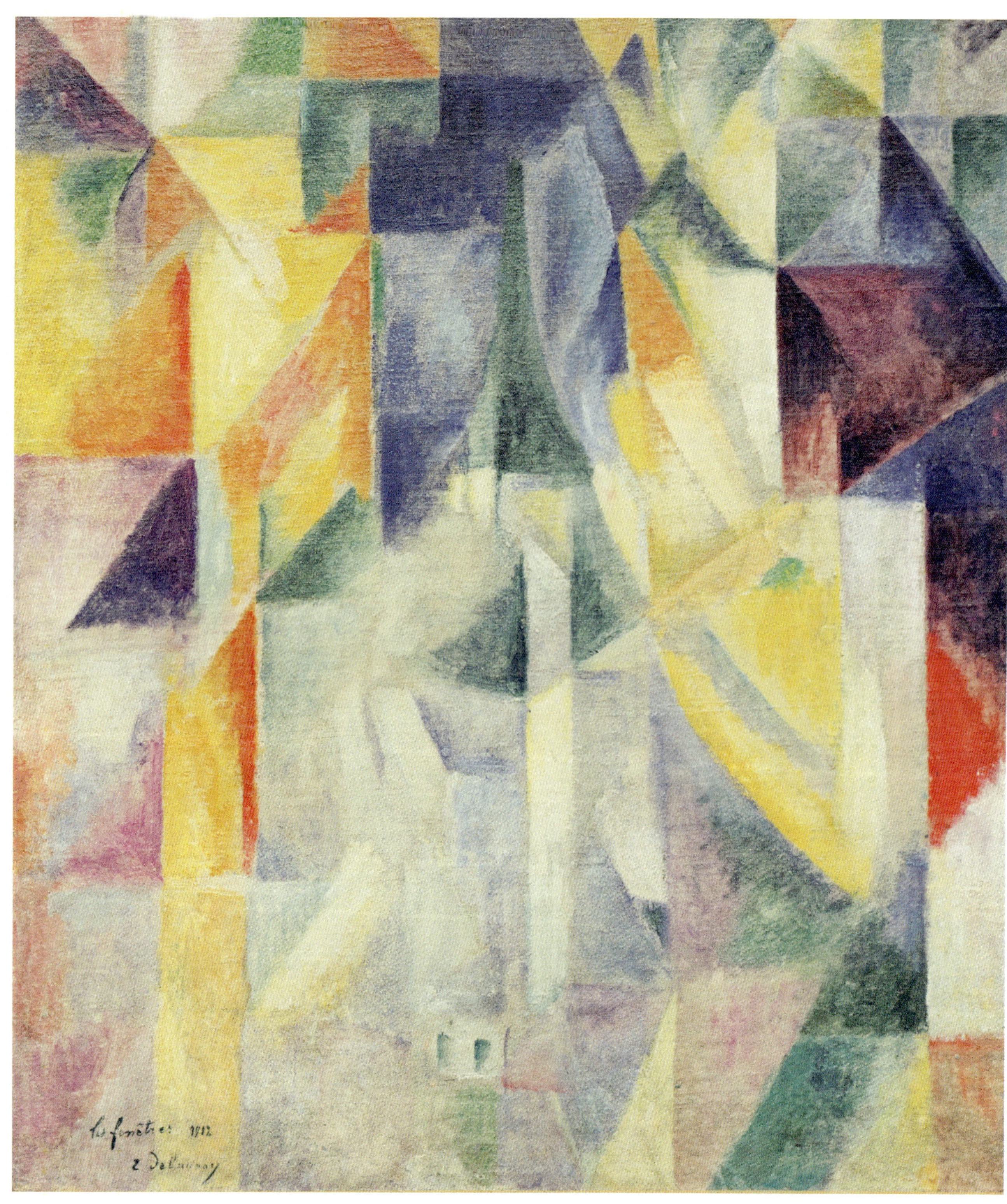

Robert Delaunay

(1885–1941)

Windows

1912
Encaustic on canvas
79.9 × 70 cm (31½ × 27½ in.)
THE MUSEUM OF MODERN ART, NEW YORK

And now look at the window opening
Spiders when hands wove the light
Beauty paleness unfathomable violet tints
O Paris
The yellow fades from red to green
Paris Vancouver Hyères Maintenon New York and
*   the Antilles*
The window opens like an orange
Lovely fruit of light

GUILLAUME APOLLINAIRE, 'WINDOWS'[4]

In common with Apollinaire (1880–1918) – the French poet, playwright and art critic – Robert Delaunay celebrated the lyricism of windows by emphasizing the delicacy of the light they transmit. He created veils of colour from dynamic, transparent planes inspired by cubism, abandoning 'the recognised artistic means such as lines, values, volumes, chiaroscuro and so on'.[5] The various hues, which were meant to be perceived simultaneously, create 'depth – not perspectival, not successive, but simultaneous depth – as well as form and movement'.[6] Although at first sight the windows appear abstract, they reveal the jumbled forms of curtains and even the Eiffel Tower. This is a poetic, atmospheric response to a mundane scene, albeit one with a touch of Parisian glamour.

Christo (Christo Javacheff)

(born 1935)

Four Store Fronts Corner

1964–65
Galvanized metal, clear and coloured Plexiglas,
masonite, canvas and electric light
Parts 1 and 2: 248 × 533 × 43 cm (97⅝ × 209⅞ × 16⅞ in.);
parts 3 and 4: 248 × 569 × 61 cm (97⅝ × 224 × 24 in.)
COLLECTION OF THE ARTIST

An early example of Christo's obsession with wrapping everything, from a bay in Sydney to the Pont Neuf in Paris and the Reichstag in Berlin, can be found in a series of minimalist installations that evoke modern shopfronts while concealing the vitrines behind swathes of fabric. These seminal works drew inspiration from the 'Arcades Project', a classic text by the German thinker Walter Benjamin, begun in 1927 and incomplete at the time of his death in 1940. Benjamin's analysis of nineteenth-century shops and arcades also examined the display of artefacts in museums, and Christo's response can in turn be seen as a comment on the role of these institutions in contemporary society. By denying gallery visitors their normal experience, the artist encourages a reconsideration of the culture of display, and of the assumptions that we make about the boundaries between commerce and education.

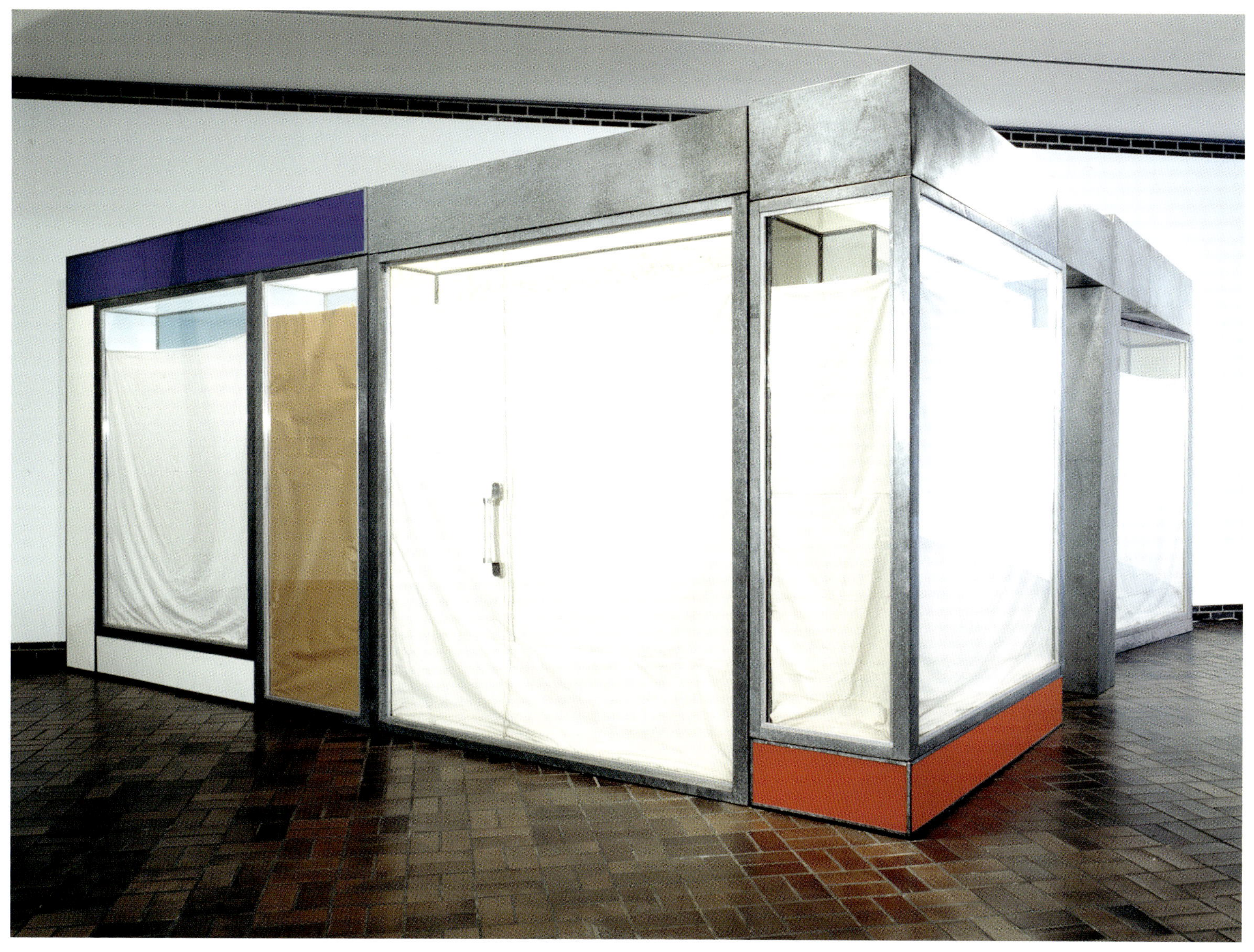

Don Eddy

(born 1944)

New Shoes for H

1973–74
Acrylic on canvas
111.7 × 121.9 cm (44 × 48 in.)
THE CLEVELAND MUSEUM OF ART

New Shoes for H, a painting of a shopfront on
Fourteenth Street in New York, presents a
bewildering kaleidoscope of images within a
fundamentally grid-like composition. An array
of shiny shoes and bags is accompanied by
imposing commercial buildings, pedestrians,
a lorry and a bus. Views through the window
are confused by fragmentary reflections on
both the surface of the glass and a mirrored
column inside the store. Even part of the sky
seems to enter the building. Don Eddy's work
still alludes to the traditional idea of the
painting as a window, but he confounds it
with a series of sharp, angled planes. It is also
significant that the title includes an abbreviated
reference to the German-born painter and
theorist Hans Hofmann (1880–1966), whose
abstract style anticipated Eddy's rigorous use
of colour and form.

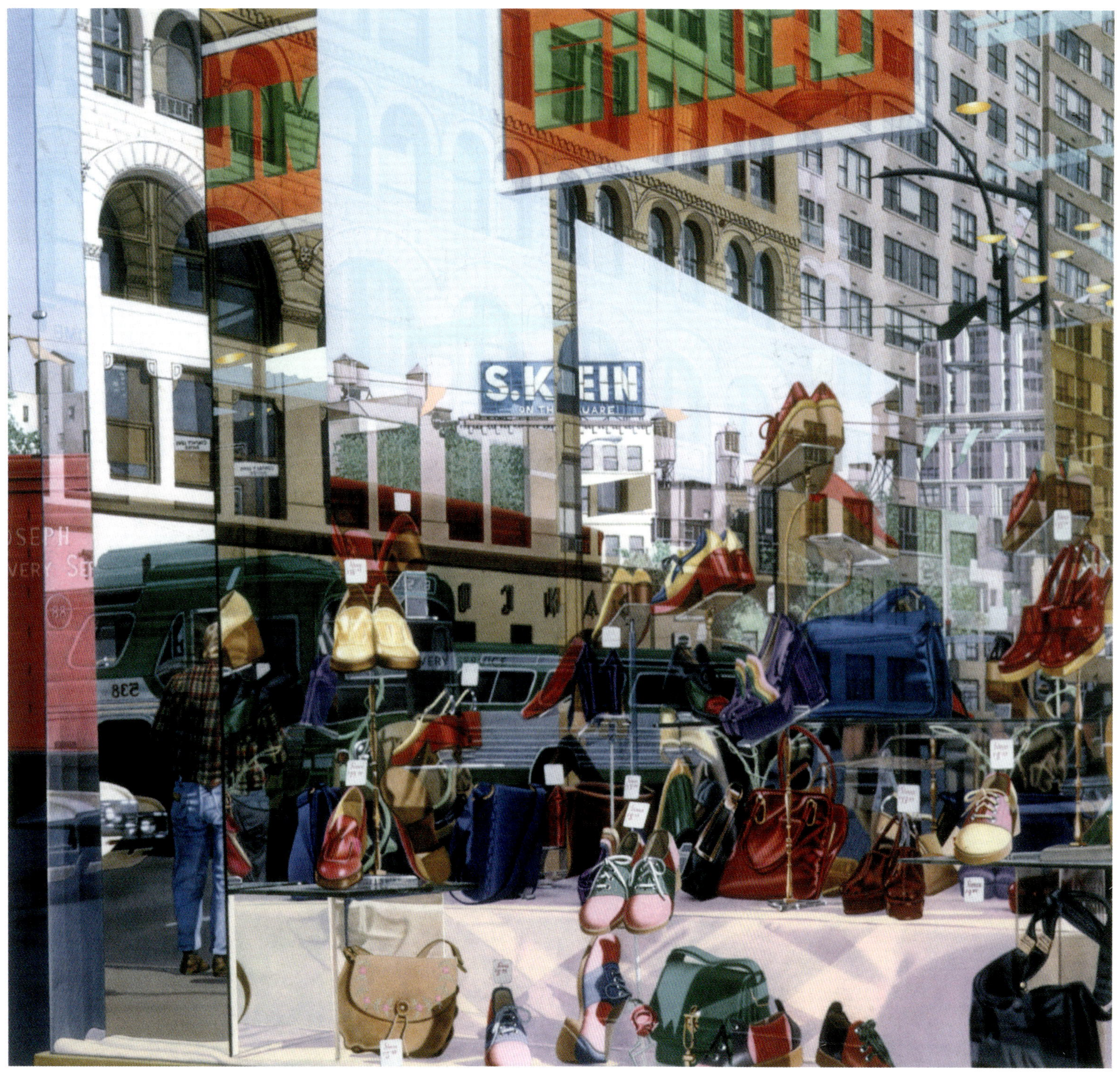

S.KLEIN
ON THE SQUARE

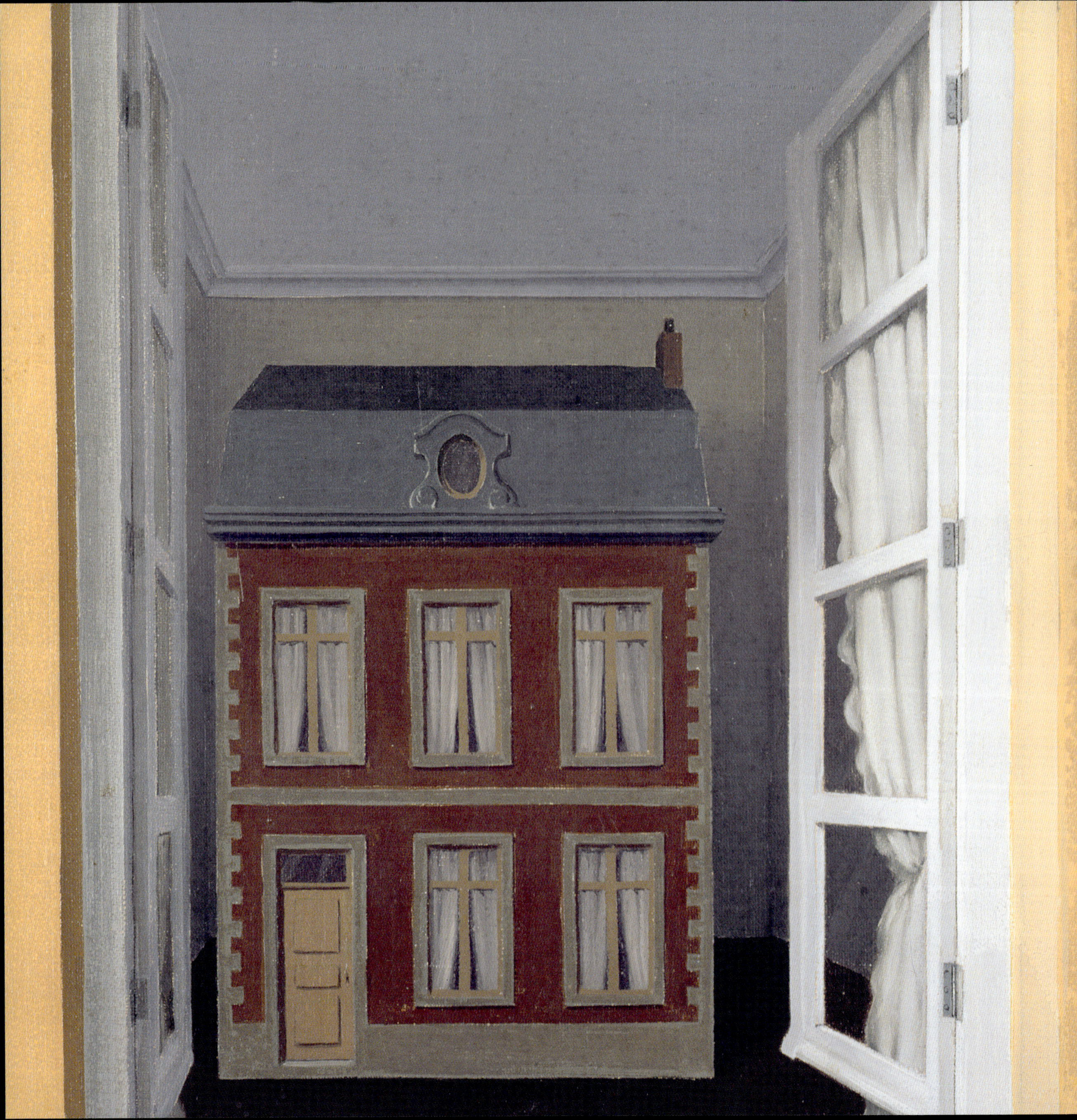

Mirror of the Soul

Caspar David Friedrich's *Woman at the Window* (page 126) is undoubtedly one of the most influential paintings of the nineteenth century, having inspired a remarkable sequence of images in which a female figure, often alone, stands in front of a window. The woman's remoteness from both the viewer and the landscape gives these works a metaphorical quality, as if the window is intended to represent aspects of human experience, above all its solitude and subjectivity. More specifically, the works also reflect the condition of women in the nineteenth and early twentieth centuries, even though that purpose may not have been foremost in the artists' minds.

Despite their complex mediation of reality, these pictures generally maintain the illusionistic qualities of Western painting, unlike the more overtly subversive approach of the Belgian surrealists Paul Delvaux and René Magritte. Both artists used windows to confuse the distinction between interior and exterior space, although with different aims: Delvaux's inner landscape is a place of nostalgia and transferred eroticism (page 134), while Magritte concerned himself with psychological and metaphysical issues (pages 136 and 137), if not without a trace of irony.

The use of the window as a metaphor for desire and emotional attachment is illustrated by two otherwise contrasting images. Both Fra Filippo Lippi's *Portrait of a Woman with a Man at a Casement* (page 139) and Claude Monet's *Red Cape* (page 141) combine a sense of intimacy with a measure of physical separation. In Lippi's case the composition may reflect the recent death of the woman, while Monet's canvas is a record of a fleeting moment on a winter's day, but each painting appears to be charged with longing.

Although most of the pictures in this chapter are concerned with looking through windows, there are a few examples, such as Karl Schmidt-Rottluff in his studio (pages 142–43), in which the human subject ignores the view, even when he or she shares its expressive colours and tones. In other cases the window provides no view at all, as in Edvard Munch's characteristically bleak *Moonlight I* (page 145) and Mark Rothko's murals for the Seagram Building in New York (page 147), images in which the emotional darkness is conveyed through appropriately sombre hues.

Windows do not always represent 'states of the soul', as the writer Aldous Huxley suggested of Giovanni Battista Piranesi's 'Prisons of the Imagination' (page 148).[1] However, over the centuries the window has provided powerful metaphors for the inner world of memory and experience, and, as Chiharu Shiota's installation of 2005 indicates (page 151), this potential has persisted up to the present day.

Caspar David Friedrich
(1774–1840)

Woman at the Window

1822
Oil on canvas
44 × 37 cm (17¾ × 14⅝ in.)
ALTE NATIONALGALERIE, BERLIN

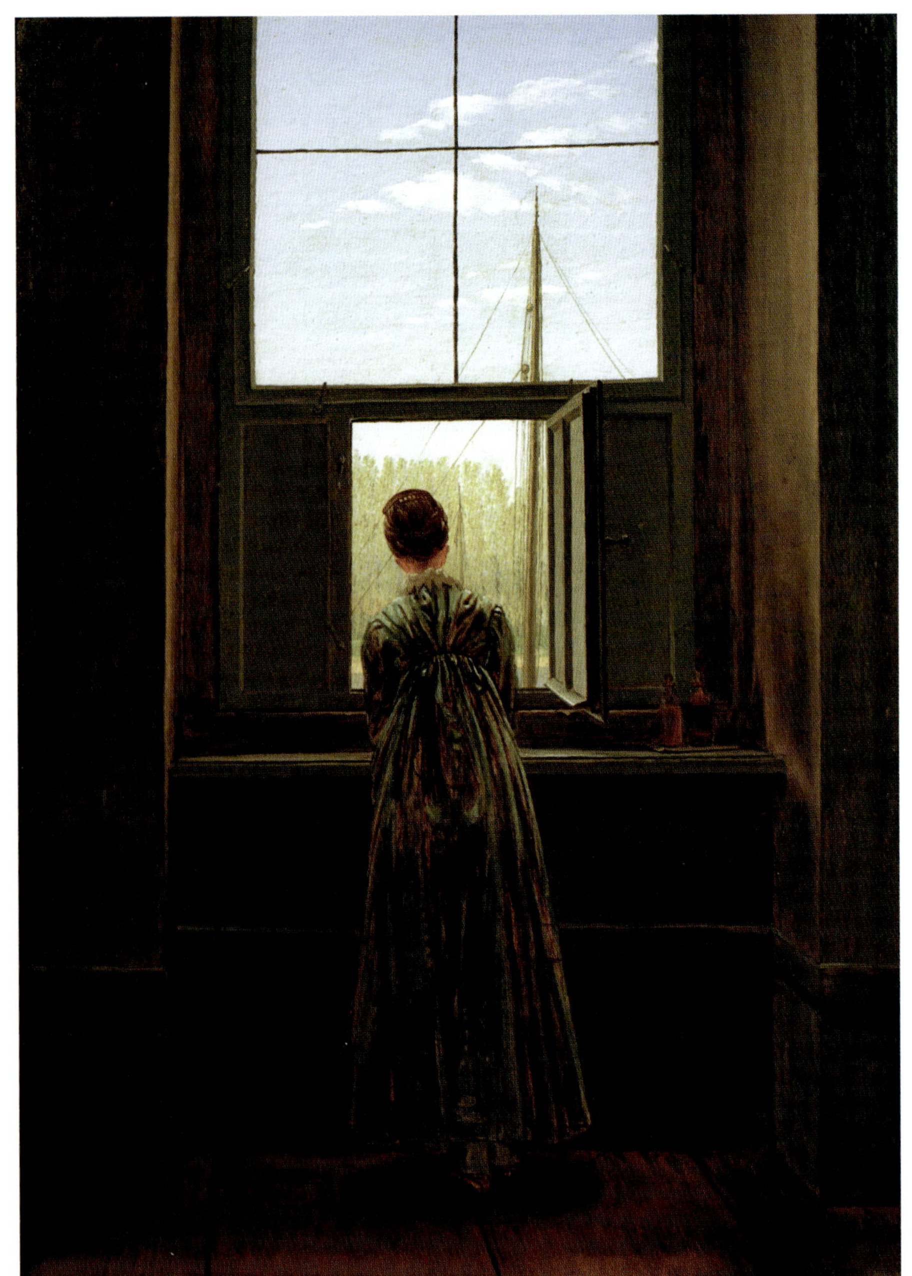

In this enigmatic canvas the window offers a view of the River Elbe in Dresden, with its boat masts and poplar-lined banks, and yet most of the scene is blocked from both the viewer and the artist. The cross window and triptych-like shutters suggest a religious dimension, but it is hard to imagine exactly what this might be. The painting seems to offer, but ultimately withholds, an external meaning, and we are left with the impression of an intense personal significance.

The figure of the woman – modelled on the artist's wife, Caroline – is dominated by the bare studio. Subtle details, such as the bottles on the dented sill and the irregular angles of the shutters' locks, draw the eye away from the picture's main subject, the window. This painting within a painting mainly serves to emphasize the subjectivity of the whole image, its detachment from exterior reality. As one writer has put it, 'the picture-window sequesters us, like the woman, in a position of exile from, and longing for, what we can always only partially see.'[2]

Johan Christian Dahl
(1788–1857)

View of Pillnitz Castle

1823
Oil on canvas
70 × 45.5 cm (27⅝ × 17⅞ in.)
MUSEUM FOLKWANG, ESSEN

The Norwegian artist Johan Christian Dahl spent much of his career in Dresden, becoming a close friend of the city's greatest painter, Caspar David Friedrich. Indeed, in 1823 Dahl and his family moved into the house in which Friedrich lived, using a studio under the roof, where he executed this prospect across the River Elbe.

Unlike Friedrich's *Woman at the Window* (opposite), made in the same house, or *Window with a View of a Park* (page 111), Dahl's image creates a striking sense of space. The closure of the window at the top sets off the dramatic opened casement below, with the reflections in the glass effectively expanding the view. The immense sky is suffused with a poetic sunset glow, while the division of the window makes the landscape in the lower half look very much like a 'painting within a painting'. The artifice is completed by the appearance of Pillnitz Castle, which Dahl has transported in his imagination from its actual position some distance upstream.

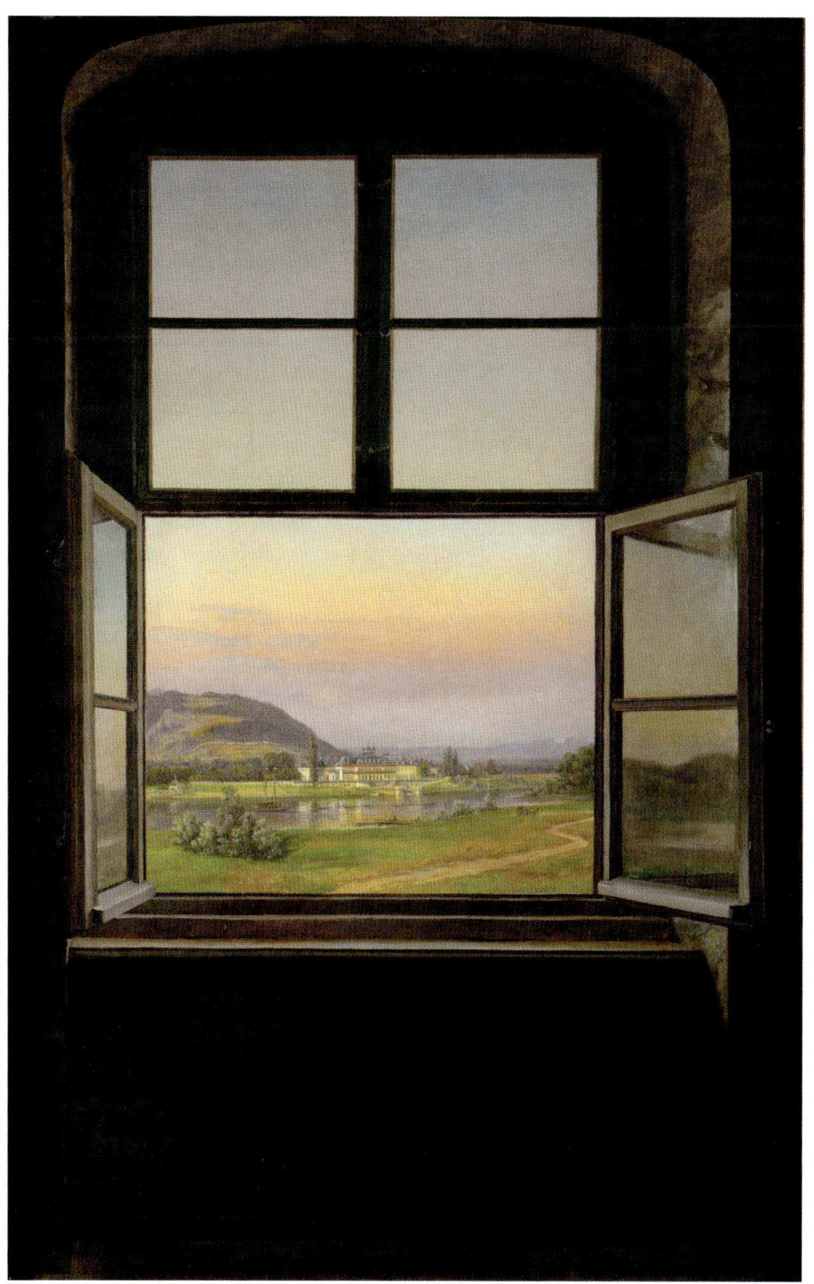

Carl Gustav Carus

(1789–1869)

Window at Oybin by Moonlight

c. 1825
Oil on canvas
27.7 × 32.8 cm (10⅞ × 12⅞ in.)
MUSEUM GEORG SCHÄFER, SCHWEINFURT

The German scientist, doctor and painter Carl Gustav Carus received an informal artistic training from Caspar David Friedrich, an experience that heavily influenced this image of a window with curtain (or upswung) tracery at the ruined monastery of Oybin in Saxony, eastern Germany. Certain features, such as the window and the figures seen from the back, mirror Friedrich's work (see, for example, page 126), even though during the 1820s Carus developed an aesthetic theory that was significantly different from that of his mentor. In *Neun Briefe über Landschaftsmalerei* (Nine Letters on Landscape Painting; 1831) Carus espoused a more scientific approach to the depiction of clouds and other phenomena, partly under the influence of the poet Johann Wolfgang von Goethe and the naturalist Alexander von Humboldt. The view through the arch at Oybin is indeed based on nature studies that Carus made on the Zittau Mountains in August 1820, and yet its principal significance is as a metaphor, a means of expressing the feelings of the artist or his imaginary subjects. Friedrich's example remained dominant in Carus's art throughout his career, whatever his writings might suggest.

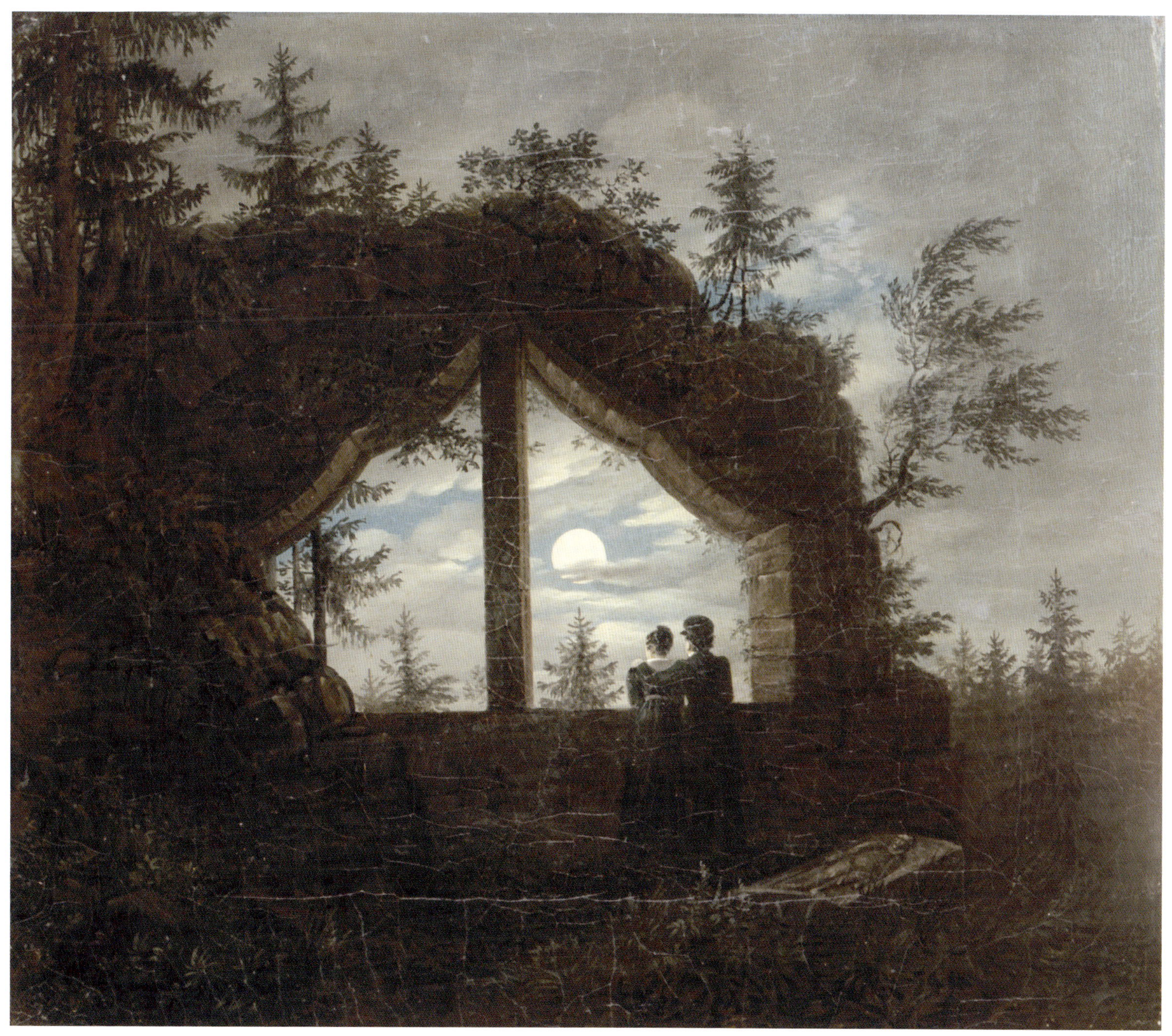

Salvador Dalí
(1904–1989)

Figure at a Window

1925
Oil on canvas
102 × 75 cm (40⅛ × 29½ in.)
MUSEO NACIONAL CENTRO DE ARTE REINA SOFIA, MADRID

This striking image, painted before Dalí had
joined the surrealist movement, shows his
younger sister, Ana Maria, looking out of the
Dalí family home in Port Lligat, a small village
near the city of Cadaqués in Catalonia, north-
eastern Spain. As well as demonstrating the
artist's self-confessed penchant for women's
backs, this canvas shows the influence of Caspar
David Friedrich (page 126), as once again there
is a sense of distance and emptiness around
the figure gazing at the water. Although the
seascape appears serene and harmonious, the
window itself is asymmetrical and apparently
unfinished on the left-hand side, as if to stress
its subjective, even whimsical quality.

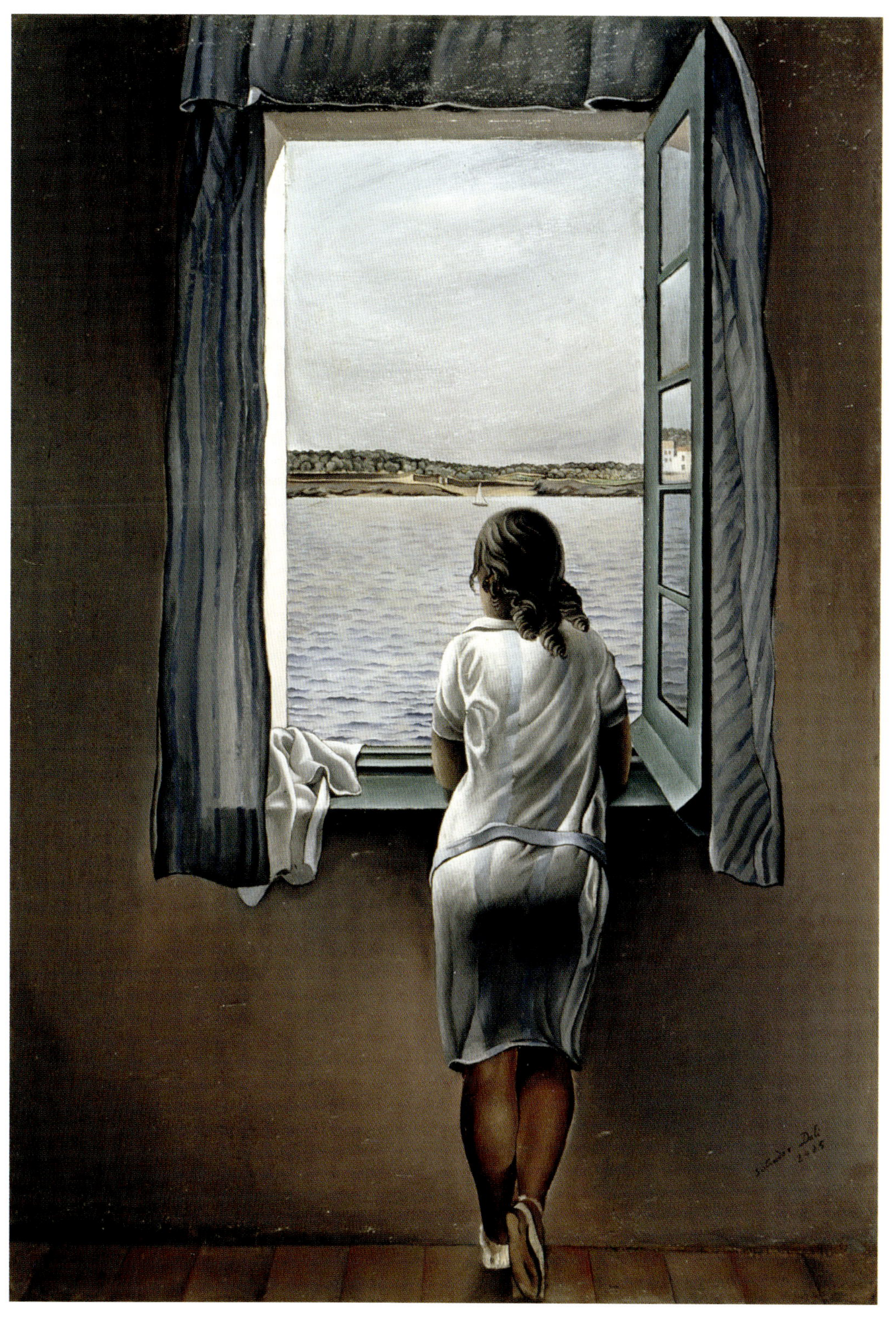

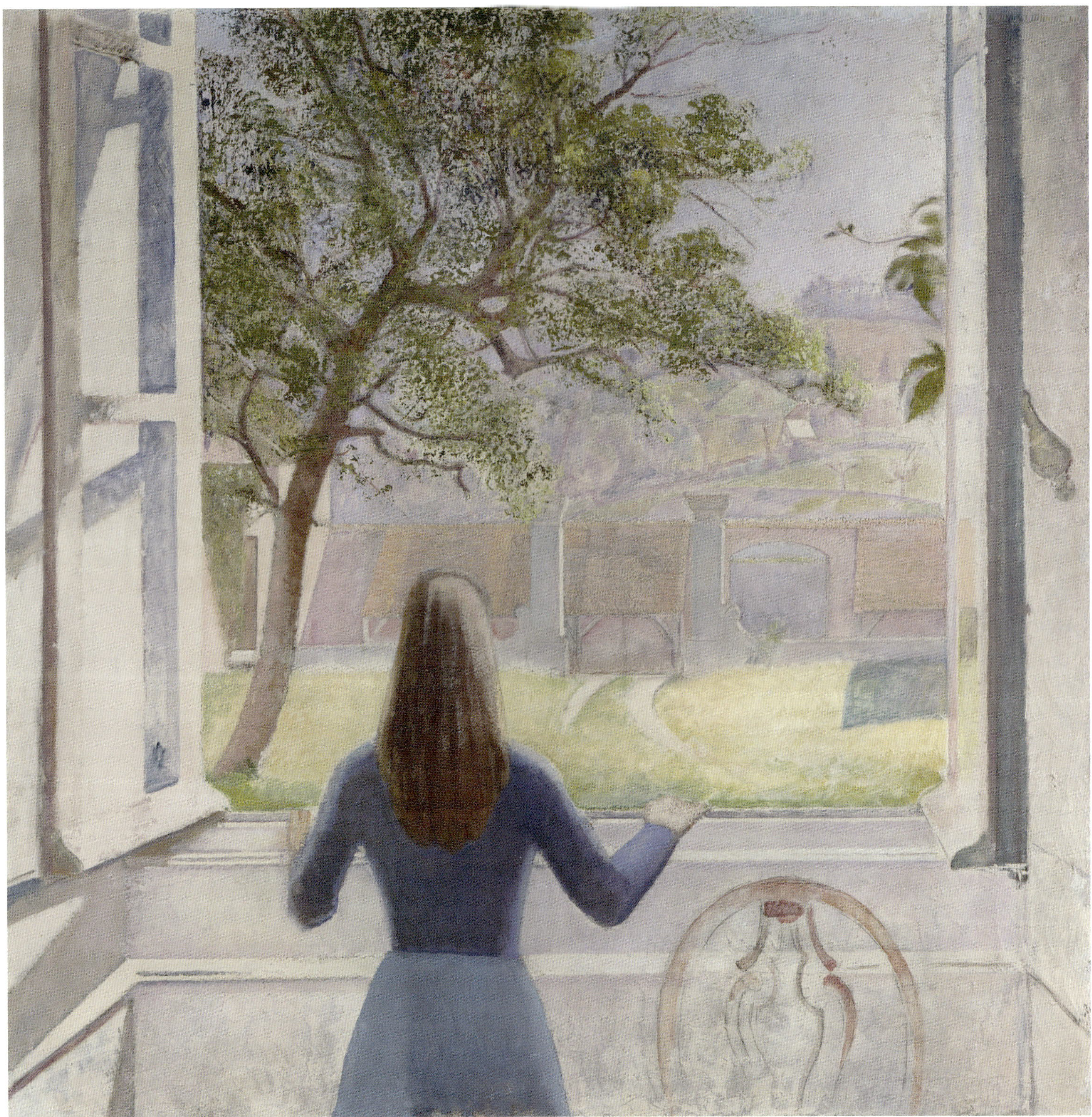

Balthus (Count Balthazar Klossowski de Rola)

(1908–2001)

Young Girl at the Window

1957
Oil on canvas
160 × 162 cm (63 × 63¾ in.)
PRIVATE COLLECTION

In common with Dalí's *Figure at a Window* (page 131), Balthus's painting draws directly on the form and content of *Woman at the Window* by Caspar David Friedrich (page 126). Here, however, there is no feeling of emptiness or thwarted desire. The wide, open window reveals the lush surroundings of Balthus's chateau at Chassy in Burgundy, central France, with the gates, adjacent buildings and trees represented in vivid detail. The daylight floods in, gilding the hair of the girl, who rests her hands on the ledge while otherwise keeping herself at a slight distance from the window. In this way, Balthus expresses a sense of longing that is close to fulfilment, a sunlit inner landscape presented through the mediating figure of the girl.

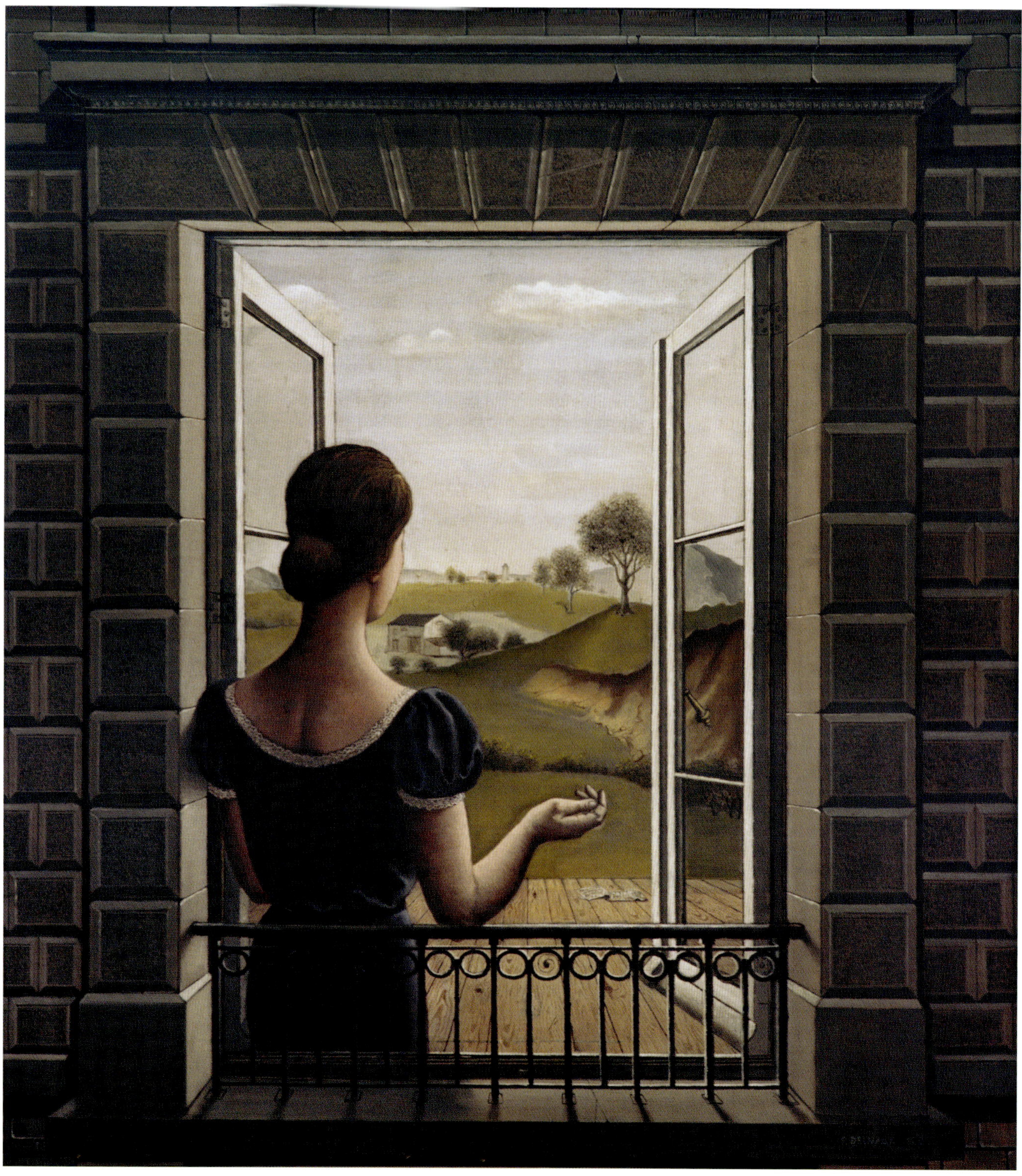

Paul Delvaux

(1897–1994)

The Window

1936
Oil on canvas
110 × 100 cm (43¼ × 39⅜ in.)

The Belgian surrealist Paul Delvaux has turned the motif of the interior landscape into something concrete and explicit. Daylight streams out of the room, casting shadows beyond the railings of the window, as the mysterious woman facing away from us raises her hands in an almost devotional pose. Delvaux uses the window to create a fantasy world, populated by a single inhabitant dressed nostalgically in the fashion of the early twentieth century. According to André Breton, the founder of the surrealist movement, Delvaux 'turned the whole universe into a single realm in which one woman, always the same woman, reigns over the great suburbs of the heart'.[3]

René Magritte

(1898–1967)

The Human Condition

1933
Oil on canvas
100 × 81 cm (39¾ × 31⅞ in.)
NATIONAL GALLERY OF ART, WASHINGTON, D.C.

In Praise of the Dialectic

1937
Oil on canvas
65.5 x 54 cm (25¼ × 21¼ in.)
NATIONAL GALLERY OF VICTORIA, MELBOURNE

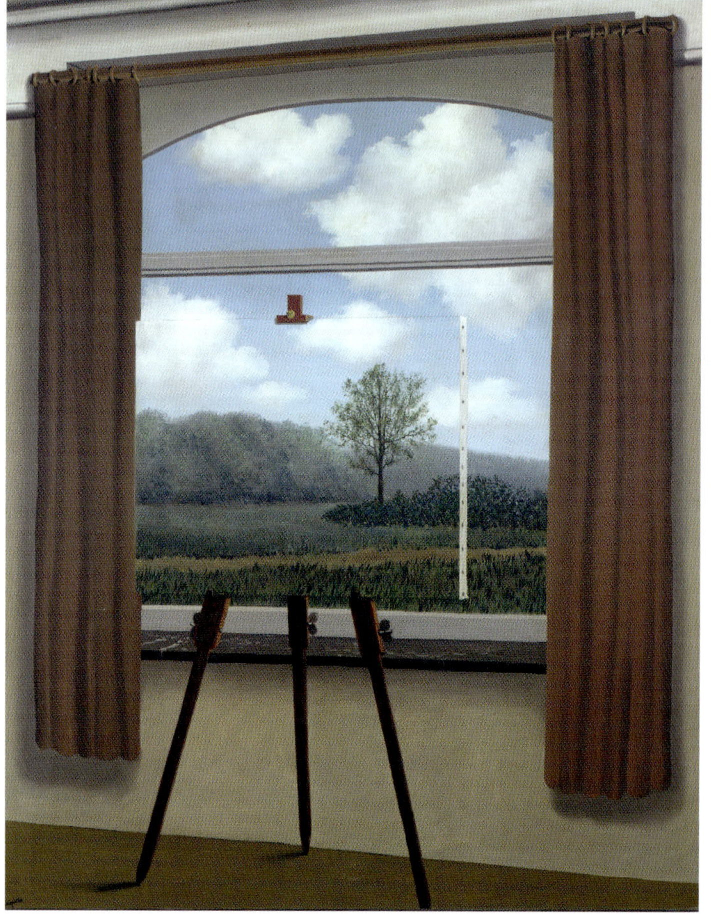

Magritte himself described how, in *The Human Condition* (left), each section of the canvas on the easel represents 'exactly that portion of the landscape' it conceals, so as to confound the normal distinction between exterior and interior suggested by the window.[4] According to the artist, 'This simultaneous existence in two different spaces is like living simultaneously in the past and in the present, as in cases of déjà vu';[5] it also emphasizes the fact that although 'we see it [the world] as being outside ourselves, … it is only a mental representation of it that we experience inside ourselves'.[6]

This dialogue of contradictions is also the subject of *In Praise of the Dialectic* (opposite), as the title of the work suggests. Here, just as in the painting by Paul Delvaux (page 134), the window presents an interior view of a piece of the outside world. However, Magritte complicates the matter by filling the room not with a lyrical landscape but with another bourgeois building, this time with its windows and curtains primly shut. The ancient conceit that the eyes are windows to the soul has been given an unexpected twist.

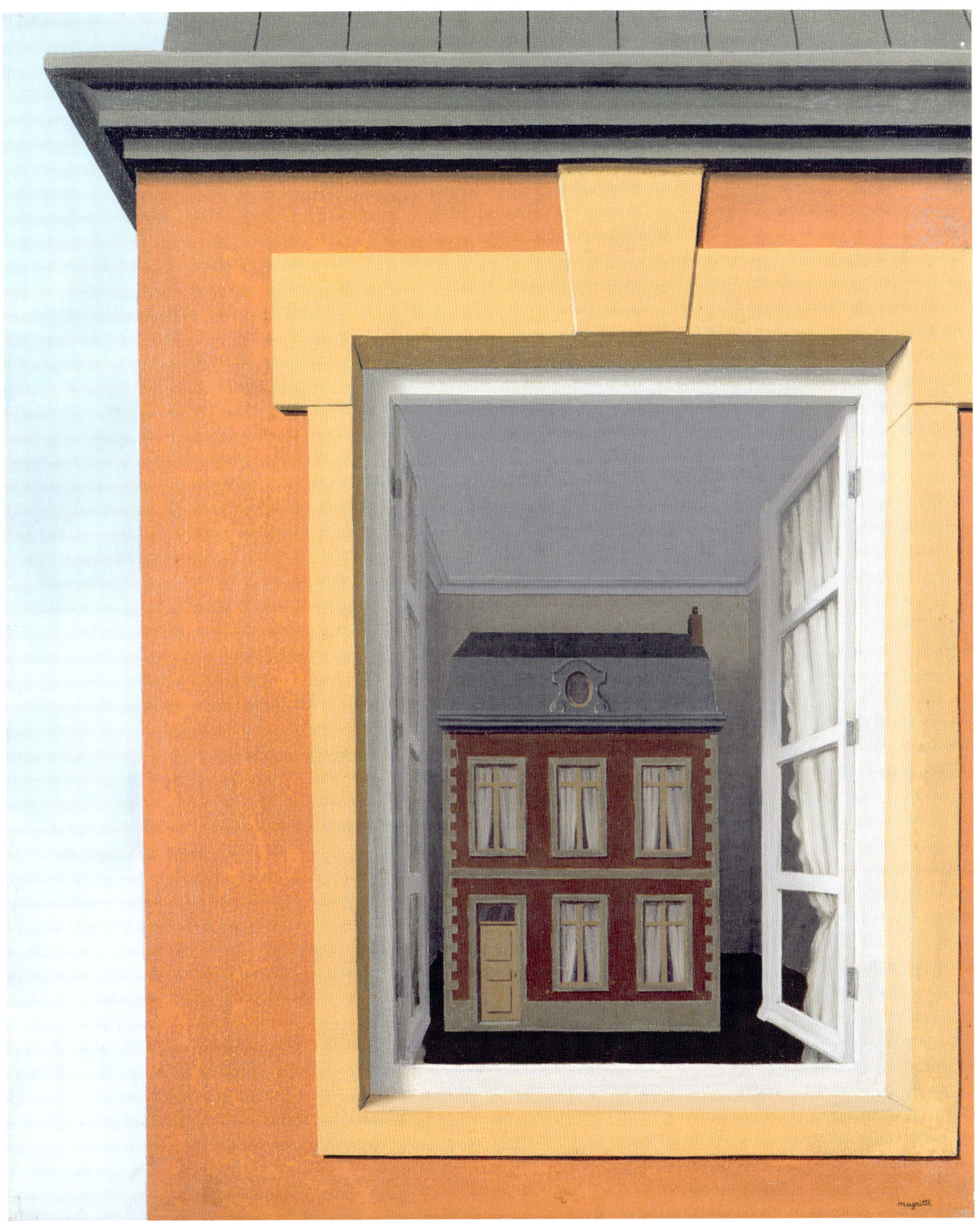

Portrait of a Woman with a Man at a Casement

c. 1440
Tempera on wood
64.1 × 41.9 cm (25¼ × 16½ in.)
THE METROPOLITAN MUSEUM OF ART, NEW YORK

It still remains unclear why this couple are sundered by a window, with the gentleman resting his hand on a coat of arms, and the lady proclaiming her loyalty through the Italian word 'Lealtà' embroidered on the cuff of her left sleeve. It has been suggested that this division, together with the greater proximity and size of the lady, indicates a disparity of social status. Alternatively, the couple could be betrothed, in which case the window might eloquently describe the chaste rituals of courtship. However, perhaps the strongest theory is that the man and woman have already been parted by death, with the window acting as an emblem of a connection that continues despite their physical separation. The panel has a tender, lyrical quality, which is enhanced by the view of gardens and perhaps a chapel or convent through the window behind the woman.

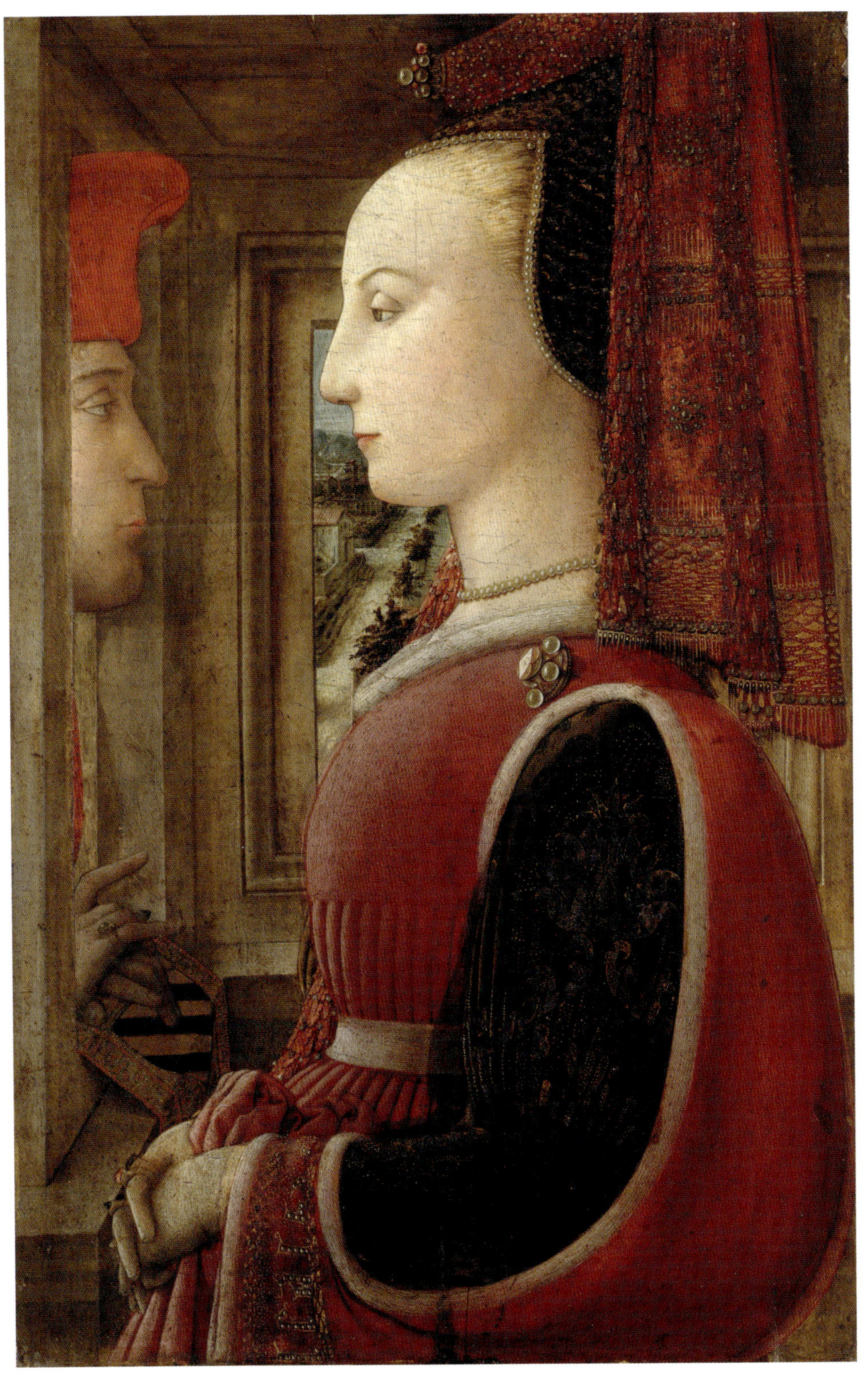

Claude Monet

(1840–1926)

The Red Cape

1868–69
Oil on canvas
100 × 80 cm (39⅜ × 31½ in.)
THE CLEVELAND MUSEUM OF ART

Here, Monet's future wife Camille is seen looking through a French window at a house in Étretat, a seaside town in Normandy. The painting depends on contrasts: rectilinear lines versus the curved forms of the woman and her umbrella; the intense red of the cape against the cool winter light; intimacy and separation. The picture was made at a difficult period in the couple's life, with Camille particularly isolated as an unmarried mother and mistress, and it is possible that the composition was intended to express this, albeit obliquely. Unfinished and never publicly exhibited during the artist's lifetime, this was one of the few early works that Monet kept until his death.

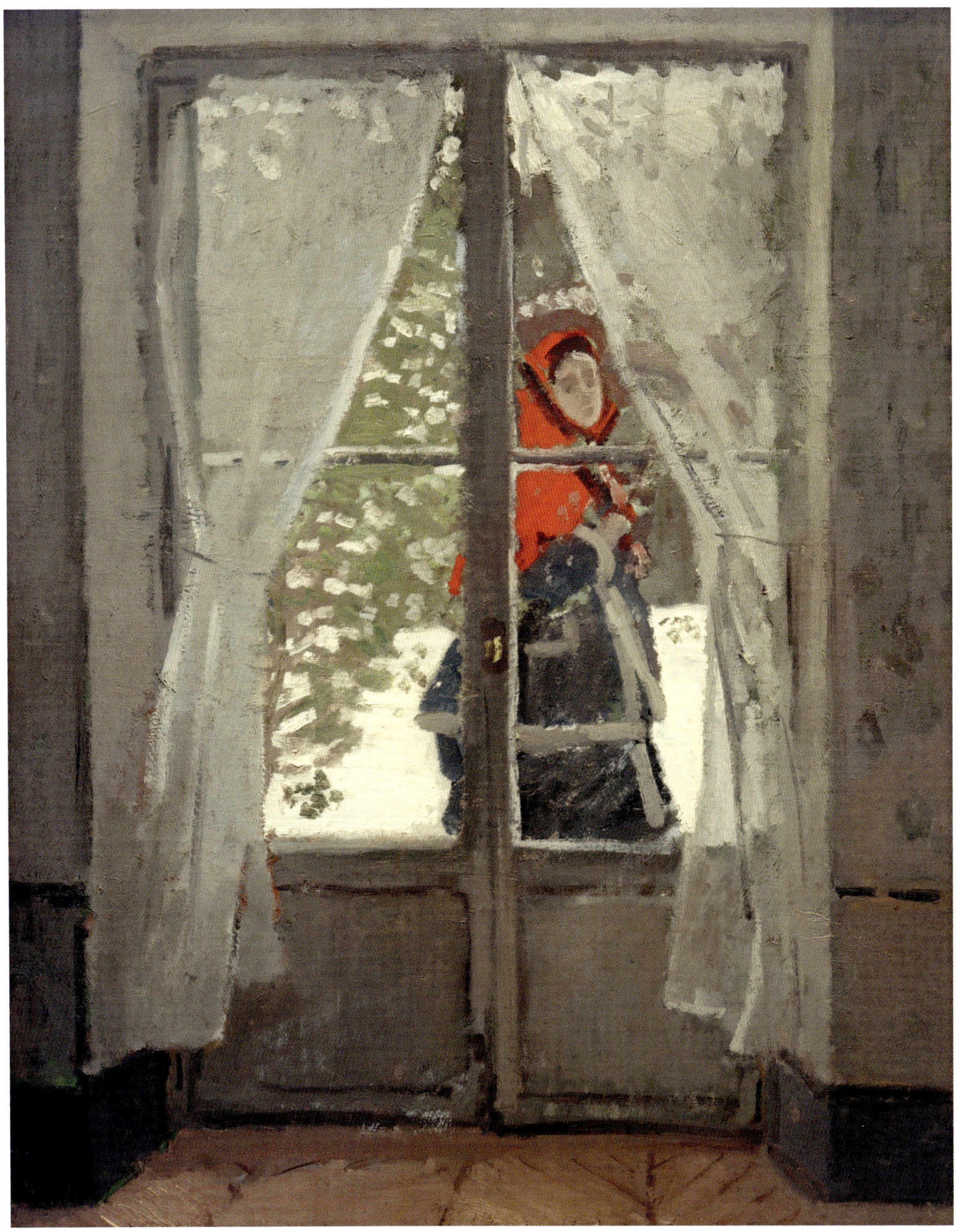

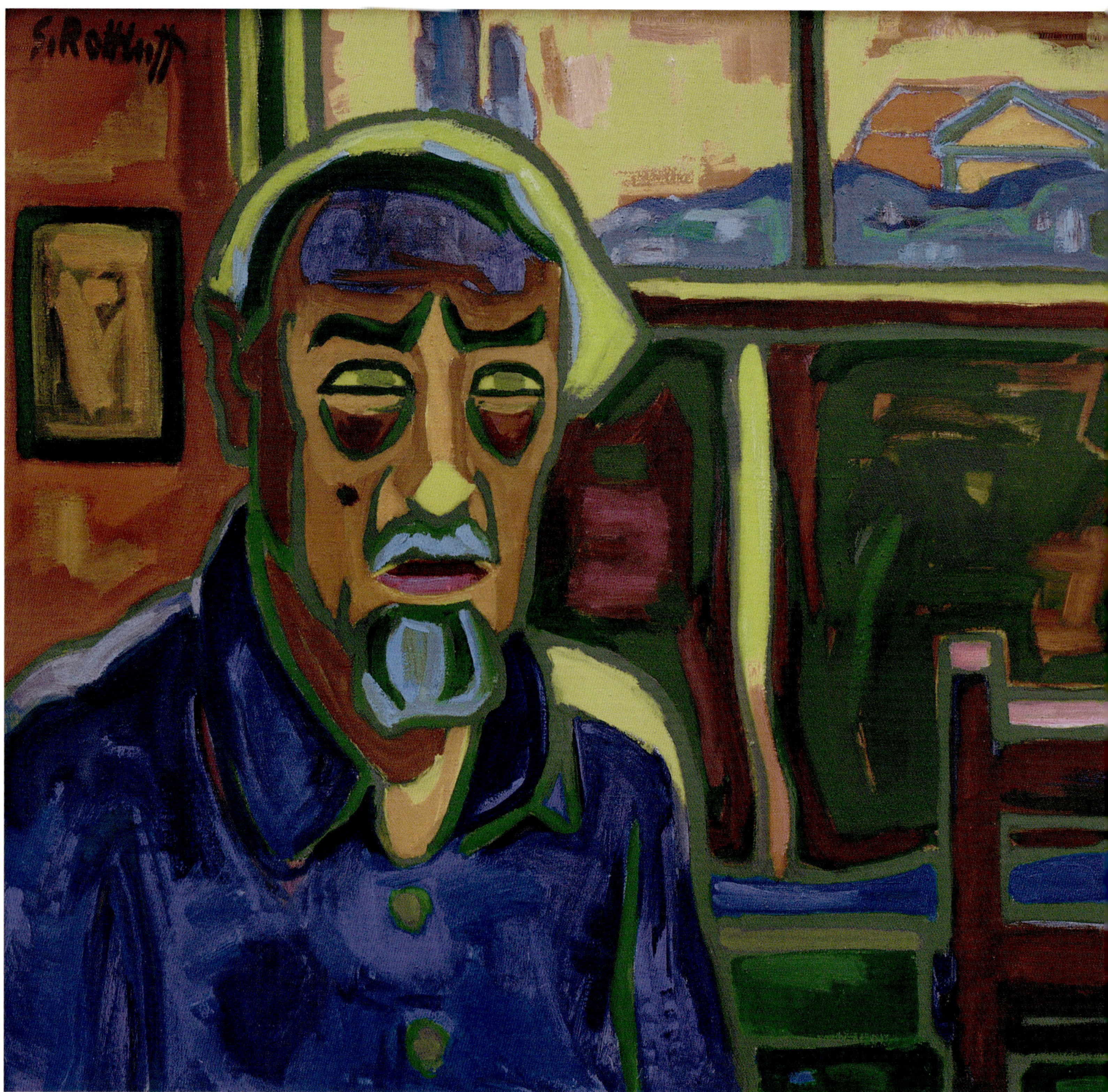

S.Rottluff

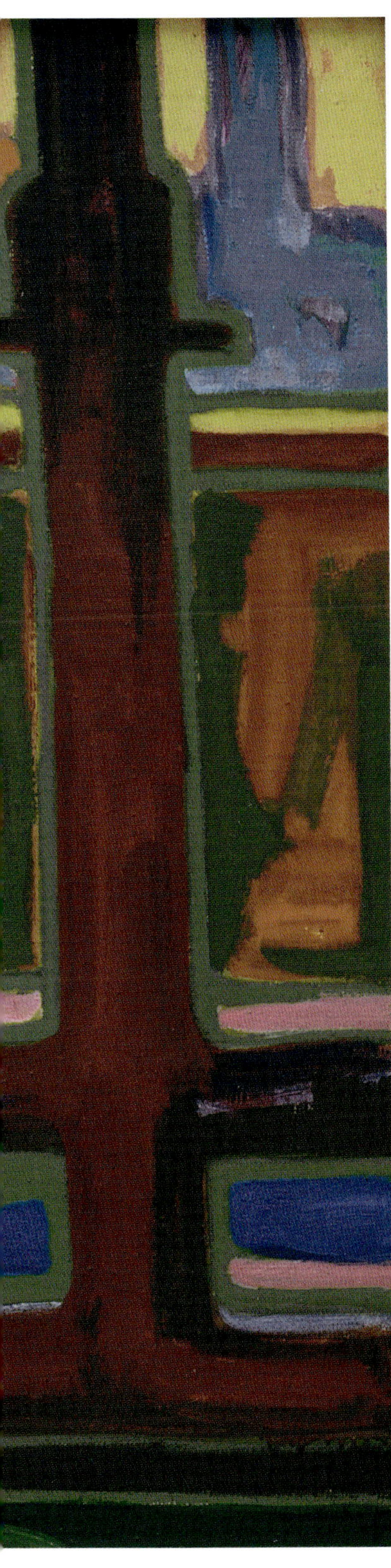

Karl Schmidt-Rottluff
(1884–1976)

In the Studio

1950
Oil on canvas
76 × 100 cm (29⅞ × 39⅜ in.)
BRÜCKE MUSEUM, BERLIN

A former member of the German expressionist group Die Brücke (The Bridge), Karl Schmidt-Rottluff was dismissed as a 'degenerate' artist by the Nazis; was prohibited first from exhibiting and then from painting; and, in 1943, lost his studio in Berlin in an air raid. This picture was made shortly after his post-war rehabilitation. The bold hues seen through the window, above all the complementary blue and yellow, correspond with those of the artist's gaunt face, while the brushwork is consistently vigorous and expressive. The world outside is apparently coloured by the painter's mood, although more strictly pictorial considerations have also determined the strong sense of pattern that dominates the composition.

Edvard Munch

(1863–1944)

Moonlight I

1896
Woodcut
Image: 40.5 × 46.7 cm (16 × 18¾ in.)
MUNCH MUSEET, OSLO

This woodcut presents a detail from a slightly earlier canvas (*Moonlight*, 1893) now in the National Museum of Art, Architecture and Design in Oslo. It gains much of its effect from the extravagant tonal contrasts, including those of the window in the top left-hand corner. The vibrant green merely emphasizes the blackness of the glass, providing a suitable backdrop for the femme fatale staring hieratically into the moonlight, as well as helping to express Edvard Munch's pathological morbidity: 'People's souls are like planets. Like a star that appears out of the gloom and meets another star – they shine brightly for a moment and then disappear completely into the darkness.'[7]

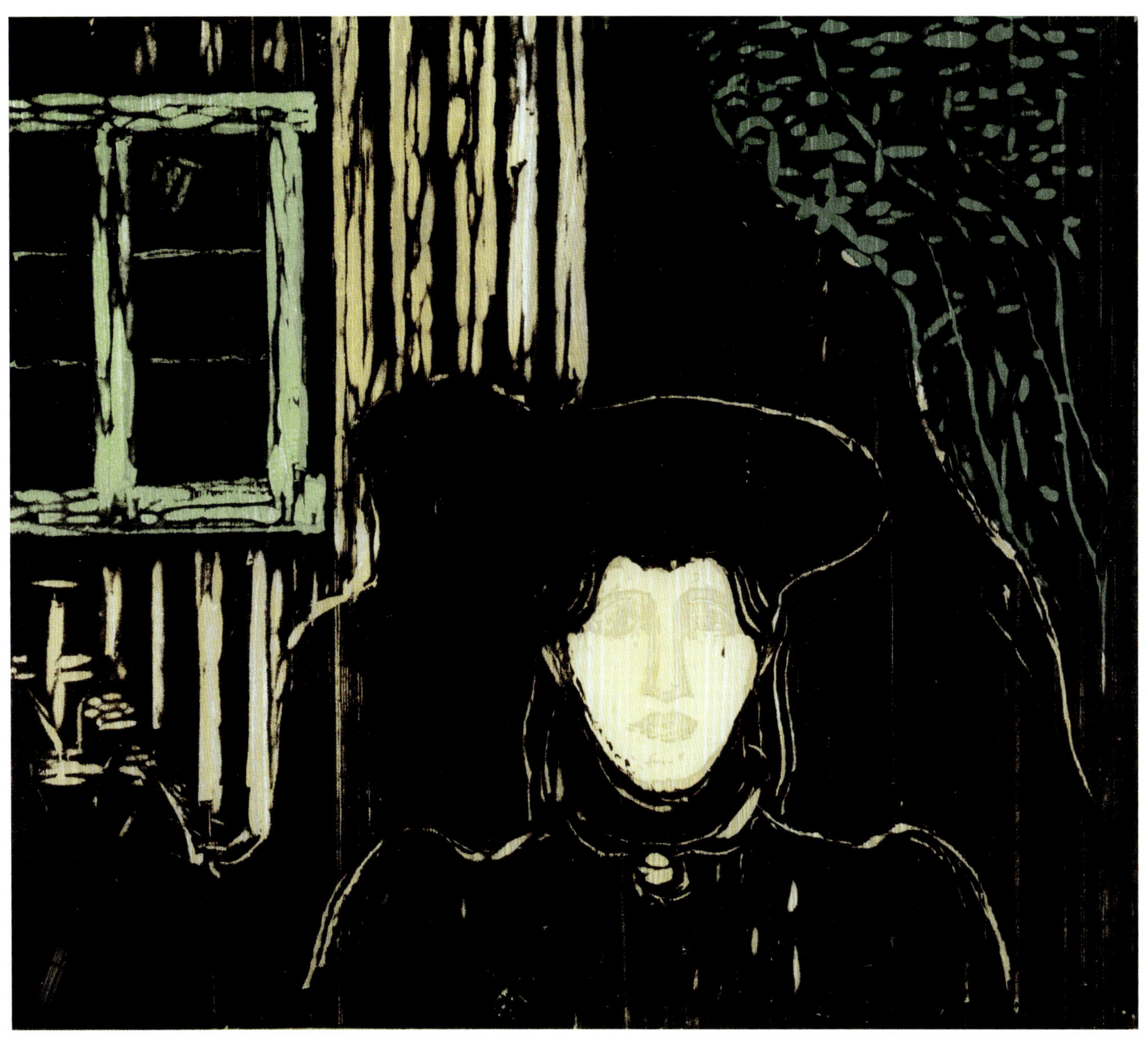

Mark Rothko

(1903–1970)

Red on Maroon (Mural, Section 4)

1959
Mixed media on canvas
266.7 × 238.8 cm (105 × 94 in.)
TATE, LONDON

In 1958 Mark Rothko received a commission to decorate the Four Seasons Restaurant in the recently completed Seagram Building, a skyscraper on Park Avenue in New York designed by the German-born architect Ludwig Mies van der Rohe. Rothko's mural-like canvases were intended to hang as a continuous frieze, with the narrower ones positioned above the doors to the room.

Although the open, rectangular compositions evoke the forms of windows, the view that they provide is of a strange, interior world determined by the artist's essentially tragic concept of the human condition. As in the case of Rothko's earlier works, the fields of colour appear to float and pulsate, with the ragged edges creating a sensation of shimmering light. The effect is, nonetheless, uniquely sombre. Significantly, the artist compared this project to the claustrophobic vestibule of the Laurentian Library in Florence, designed by Michelangelo, who, according to Rothko, 'achieved just the kind of feeling I'm after – he makes the viewers feel that they are trapped in a room where all the doors and windows are bricked up, so that all they can do is butt their heads forever against the wall'.[8]

Rothko's ambitions for the murals led him to withdraw them from the Seagram Building, which he regarded as an unsuitable location. Eventually, he bequeathed nine of the paintings to the Tate Gallery in London.

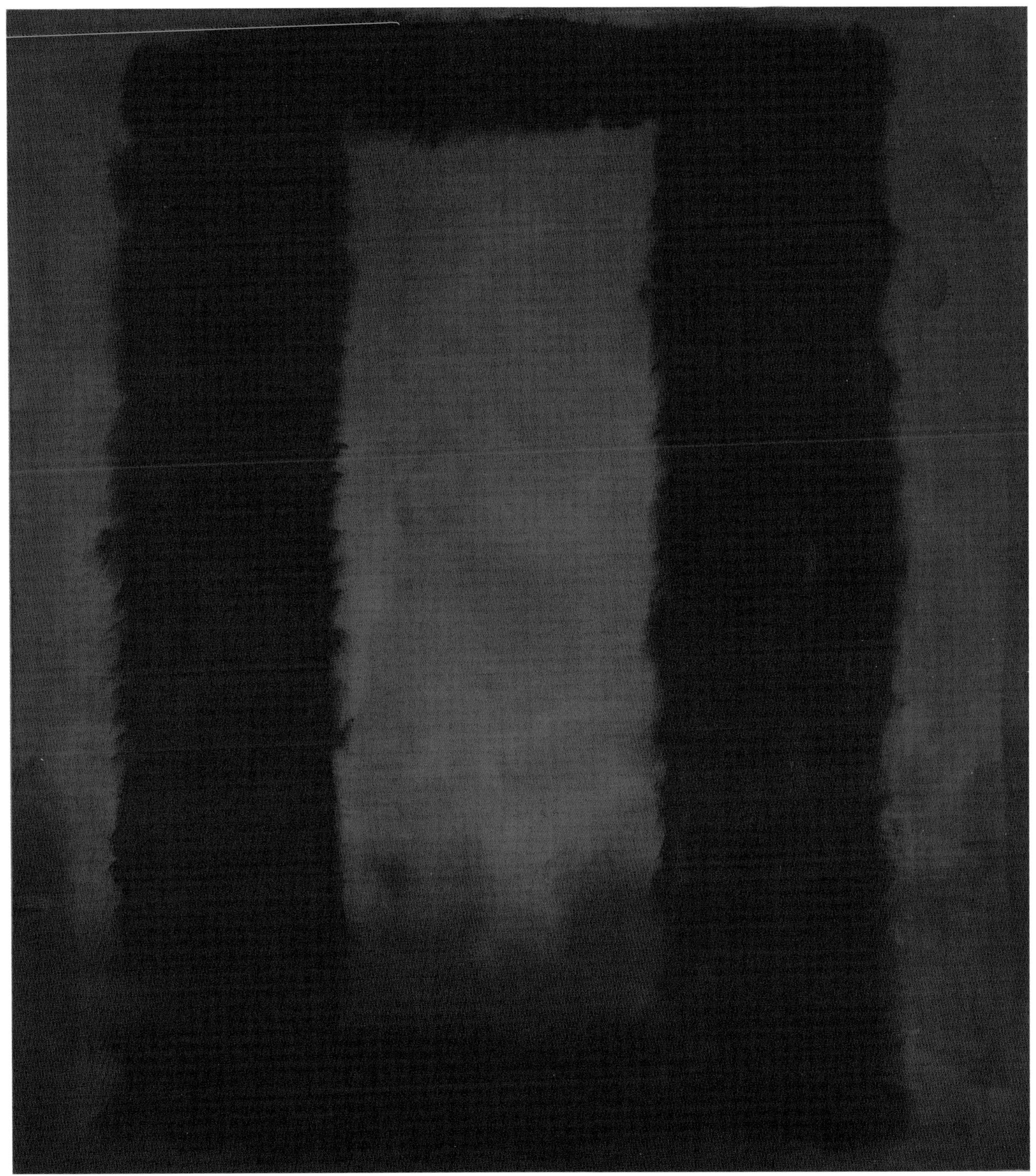

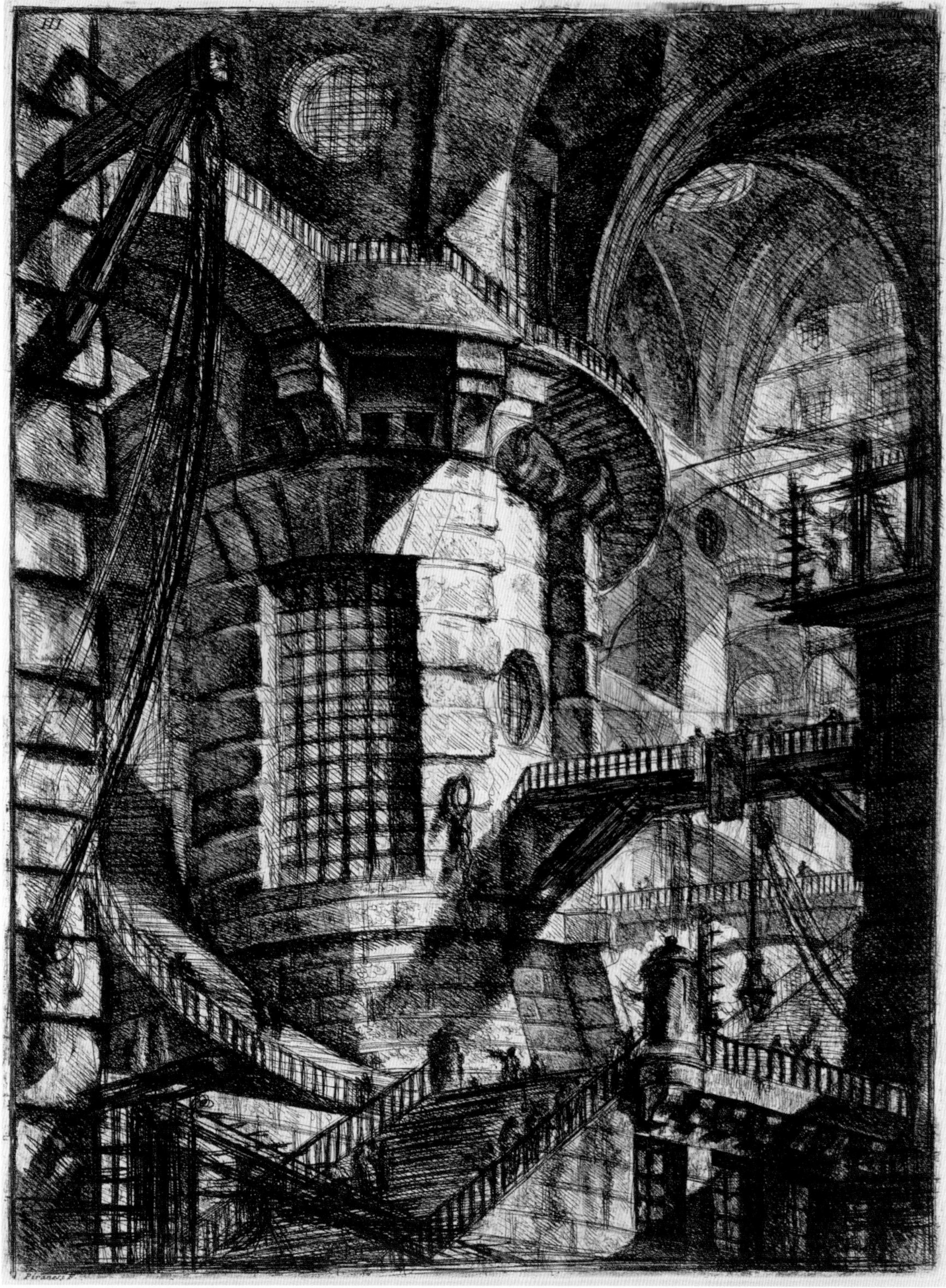

Giovanni Battista Piranesi
(1720–1778)

The Round Tower
Plate 3 of *Carceri d'invenzione*

1761 (first published 1749–50)
Etching, engraving, sulphur tint or open bite,
burnishing
55.6 × 41.8 cm (21⅞ × 16½ in.)
VARIOUS LOCATIONS

The third etching from Piranesi's series *Carceri d'invenzione* (Prisons of the Imagination) features an immense rusticated window inspired partly by ancient Roman remains, and partly by Renaissance buildings, including, perhaps, those of Michele Sanmicheli in Piranesi's native Venice. The window serves no obvious function, with bright shafts of light coming from other directions, and it is certainly consistent with Aldous Huxley's description of the prisons' 'colossal pointlessness [that] goes on indefinitely, and is co-extensive with the universe'.[9] Huxley's analysis of these images as representing 'states of the soul' is less fanciful than other accounts based on Freudian psychoanalysis or comparisons with the effects of taking opium.[10]

A more prosaic explanation is that these 'capricious inventions', as Piranesi first titled them, were derived from stage designs – including those of prisons – by the Italian architect and designer Filippo Juvarra (1678–1736) and members of the Bibiena family of Italian artists (*fl*. 1680s–1780s). It is, however, undeniable that Piranesi's dramatic and emotional range far exceeded that of any of his predecessors.

Chiharu Shiota
(born 1972)

House of Windows

2005
Reclaimed wooden windows
500 × 450 × 300 cm (196⅞ × 177⅛ × 118⅛ in.)
THIRD FUKUOKA ASIAN ART TRIENNALE

The Japanese artist Chiharu Shiota, who lives
in Germany, has created a series of installations
made out of multiple layers of windows taken
from building sites in East Berlin after the fall
of Communism. Intensely illuminated, this
structure transfigures mundane objects, its
flimsy, unsubstantial nature creating an
impression of something immaterial and
spiritual. These plain, ordinary windows have
become metaphors for countless dreams and
aspirations – the fleeting experiences of those
who once gazed out of them.

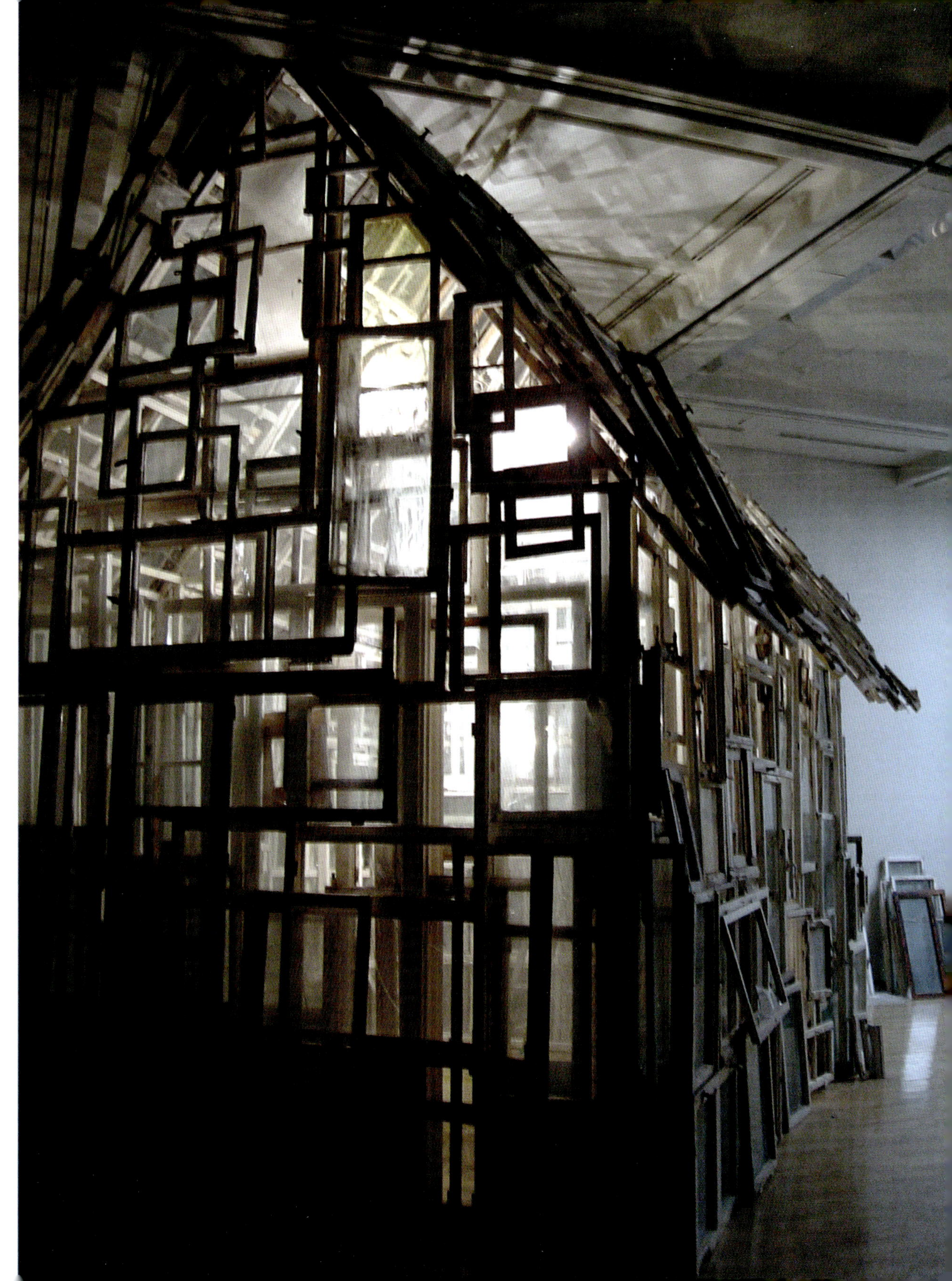

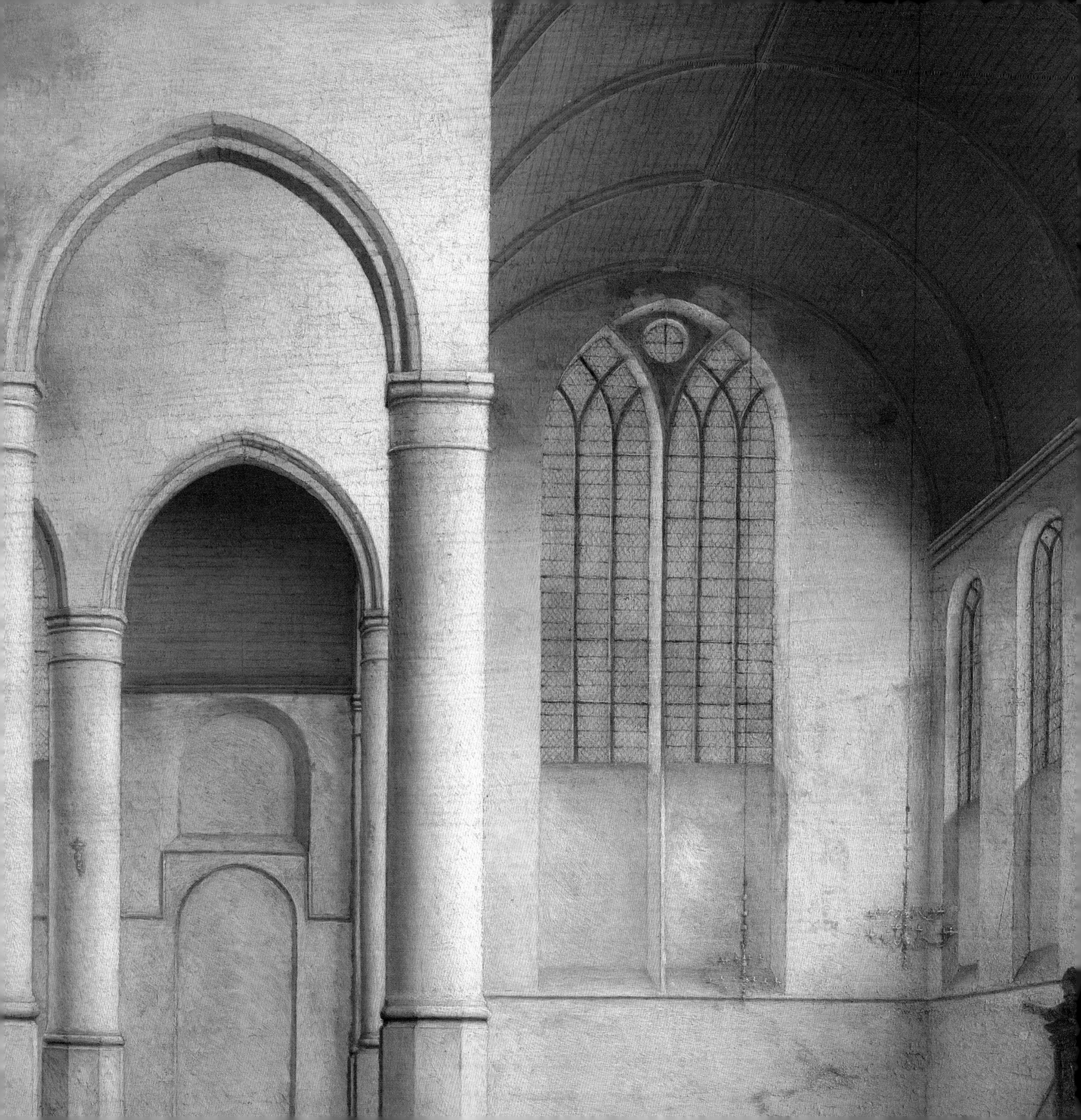

The Architecture of Light

In many works of art the architecture of windows is more than just supplementary to the main theme. The Danish artist Vilhelm Hammershøi, for example, favoured subjects that possessed linear, 'architectural' qualities, which he found in abundance in a domestic window (page 154). While Hammershøi's interests were principally aesthetic, the Renaissance painter Antonello da Messina used mullions, window seats and clerestories as a kind of extended portrait, characterizing St Jerome as both a gentleman-scholar and a priest (page 157).

The light that passes through Antonello's windows and door also defines an architectural space of breathtaking realism, a supreme example of the Albertian concept of painting (see pages 8–9). In contrast, the medieval stained glass of the Sainte-Chapelle in Paris (page 159) achieves an effect of intense luminosity accompanied by an absence, or near absence, of pictorial space – an aesthetic dimly reflected, in a secular context, in a contemporary photogram (page 161). Ultimately, stained glass dwindled in importance as a result of both religious and artistic developments: the iconoclasm of the Reformation, the effects of which can be seen in Pieter Saenredam's painting (pages 162–63); and the taste for *trompe l'œil*, which began in the Renaissance and reached its peak during the seventeenth century (pages 164 and 167).

Windows are, of course, also intended to be seen from the outside, and the streetscapes by Jan Vermeer (page 168) and Bernardo Bellotto (pages 170–71) present a variety of scale as well as design. In contrast to the vernacular, domestic style of Vermeer's *Little Street*, Bellotto's canvas includes a Renaissance public building, the Scuola di San Marco in Venice, with elaborate, if relatively small, classical windows.

Good natural light is essential to making and exhibiting works of art. Hubert Robert's view of the Grande Galerie at the Louvre (page 173) is an example of a picture with an agenda, in this case an argument for introducing skylights into a museum. Robert's work may be compared to Frédéric Bazille's canvas of his own up-to-date atelier (page 175), which in turn contrasts with Vincent van Gogh's brilliant view of his barred asylum window (page 176).

In the twentieth century new building and glass-production techniques enabled windows to play a much more prominent role in architecture, as can be seen in the two final works (pages 178–79 and 181). These are paintings of aspects of the American dream – respectively, the convenience and freedom represented by the motel, and the skyline of a modern metropolis – but each has an unsettling, even disturbing quality, as if the dream might at any moment turn into a nightmare.

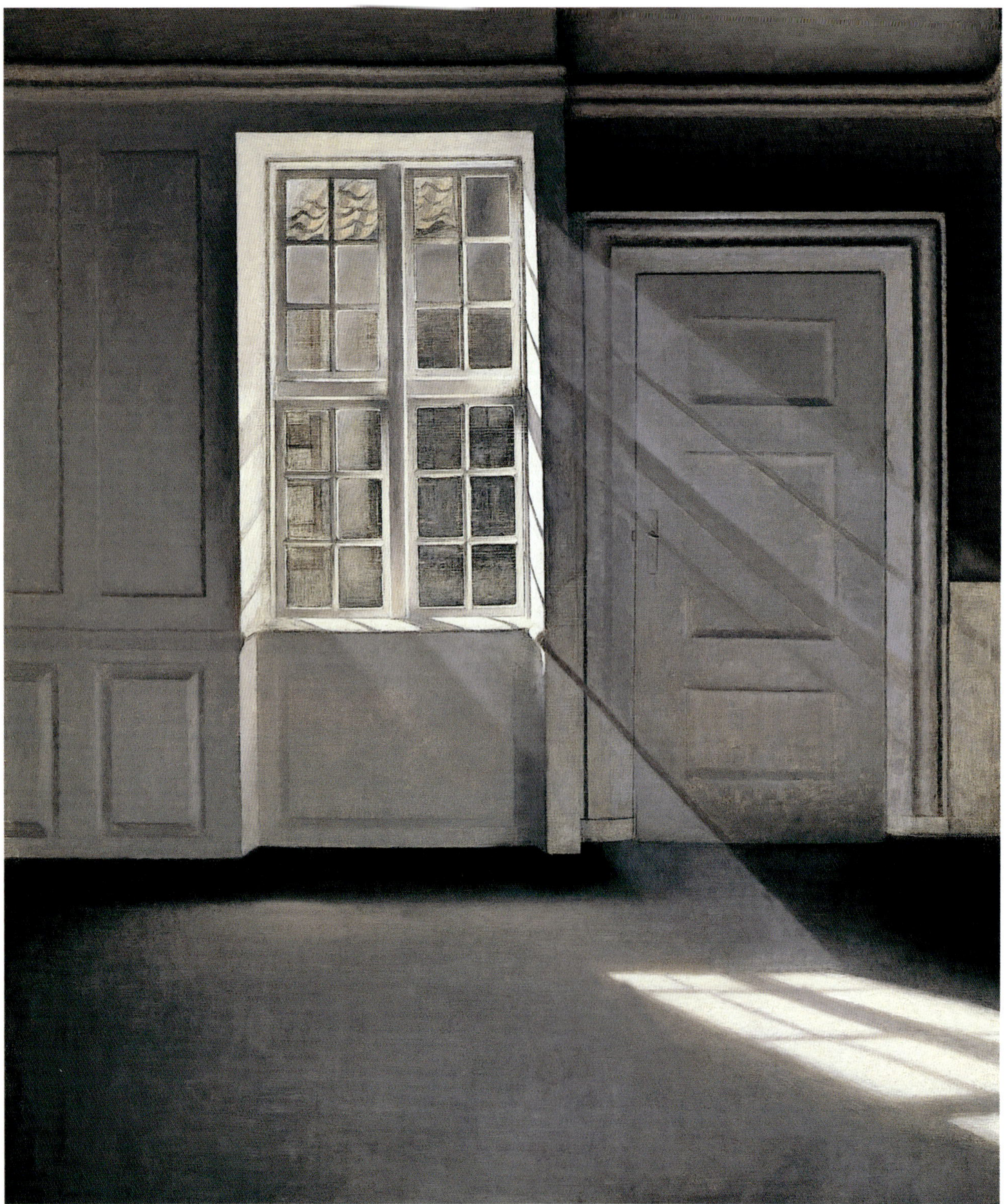

Vilhelm Hammershøi

(1864–1916)

Sunbeams or Sunshine. Dust Motes Dancing in the Sunbeams

1900
Oil on canvas
70 × 59 cm (27½ × 23¼ in.)
ORDRUPGAARD, COPENHAGEN

Vilhelm Hammershøi's depiction of his home in Copenhagen ignores such frivolous details as window handles and curtains, let alone the flowers that can be seen in photographs of his apartment. The glass reveals little of the courtyard beyond the panes, many of which have been made opaque by the reflection of light. Instead, the canvas is dominated by the brilliant sunbeams, illuminating motes of dust and casting the outline of the window on to the embrasure and the floor. Despite this emphasis on the effects of sunshine, a strong linear pattern is created by such features of the room as the window frame, the cornice and the panelling, as well as by the rays themselves. As Hammershøi himself explained: 'What makes me choose a motif are … the lines, what I like to call the architectural content of an image. And then there's the light, of course. Obviously, that's also very important, but I think it's the lines that have the greatest significance for me.'[1] Here, the elegant domestic architecture and poetic light effects have been perfectly integrated.

Antonello da Messina

(*c.* 1430–1479)

St Jerome in His Study

c. 1475
Oil on lime
45.7 × 36.2 cm (18 × 14¼ in.)
THE NATIONAL GALLERY, LONDON

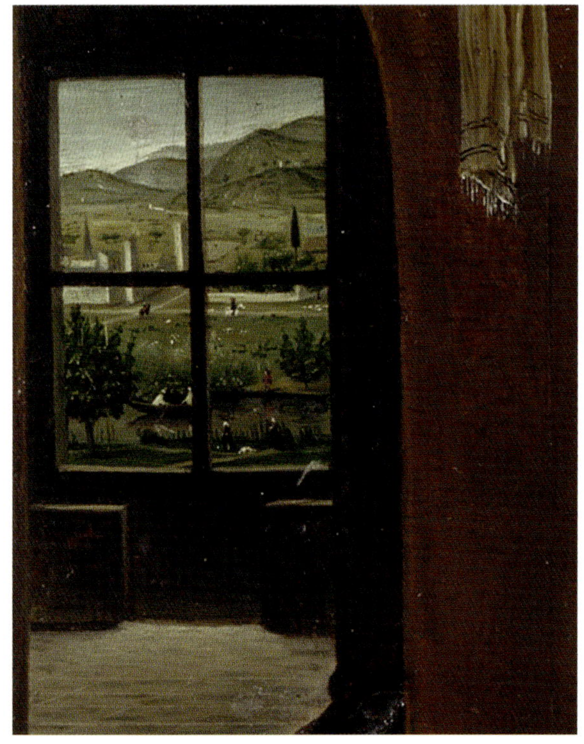

Antonello da Messina was a Sicilian who travelled throughout Italy but was inspired above all by Netherlandish art. He used the medium of oil paint to create subtle light effects, such as the daylight shining on the tiled floor at the back of this interior. The fenestration is precisely differentiated: secular on the ground floor and ecclesiastical above. The cross window (see detail, left), with its view of a walled city, creates a domestic atmosphere, while on the right another rectangular opening illuminates an arcaded Renaissance library. The cusped, bipartite (or 'bifore') windows at the top are a feature of medieval architecture, especially in Italy, derived from late classical and Byzantine prototypes. Here, Antonello represents a magnificent clerestory, part of a composite setting reminding us that Jerome was not only a great scholar but also a Doctor of the Church.

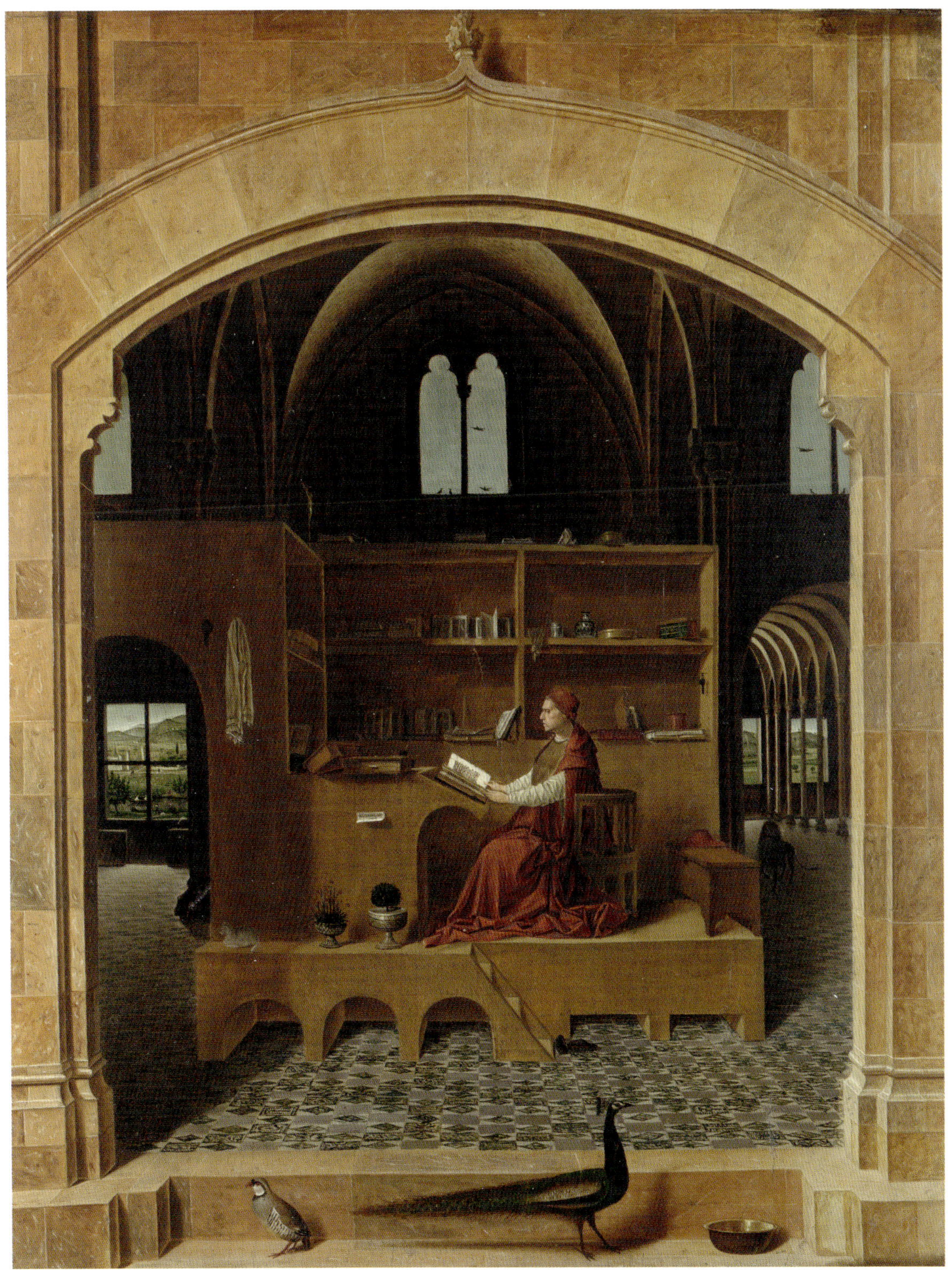

Sainte-Chapelle, Paris
Stained glass, upper chapel

1242/43–1248 (restored 19th century)

The upper chapel of the two-storey Sainte-Chapelle in Paris is distinguished by the remarkable scale of its windows, which occupy much of the building's surface. The architects achieved this feat by using concealed iron ties and deep external buttresses, allowing them to reduce the masonry of the walls to slender mullions reaching up to the elegant ribbed vault. The glass depicts a wide range of subjects, including, in the windows of the nave, scenes from such Old Testament texts as the book of Judith (right), and, at the centre of the apse (opposite), the Passion. The latter was a theme well suited to the function of this royal chapel, which housed such relics as the Crown of Thorns and a fragment of the True Cross, themselves the subject of a window near the south-west corner. Above all, the glass creates an overwhelming sensation of colour and light, drawing attention away from the rational, regular forms of the architecture. The ongoing restoration of the windows, scheduled for completion in 2014, has been facilitated by a generous grant from the VELUX Foundations in Denmark.

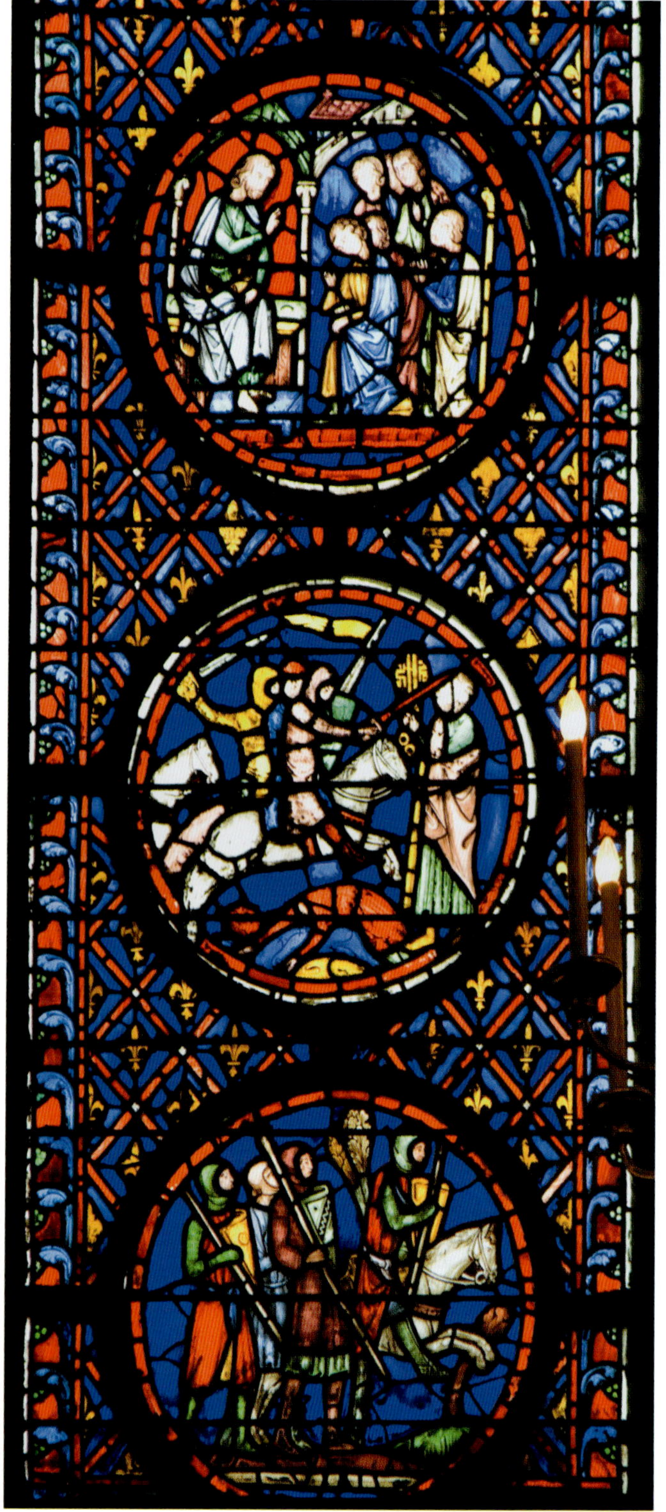

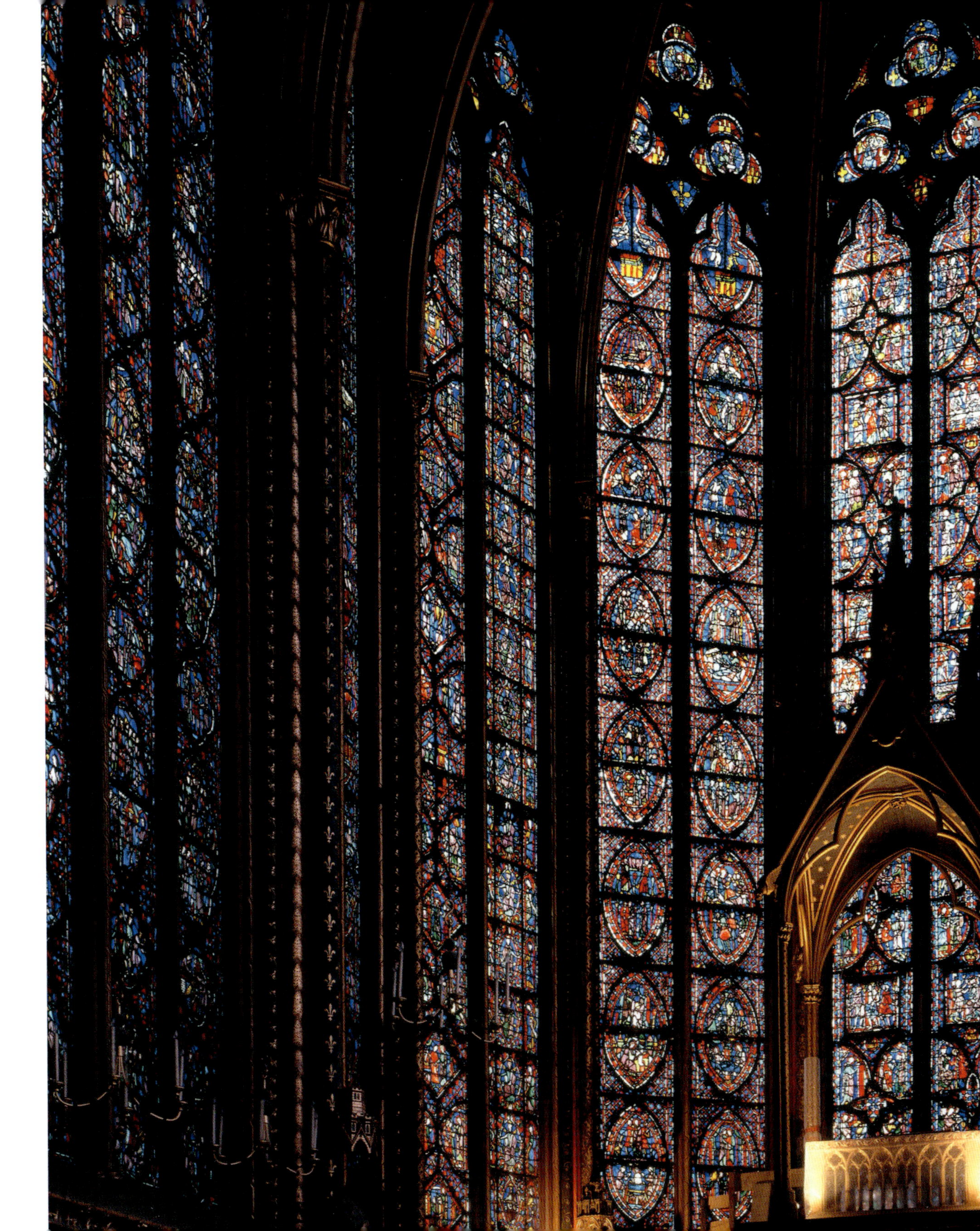

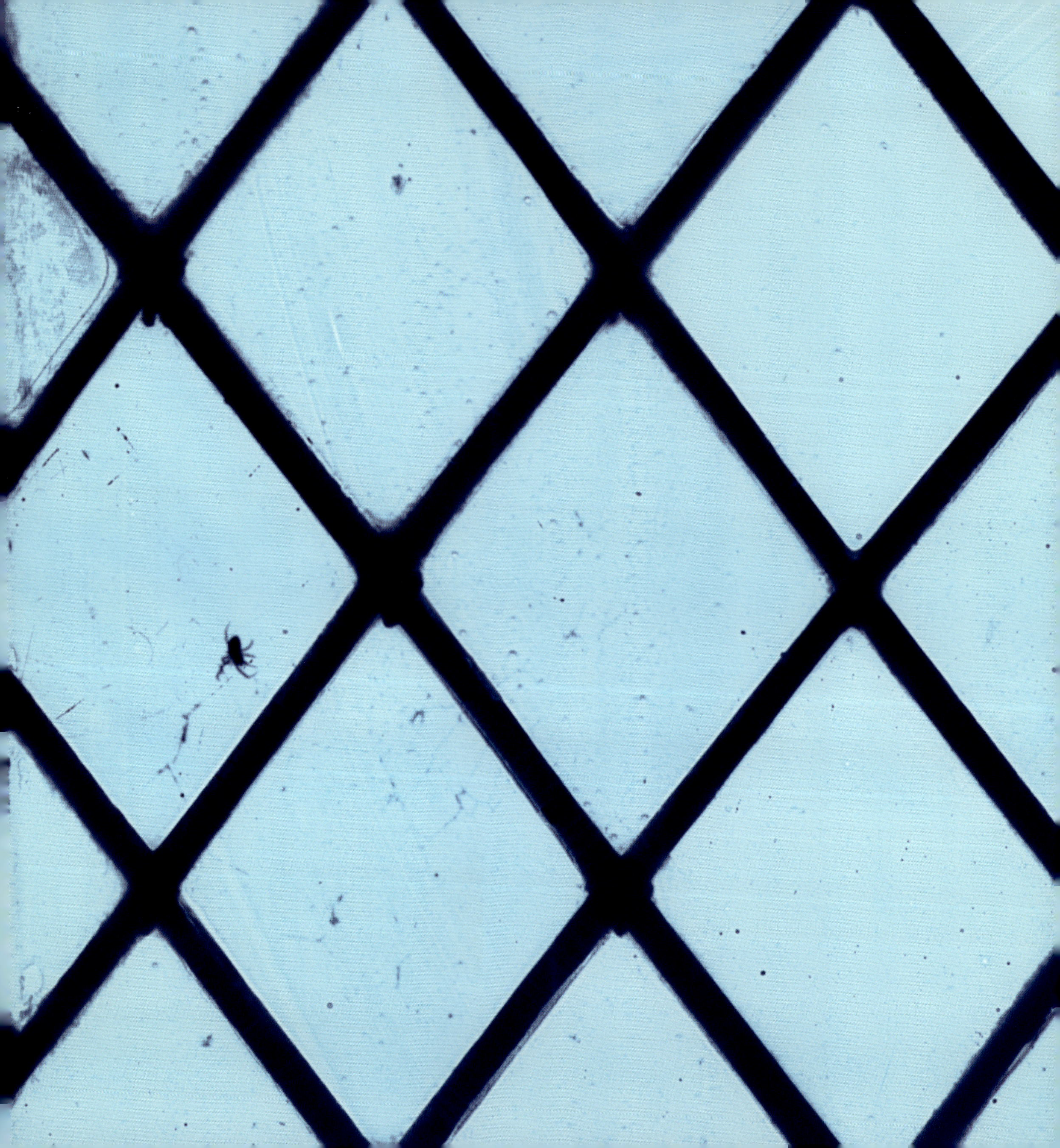

Floris Neusüss

(born 1937)
In collaboration with Renate Heyne

Homage to William Henry Fox Talbot: His 'Latticed Window' in Lacock Abbey as a Photogram, Lacock Abbey

2010
Dye destruction prints
320 × 237 cm (126 × 93¼ in.)
COLLECTION OF THE ARTIST

The German artist Floris Neusüss has pared down his subject to its essentials. The mullions and transom of the window have been reduced to a silhouette against the light, with little sense of the surrounding walls or of a view beyond the glass. This apparent simplicity is actually intended as a form of homage to an icon of photography. In 1835 William Henry Fox Talbot used a piece of silvered paper to reproduce the same subject, a window in the south gallery of his house, Lacock Abbey. The result was a small photographic negative – the first of its kind – of the light passing between the latticed, lead glazing bars; Neusüss, however, has used modern technology to make a life-size, positive print. Neusüss's version is also far more detailed than its predecessor, recording the imperfections of the glass and even a spider hanging from its thread (see detail, opposite). Despite these subtleties, it is a highly reduced, two-dimensional image – a work that ignores the heritage of the Renaissance and, indeed, many of the conventions that still determine contemporary photography.

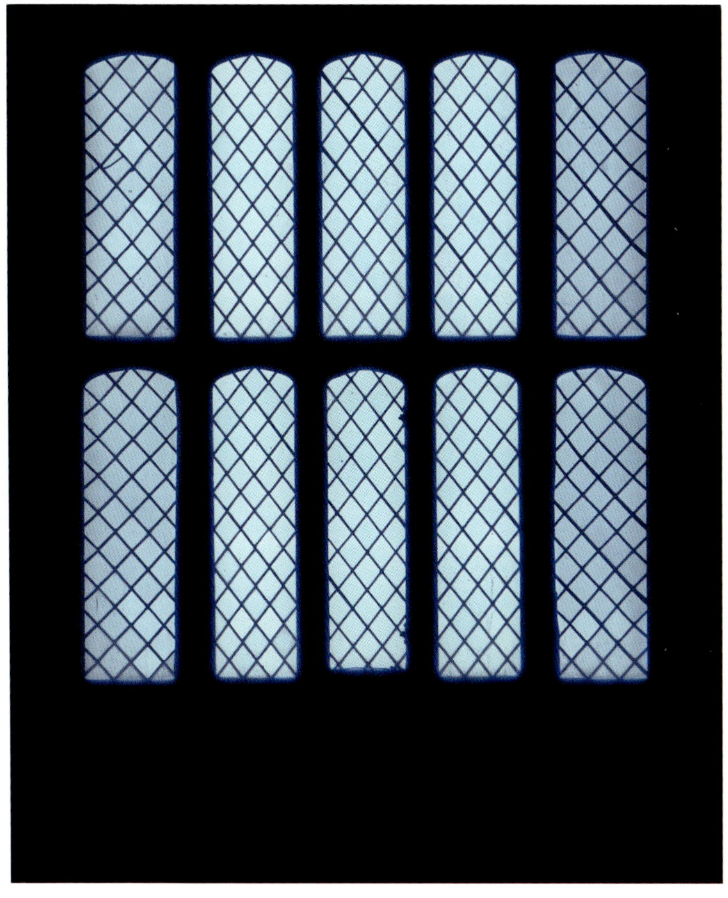

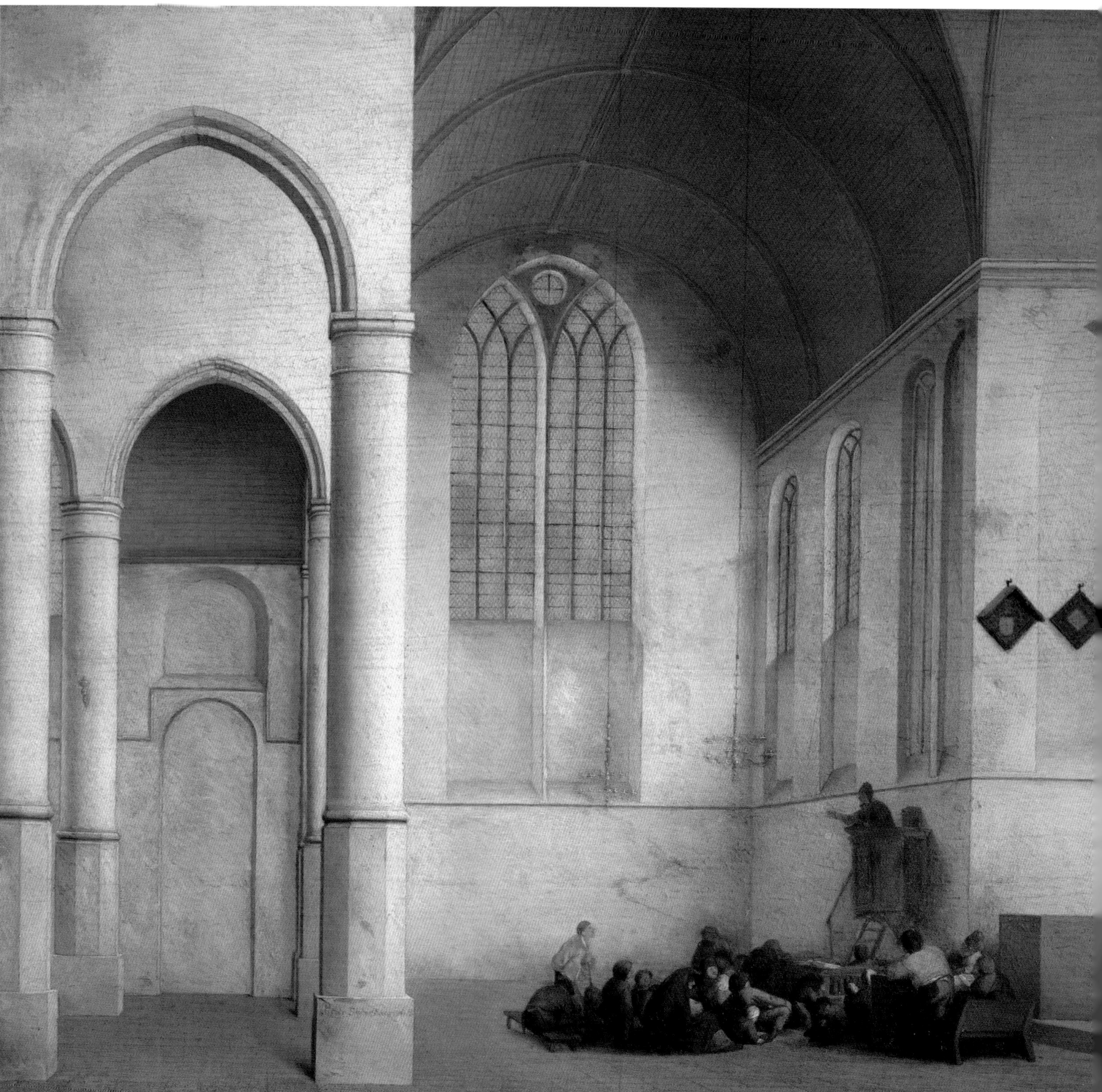

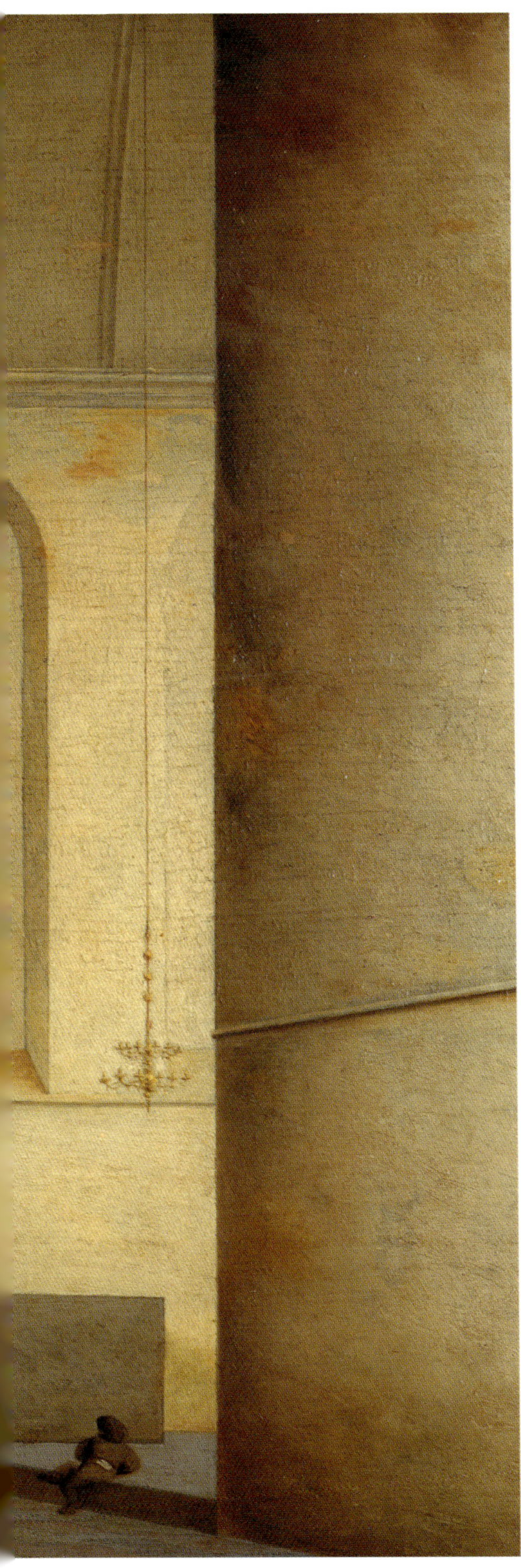

Pieter Saenredam

(1597–1665)

Figures attributed to Adriaen van Ostade

North transept and adjoining areas of the choir (right) and nave (left) of St Odulphuskerk, Assendelft

c. 1633
Oil on panel
46 × 64 cm (18⅛ × 25¼ in.)
GALLERIA SABAUDA, TURIN

As a result of Protestant iconoclasm, the windows of this Dutch Gothic church are unadorned, providing a lucid setting for the sermon, which is probably being delivered by a relative of the artist. Here, the emphasis is very much on the Word rather than the image. The painter is alive to the structure's architectural qualities; its space, vividly illuminated through the clear glass; and its physical lightness and height, to which the soaring windows are integral. Although the openings have been completely or partially blocked up, the slender, two-light window in the transept, with its small oculus at the top, remains particularly impressive.

Pieter Saenredam was a pioneer of a new type of church painting, replacing distant viewpoints and an emphasis on perspectives along the nave with a more intimate, informal approach. This does not mean that his pictures are totally realistic, as is demonstrated by a comparison of this panel with a preparatory drawing. Saenredam has simplified and moved certain details, such as the pulpit, while the interior is shown from an angle that was probably impossible. This cannot be tested, however: the building was demolished in 1852.

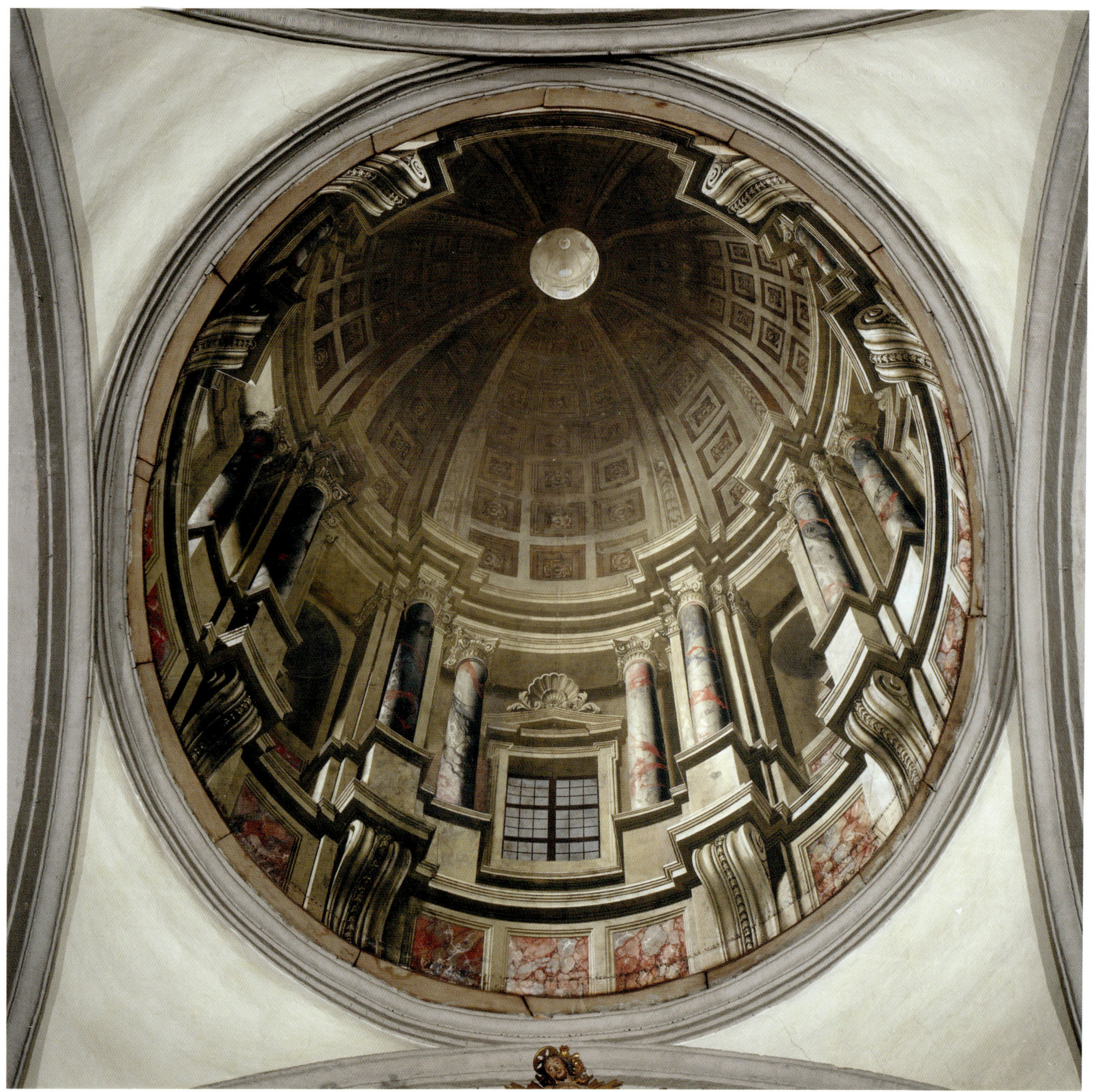

Andrea Pozzo
(1642–1709)

Painted canvas with illusionistic architecture in the Church of Saints Flora and Lucilla, Arezzo

1702

Andrea Pozzo's canvas cupola is a striking example of *trompe l'œil*, made in Rome for a Benedictine abbey church in Tuscany. The drum, or lower part, of the dome includes a remarkable image of a rectangular window with an elaborate Baroque frame and architrave surmounted by an exquisite shell moulding, while other unseen openings are implied in both the drum and the lantern at the top. There is relatively little interest in the windows per se, and certainly none in the glass, but, as concentrated sources of light, they define the architecture's distinctive qualities: its plasticity and striking variation of colour and texture.

A Peepshow with Views of
the Interior of a Dutch House

c. 1655–60
Oil and egg on wood
58 × 88 × 60.5 cm (22⅞ × 34⅝ × 23⅞ in.)
THE NATIONAL GALLERY, LONDON

When the observer looks through peepholes in either side of this unusual object – a box covered on the inside with images of the interior of a Dutch house – the effect of perspective creates a coherent sequence of spaces articulated by paintings, doors and windows. These include, on the left, a cross window with a finely moulded mullion and transom, and, to the right, in an end room beyond a bed chamber, a minute depiction of stained glass featuring a coat of arms and a standing figure probably holding a cross. Other windows, not visible in this image, present a range of designs, as well as offering glimpses of the outside world. The variety of domestic fenestration in the Netherlands of the mid-seventeenth century may not be the peepshow's principal theme, but the attention paid to this subject enhances the startling illusion of reality.

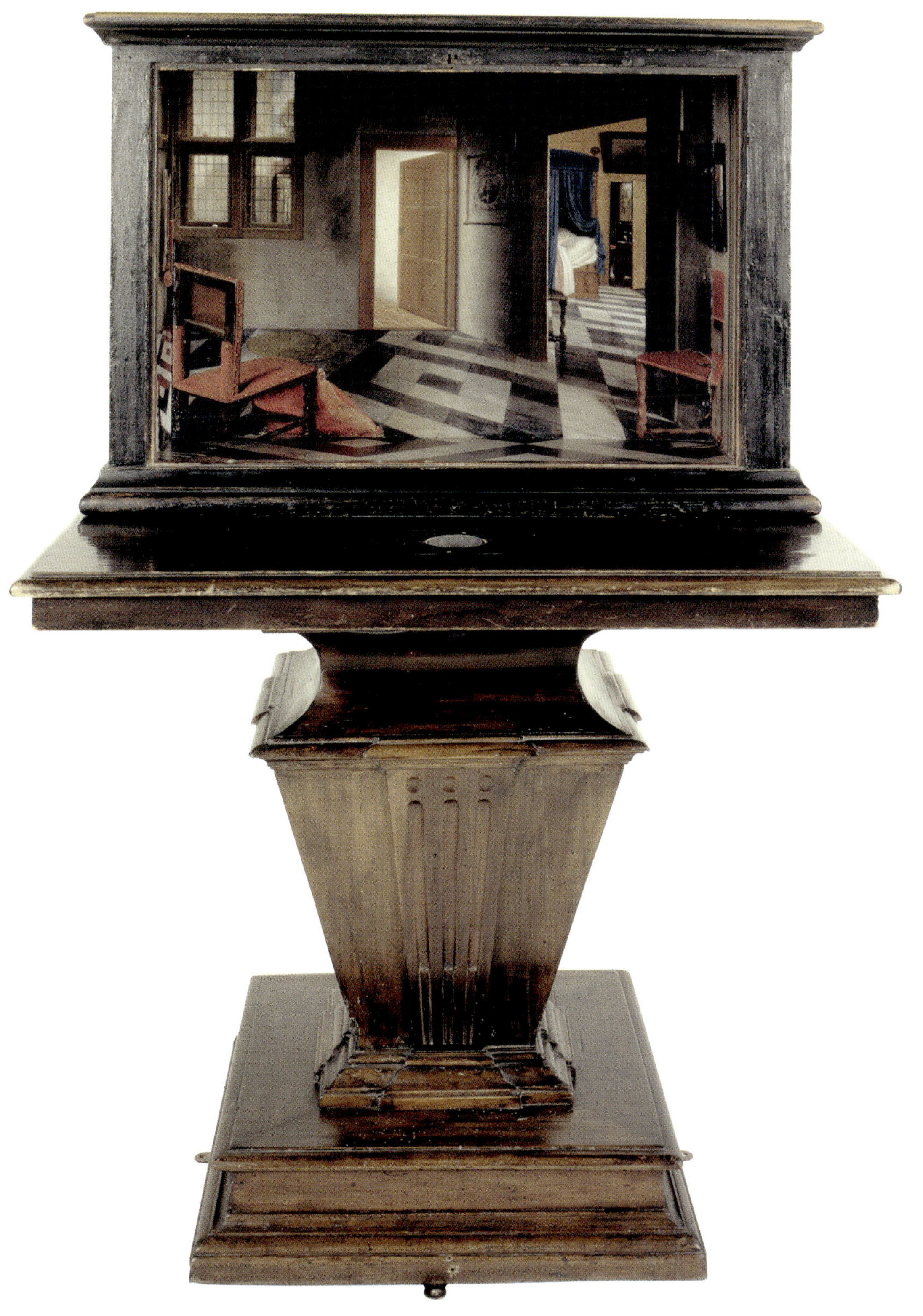

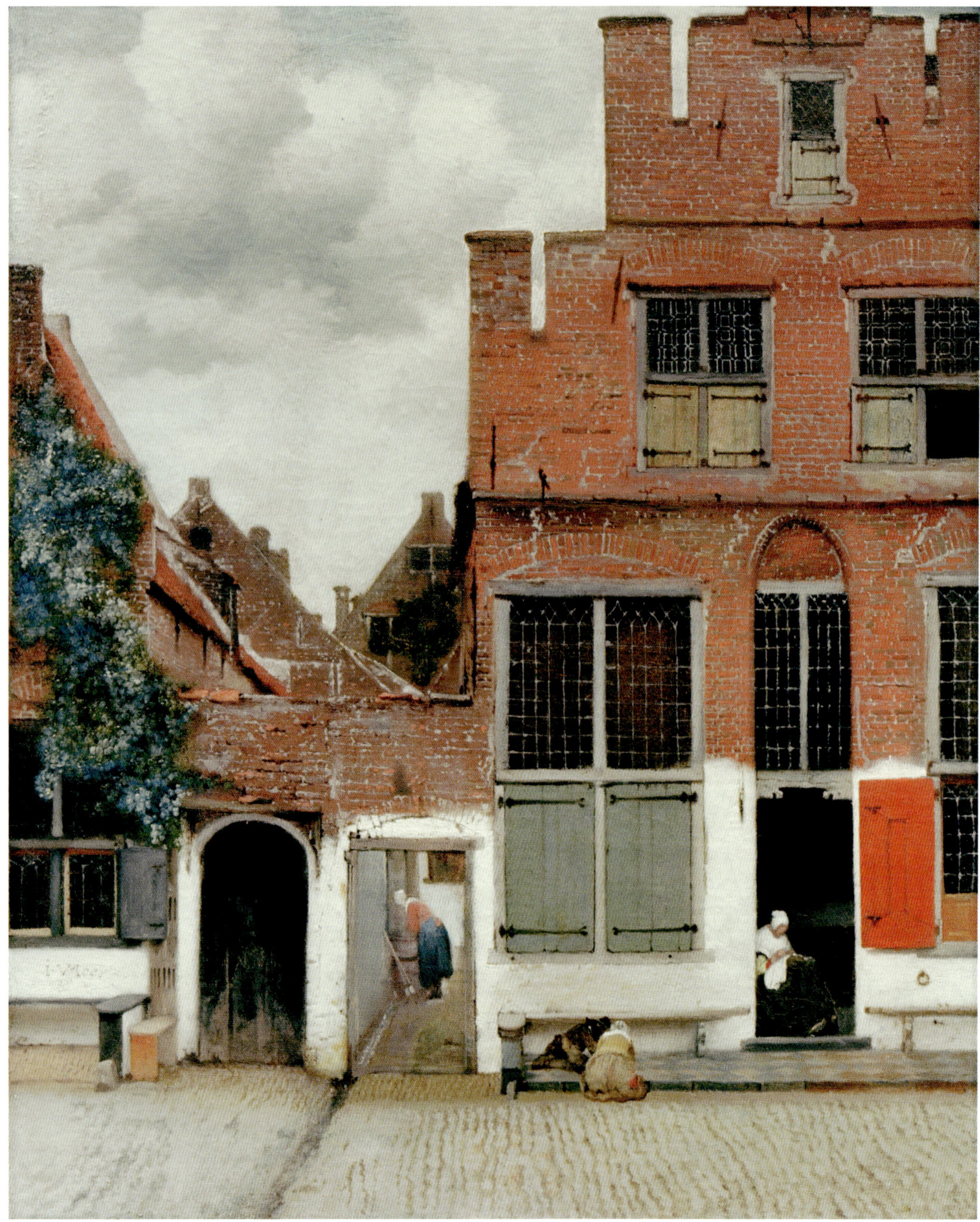

Jan Vermeer

(1632–1675)

The Little Street

c. 1658
Oil on canvas
54.3 × 44 cm (21⅜ × 17⅜ in.)
RIJKSMUSEUM, AMSTERDAM

The leaded cross windows in these sixteenth-
century dwellings are similar to those that
illuminate Vermeer's interiors so delicately
(pages 29 and 75), but this streetscape affords
no glimpses of his enigmatic private world.
Indeed, the panes are rectangles of blackness,
in contrast to the lighter tones of the walls and
shutters. The latter take the place of glass in
the lower parts of the upper windows, while on
the ground floor the façade is enlivened by an
opened red shutter, which adds an element of
asymmetry as well as a patch of colour. In order
to accommodate it, Vermeer has increased
the space between the door and the window.
This is not the only factual inaccuracy in the
painting, which is probably a composite of the
view from Vermeer's own house and another
street in Delft. For all its apparent realism,
The Little Street is a work that puts evocation
above topographical correctness.

Bernardo Bellotto
(1721–1780)

View of the Rio dei Mendicanti
and the Scuola di San Marco, Venice

c. 1741
Oil on canvas
41.9 × 59.9 cm (16½ × 23½ in.)
GALLERIE DELL'ACCADEMIA, VENICE

This unusual view of the Campo Santi Giovanni
e Paolo in Venice is angled so as to omit almost
entirely its most famous building. Instead of
the church from which the square gets its
name, we are presented with the Palazzo
Dandolo, seen in the foreground on the right,
and, in the distance, the Scuola di San Marco,
headquarters of the religious confraternity of the
same name. The palace's arched fenestration
and small attic openings are shown obliquely so
as to emphasize their depth, creating a sense of
privacy and shade that contrasts with the lively
social activity being conducted from the sunlit
balconies. Meanwhile, the Scuola's glinting
windows, richly adorned with columns and
segmental and triangular pediments, correspond
with other classical features, such as the curved
lunettes above them. This is a façade that
eschews large expanses of glass but displays
the rhythmic variety and richness of texture
so characteristic of Venetian architecture.

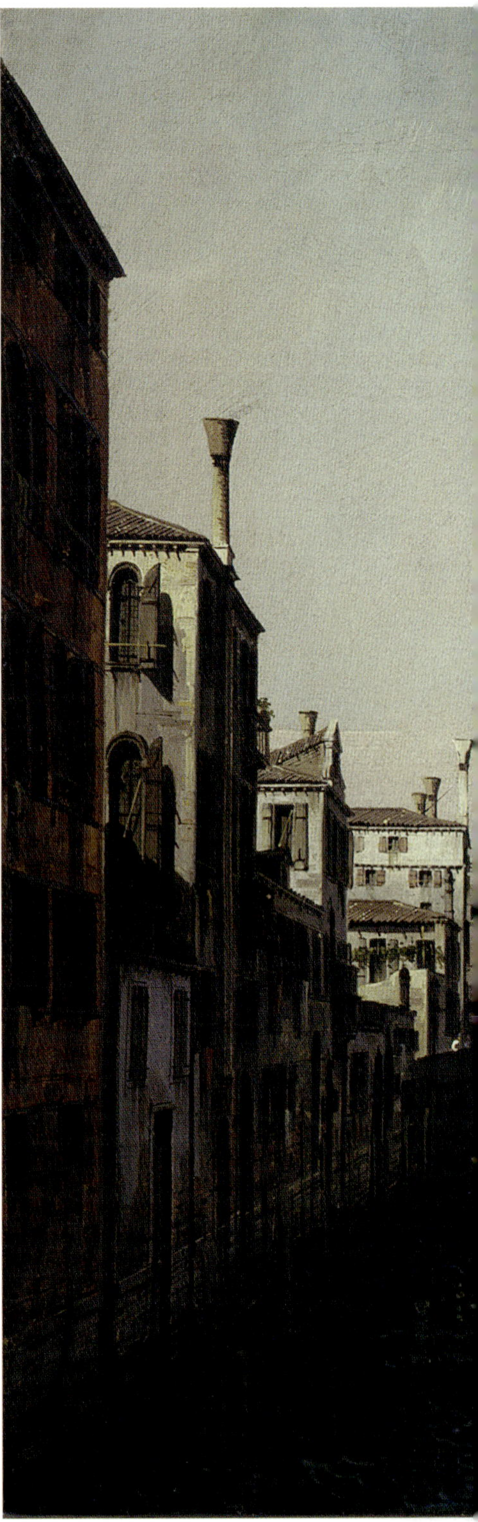

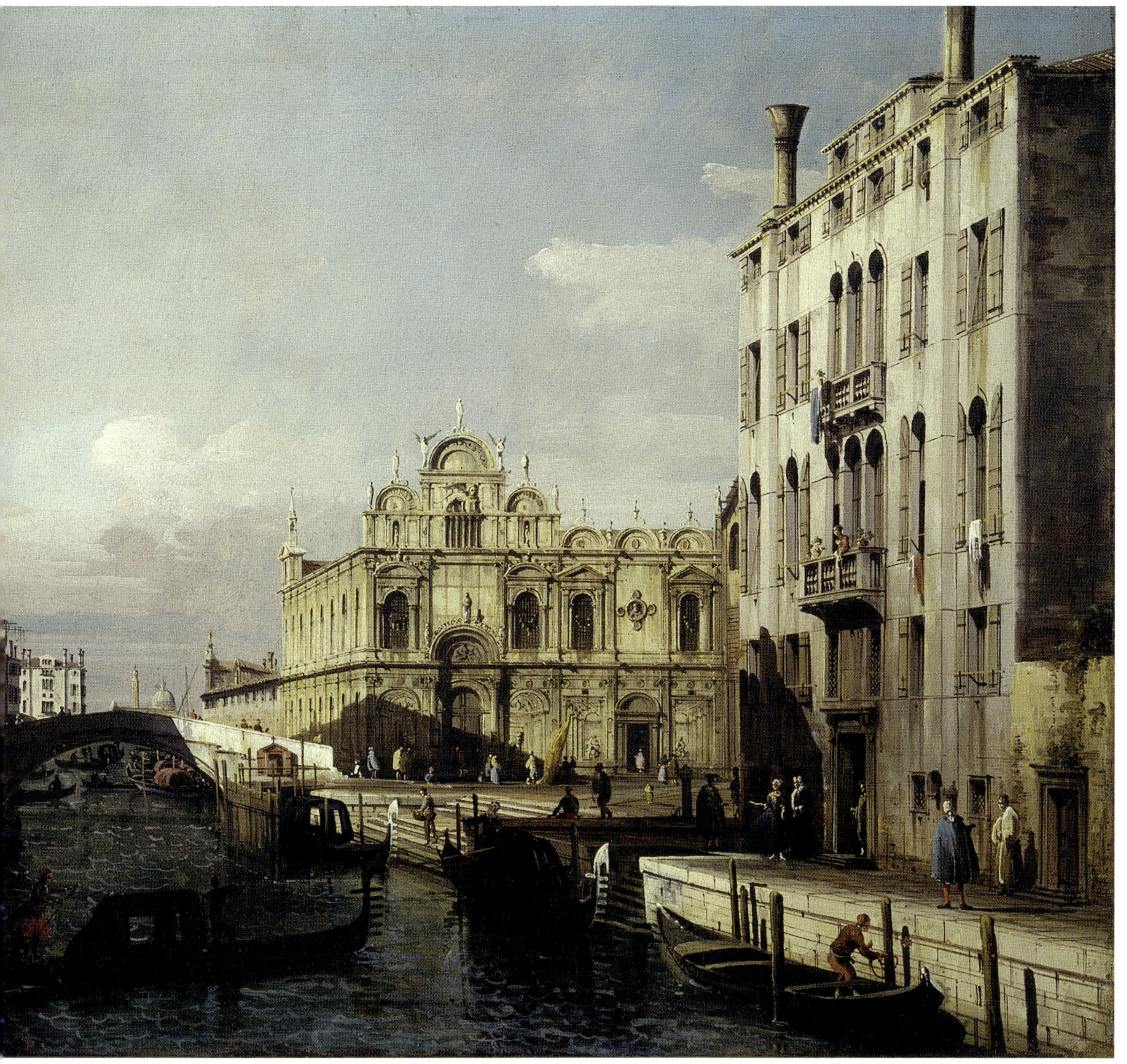

Hubert Robert

(1733–1808)

Project for the Transformation of the Grande Galerie of the Louvre

1796
Oil on canvas
115 × 145 cm (45¼ × 57⅛ in.)
MUSÉE DU LOUVRE, PARIS

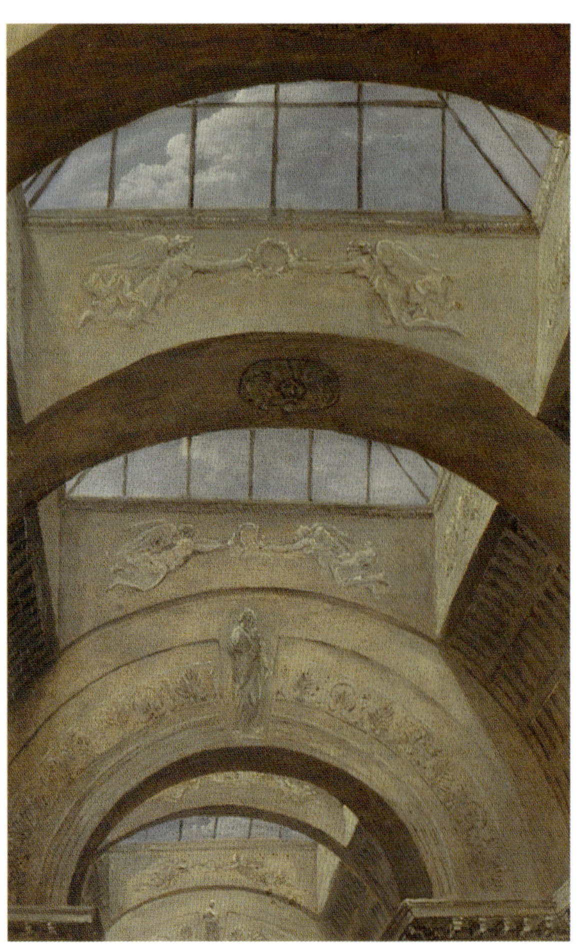

Even before the start of the French Revolution in 1789, plans had been made to create a public museum at the Palais du Louvre in Paris, although it was not actually opened until 1793. Hubert Robert's image is one of a series representing the proposed remodelling of the Grande Galerie, the long wing that connected the Louvre and the Palais des Tuileries. The classical coffered roof is broken up by ambitious skylights (see detail, left), which would have created generous, even illumination for the collection, as well as liberating wall space by removing the need for side windows. Such a design for a picture gallery was sanctioned by the writings of the Roman architect Vitruvius (see page 7), as well as by smaller-scale contemporary buildings; it was also favoured by most members of the pre-Revolutionary committee that had originally examined the proposal, including Robert himself. Indecision and upheaval intervened, and the proposal remained unexecuted. However, glass roofing later became a feature of many museum buildings, including the Grande Galerie itself, albeit to a different design.

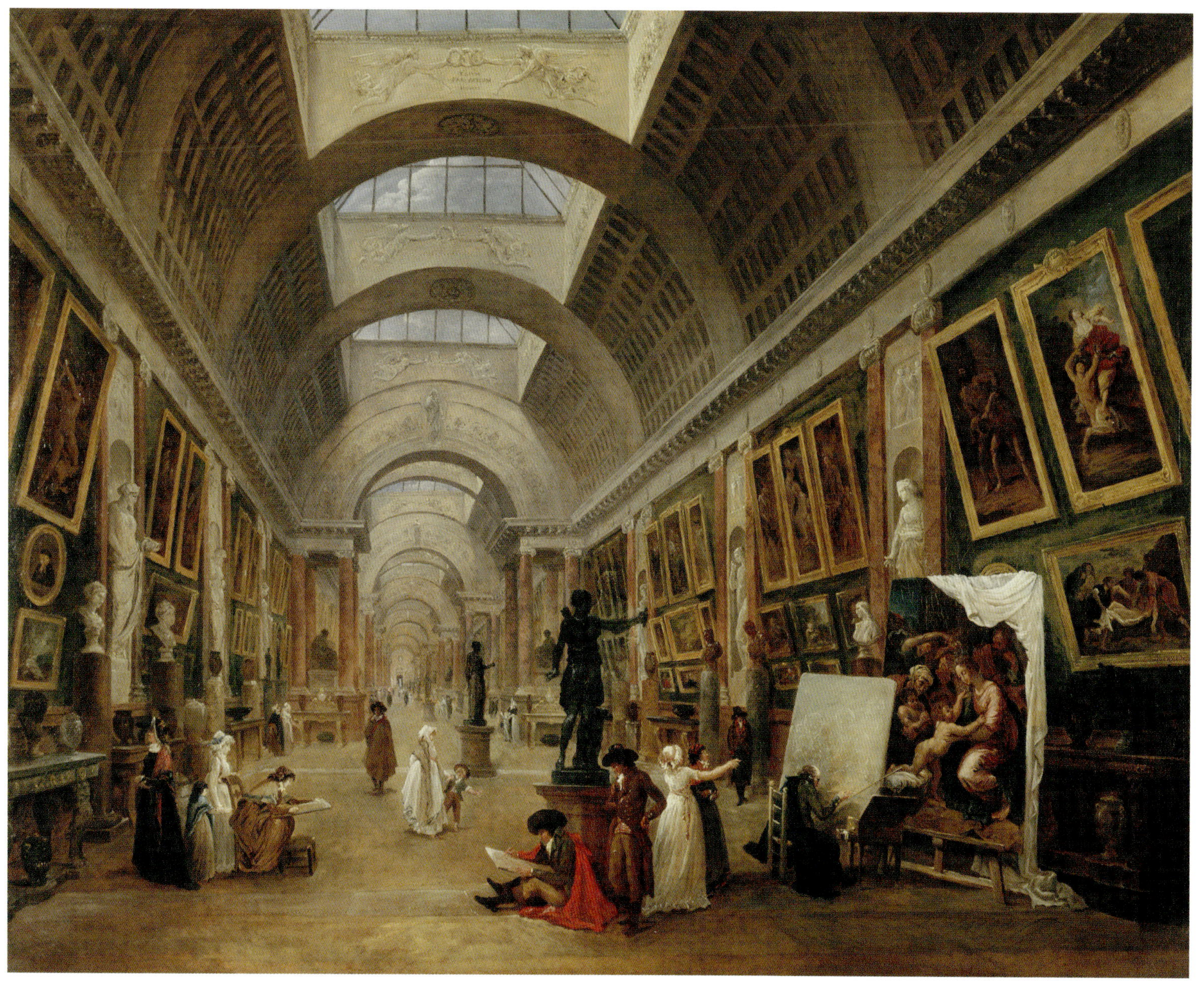

Frédéric Bazille
(1841–1870)

Bazille's Studio

1870
Oil on canvas
98 × 128 cm (38⅝ × 50⅜ in.)
MUSÉE D'ORSAY, PARIS

Although the Impressionists are renowned
for their practice of bright, *plein-air* (outdoor)
painting, they also worked more conventionally
in soberly lit studios. Here, the elegant, north-
facing window, partly curtained and framing
a grey Parisian sky, was designed to provide
an even light throughout the day. Its generous
proportions are echoed by those of the room,
which allowed Bazille (in the centre of the
picture, palette in hand, painted by Edouard
Manet) both to display his works advantageously
and to entertain his friends, who in this
instance include Manet (wearing a hat, looking
at the canvas on the easel) and, possibly,
Renoir and Monet. Bazille, the wealthy son
of a French senator, did not need to economize.

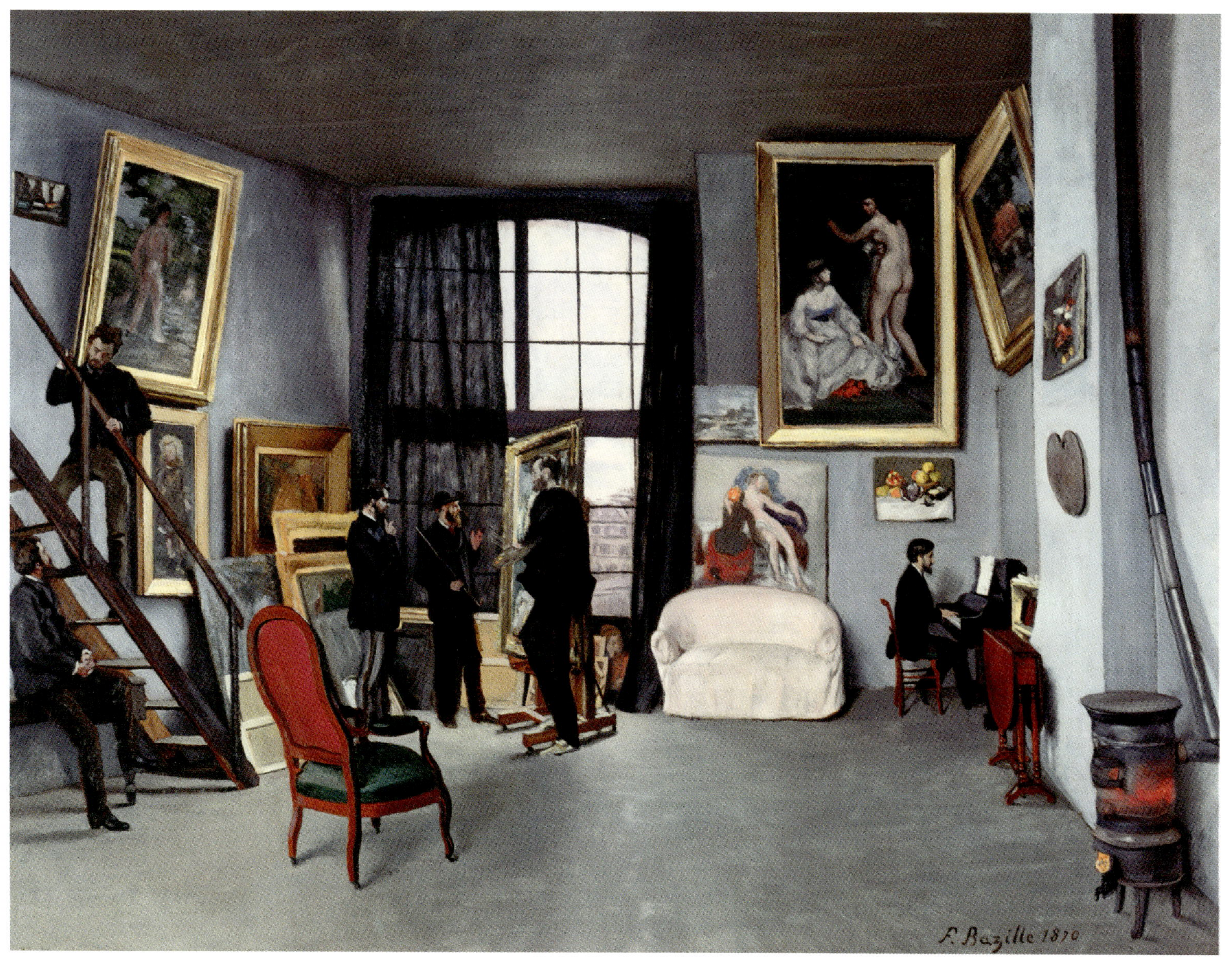

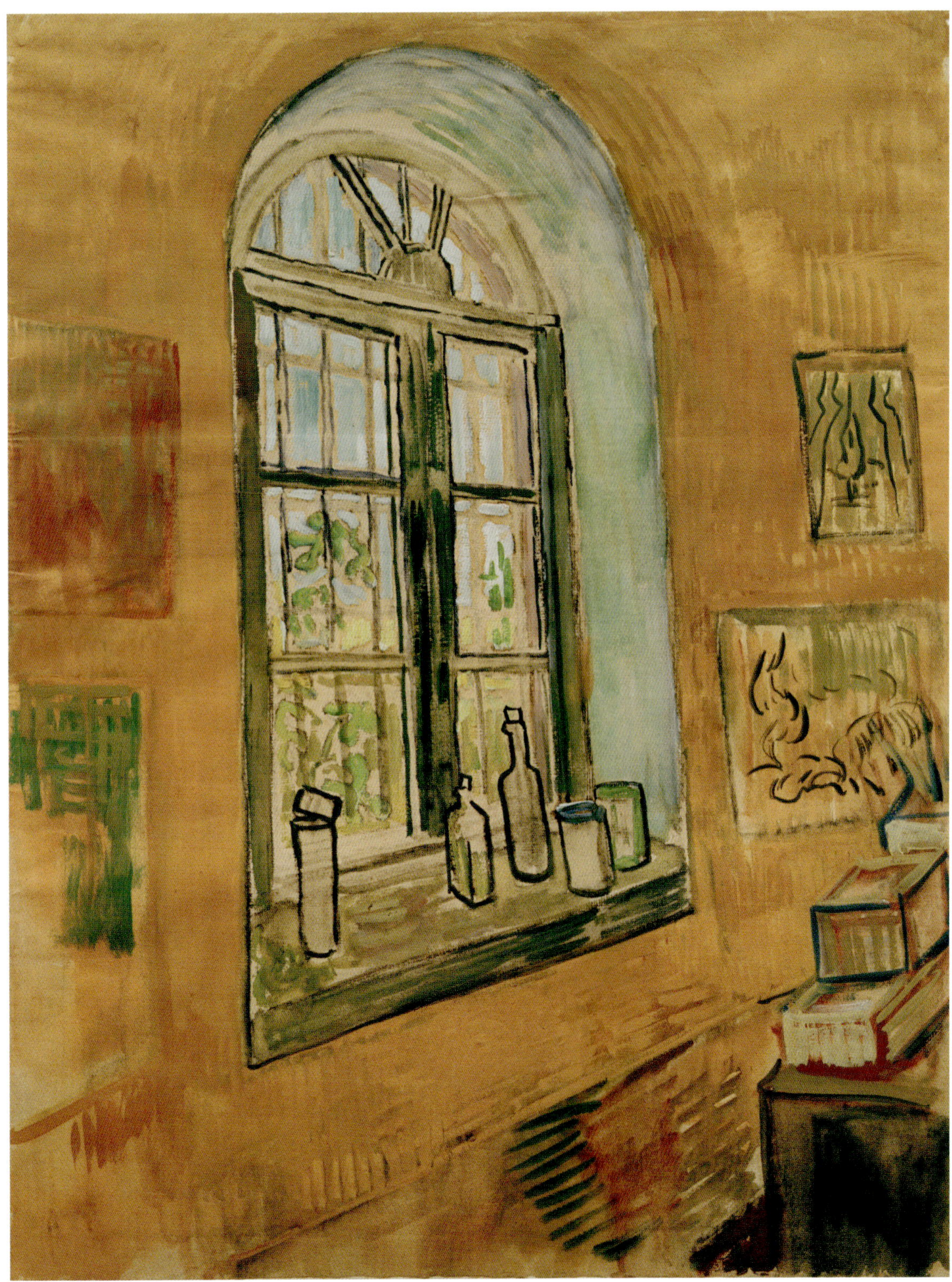

Vincent van Gogh

(1853–1890)

Window in the Studio

1889
Gouache with black chalk on pink laid paper
62 × 47 cm (24⅜ × 18½ in.)
VAN GOGH MUSEUM, AMSTERDAM

When Vincent van Gogh hospitalized himself at the Saint-Paul-de-Mausole asylum in Saint-Rémy, near Arles, in 1889, he continued to work in a cell next to his bedroom. This unconventional studio had a small barred window, which was not only a source of light but also, for a while, the vantage point from which he painted the outside world. The bars miraculously disappear from most of the pictures he made at this time, and even here they seem relatively insignificant. More prominent is the arched light at the top of the window, its shape emphasized by the curved strokes around it. Meanwhile, the transparent vessels on the sill, together with the patches of colour on the wall, accentuate the warm southern light flooding the room. Van Gogh has managed to erode the conventional distinction between studio and *plein-air* painting.

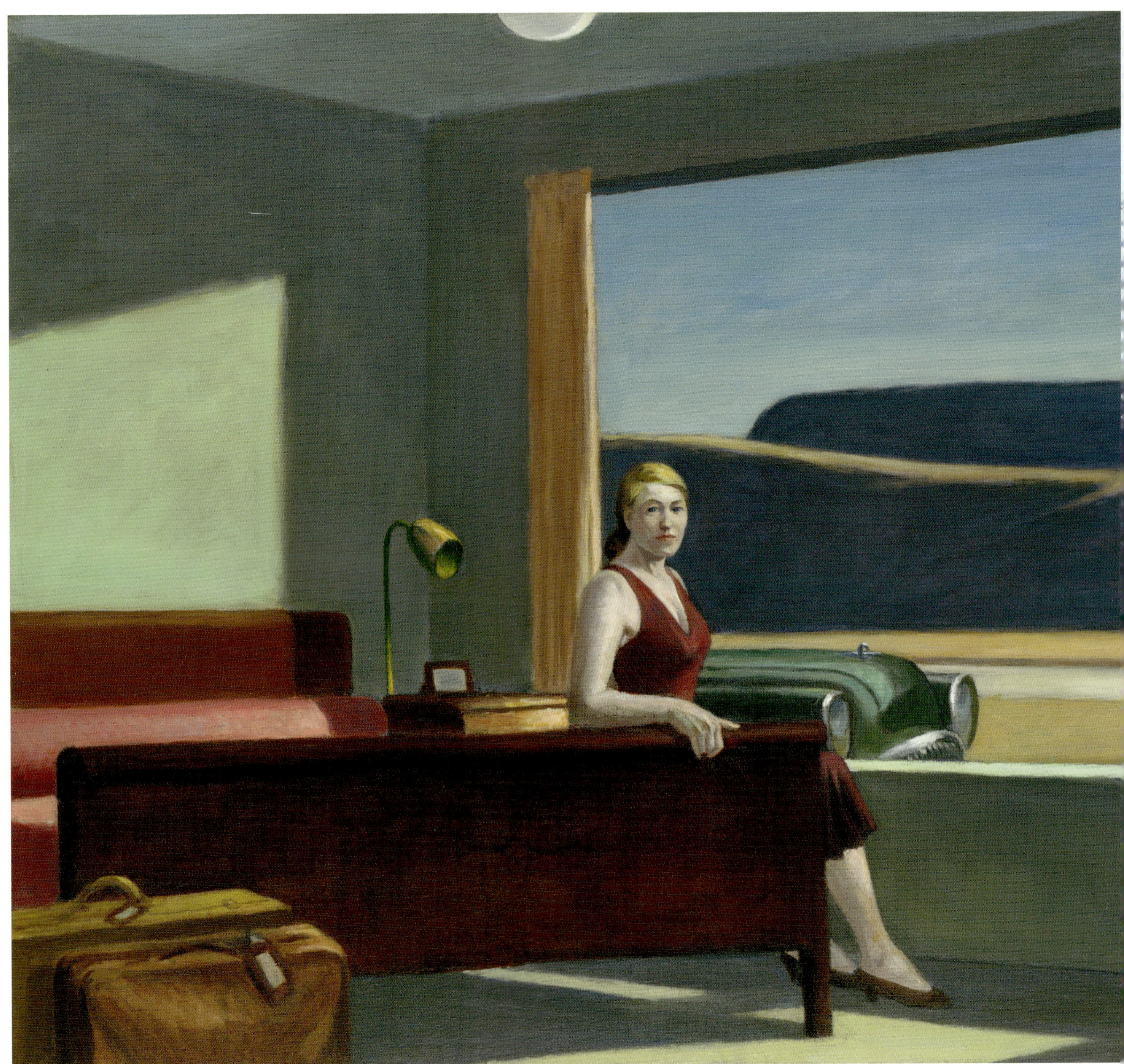

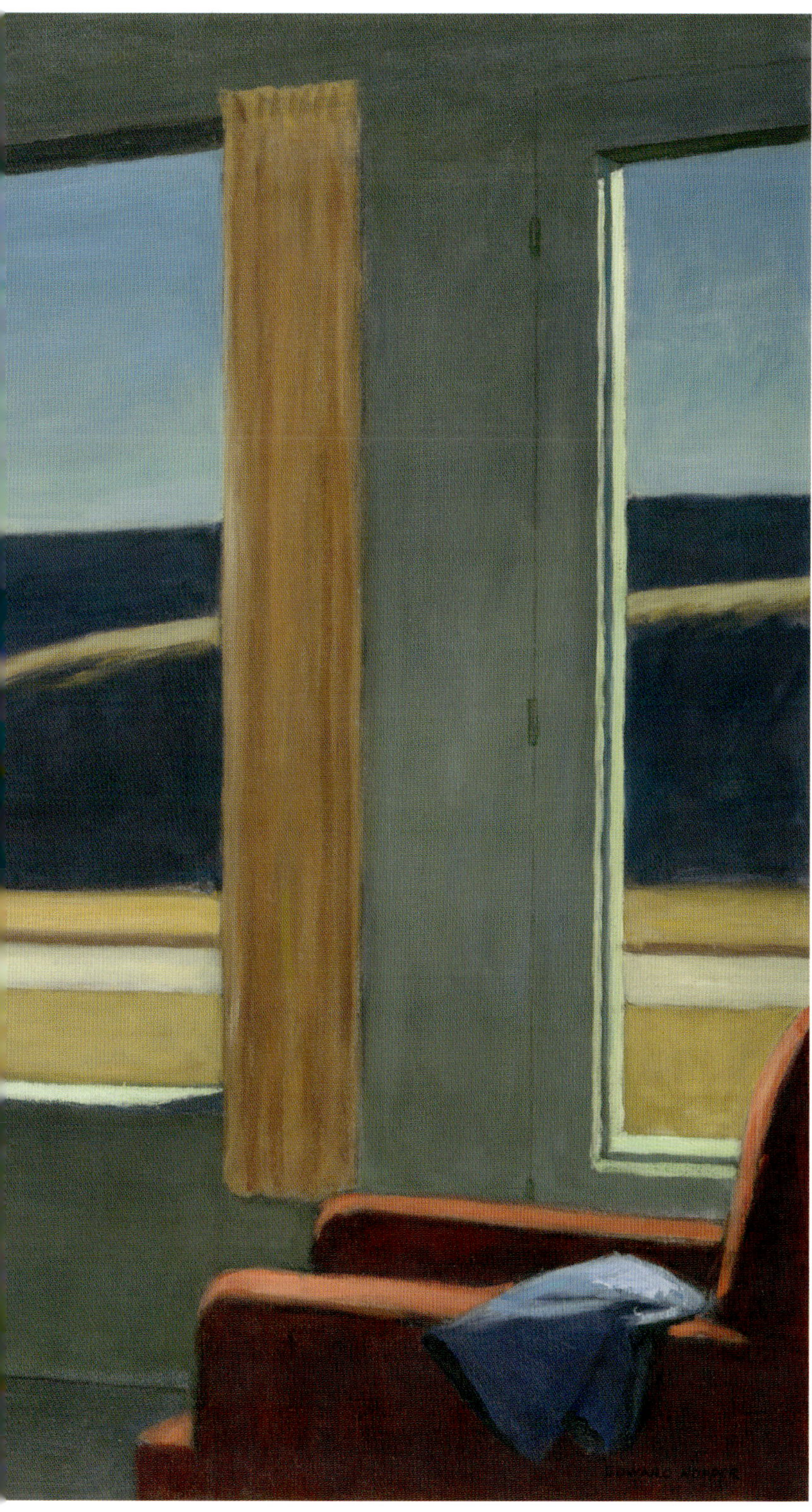

Edward Hopper
(1882–1967)

Western Motel

1957
Oil on canvas
77.8 × 128.3 cm (30⅜ × 50½ in.)
YALE UNIVERSITY ART GALLERY, NEW HAVEN, CONNECTICUT

Edward Hopper's state-of-the-art motel is
dominated by the plate-glass window, sitting
flush with the wall, into which the bonnet of
a green Buick apparently erupts, as if springing
from the woman's chest. Other features, such
as the orange of the curtains, create a visual
link with the arid landscape outside. The
feeling of openness, together with the merging
of interior and exterior, is exaggerated by
the absence of any attempt to render the
physical qualities of the glass, as well as by
the window's impossibly elongated shape.

For all its sensation of freedom, this cannot
be described as a happy image. Hopper's wife,
Jo, stares blankly at her artist-husband (and at
us), and we are left with the impression that it
is perhaps only the man who is really at liberty.
Certainly, the car with which the woman is
so sensuously linked was in fact a source of
contention. Jo was hardly ever allowed to get
behind the wheel: she was, by all accounts,
not a very good driver.

Charles Sheeler

(1883–1965)

New York No. 2

1951
Oil on canvas
68.6 × 46.4 cm (27 × 18¼ in.)
MUNSON-WILLIAMS-PROCTOR ART INSTITUTE, UTICA, NEW YORK

The Precisionist painter and photographer
Charles Sheeler has produced a memorable
image of shiny New York skyscrapers, with
their non-load-bearing walls and endless,
blank windows. The overlapping planes,
reminiscent of both superimposed
photographic transparencies and cubist
paintings, create unsettling optical effects.
A palpable air of menace hangs over the
city, emphasized by the abrupt shifts of tone
and the claustrophobia of the converging
lines and cropped composition. The modern
metropolis has taken on a disturbing persona.

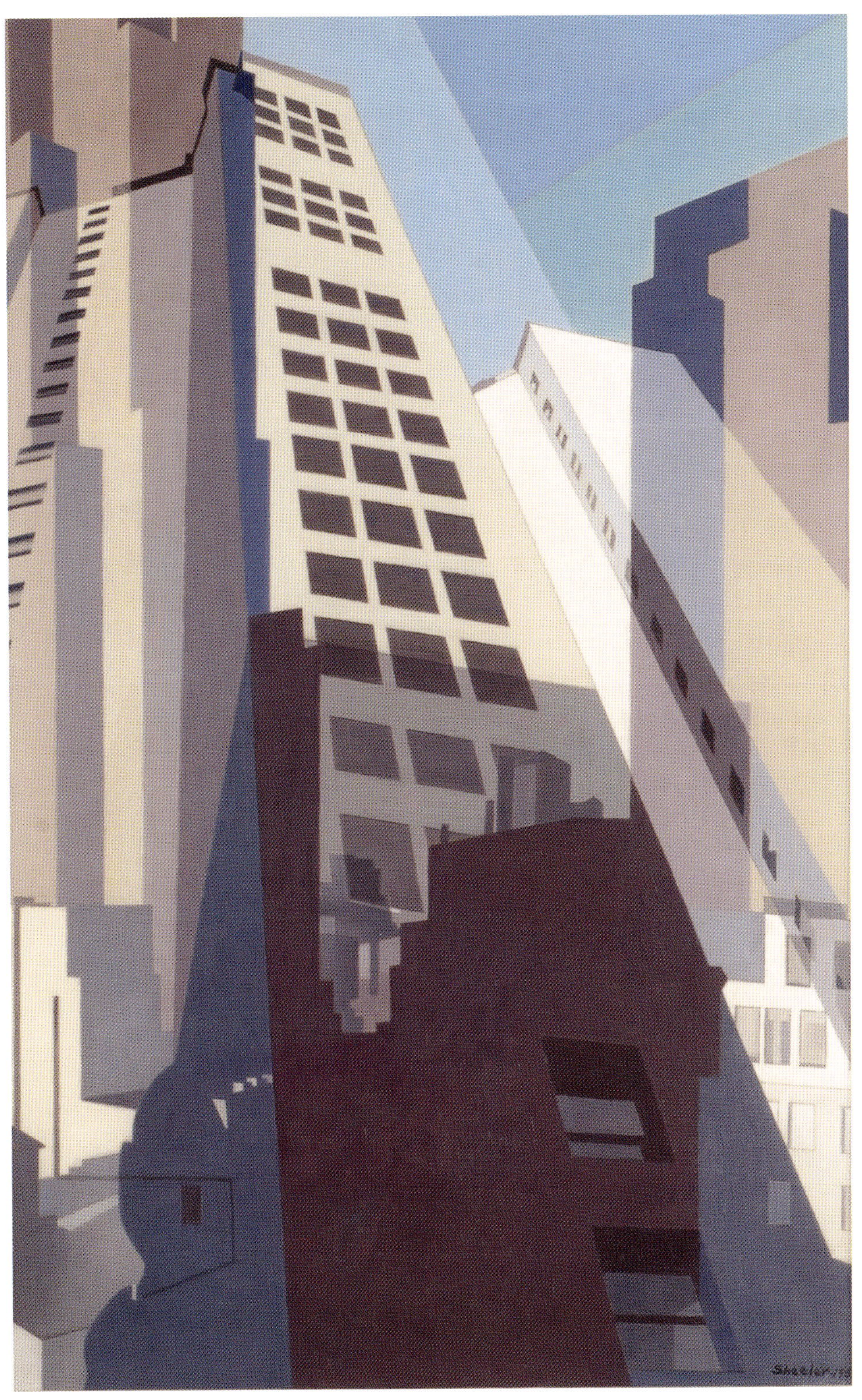

Notes

Introduction

1 Marcus Vitruvius Pollio, *The Ten Books on Architecture*, trans. Morris Hicky Morgan, Cambridge, Mass. (Harvard University Press) 1914, book II, chap. 1, p. 38.
2 *Ibid.*, p. 39.
3 Leon Battista Alberti, *On Painting and On Sculpture: The Latin Texts of De Pictura and De Statua*, ed. and trans. Cecil Grayson, London (Phaidon) 1972, book I, para. 19, p. 55.
4 Quoted in 'Ugo Rondinone', The Institute of Contemporary Art, Boston, icaboston.org/exhibitions/exhibit/rondinone, accessed June 2011.

Status and Style

1 Quoted in *David Hockney: Paintings and Prints from 1960*, exhib. cat., ed. Penelope Curtis, Tate Liverpool, April 1993 – February 1994, p. 29.

Revelations

1 Quoted in Christopher Masters, *Dalí*, London (Phaidon) 1995, p. 116.
2 *Ibid.*
3 *Ibid.*
4 Pseudo-Matthew 2:3–4, quoted in Giuseppe Basile, ed., *Giotto: The Frescoes of the Scrovegni Chapel in Padua*, Milan (Skira) 2002, p. 449.

5 Quoted in P.F. Brown, *Venetian Narrative Painting in the Age of Carpaccio*, New Haven, Conn., and London (Yale University Press) 1988, p. 161.
6 Quoted in Simon Schama, *Citizens: A Chronicle of the French Revolution*, London (Viking) 1989, p. 359.

Windows on the World

1 Quoted in Robert L.S. Cowley, *Marriage À-la-mode: A Review of Hogarth's Narrative Art*, Manchester (Manchester University Press) 1983, p. 30.
2 Banksy, *Wall and Piece*, London (Century) 2005, p. 237.
3 Quoted in *Berthe Morisot: Impressionist*, exhib. cat. by Charles F. Stuckey *et al.*, Washington, D.C.; Fort Worth, Tex.; and South Hadley, Mass., 1987–88, p. 65.
4 Translation from the French quoted in *The Window in Twentieth-Century Art*, exhib. cat. by Suzanne Delehanty, Purchase, NY, Neuberger Museum of Art, September 1986 – January 1987; Contemporary Arts Museum Houston, April–June 1987, p. 29. Originally published as 'Les Fenêtres' in Guillaume Apollinaire, *Calligrammes: poèmes de la paix et de la guerre 1913–1916*, 1918.
5 Quoted in Douglas Cooper, *The Cubist Epoch*, London (Phaidon) 1970, p. 82.
6 *Ibid.*, p. 84.

Mirror of the Soul

1 Aldous Huxley, *Themes and Variations* [1950], quoted in *Piranesi*, exhib. cat. by John Wilton-Ely, London, Hayward Gallery, April–June 1978, p. 133.
2 Joseph Leo Koerner, *Caspar David Friedrich and the Subject of Landscape*, London (Reaktion) 1990, p. 113.
3 André Breton, *Surrealism and Painting*, trans. Simon Watson Taylor, London (Macdonald) 1972, p. 80.
4 Quoted in Richard Calvocoressi, *Magritte*, rev. edn, Oxford (Phaidon) 1984, cat. 33.
5 *Ibid.*
6 Quoted in A.M. Hammacher, *René Magritte*, tr. James Brockway, London (Thames & Hudson) 1974, p. 108.
7 Quoted in Ragna Stang, *Edvard Munch: The Man and the Artist*, tr. Geoffrey Culverwell, London (Gordon Fraser Gallery) 1979, p. 148.
8 Quoted in *Rothko: The Late Series*, exhib. cat., ed. Achim Borchardt-Hume, London, Tate Modern, September 2008 – February 2009; Sakura, Kawamura Memorial Museum of Art, February–June 2009, p. 49.
9 Quoted in *Piranesi*, p. 133.
10 *Ibid.*

The Architecture of Light

1 Quoted in *Hammershøi*, exhib. cat. by Felix Krämer *et al.*, London, Royal Academy of Arts, June–September 2008; Tokyo, The National Museum of Western Art, September–December 2008, p. 23.

Further Reading

In addition to the monographs and other publications cited in the notes section of this book (pages 182–83), the reader's attention is drawn to the following literature specifically concerned with the theme of the window:

Shirley Neilsen Blum, *Henri Matisse: Rooms with a View*, London (Thames & Hudson) 2010

Samuel Y. Edgerton, *The Mirror, the Window, and the Telescope: How Renaissance Linear Perspective Changed Our Vision of the Universe*, Ithaca, NY, and London (Cornell University Press) 2009

Lorenz Eitner, 'The Open Window and the Storm-Tossed Boat: An Essay in the Iconography of Romanticism', *Art Bulletin*, 37, December 1955, pp. 281–90

Carla Gottlieb, *The Window in Art: From the Window of God, to the Vanity of Man – A Survey of Window Symbolism in Western Painting*, New York (Arabis) 1981

Oliver Kase, 'Offene und geschlossene Fenster: Mimesis-Korrekturen im Atelierbild, 1806–1836', *Zeitschrift für Kunstgeschichte*, 69, 2006, pp. 217–50

Rodolphe Rapetti, 'Paris Seen from a Window', in *Gustave Caillebotte: Urban Impressionist*, exhib. cat. by Anne Distel *et al.*, Paris, Chicago and Los Angeles, 1994–95

Rooms with a View: The Open Window in the 19th Century, exhib. cat. by Sabine Rewald, New York, The Metropolitan Museum of Art, April–July 2011

J.A. Schmoll gen. Eisenwerth, 'Fensterbilder: Motivketten in der europäischen Malerei', in *Beiträge zur Motivkunde des 19. Jahrhunderts*, ed. Ludwig Grote, Munich (Prestel), 1970, pp. 13–165

Rolf Selbmann, *Eine Kulturgeschichte des Fensters von der Antike bis zur Moderne*, Berlin (Reimer) 2010

Walter Wells, *Silent Theater: The Art of Edward Hopper*, London and New York (Phaidon) 2007, esp. Chapter 8, 'Variations at the Window', pp. 102–15

The Window in Twentieth-Century Art, exhib. cat. by Suzanne Delehanty, Purchase, NY, Neuberger Museum of Art, September 1986 – January 1987; Contemporary Arts Museum Houston, April–June 1987

Index

Page numbers in *italic* refer to the illustrations.

A

Alberti, Leon Battista 17, 153
    De pictura 9
Antonello da Messina: *St Jerome in His Study* 153, 156, *156*, *157*
Apollinaire, Guillaume: 'Windows' 119
Arena Chapel, Padua: Giotto frescoes 47, 58

B

Balthus (Count Balthazar Klossowski de Rola): *Young Girl at the Window* 132, *133*
Banksy: graffiti in Park Street, Bristol 81, 98, *99*
Barbaro, Daniele 32
Barbaro, Marc'Antonio 32
Baudelaire, Charles 103
Bazille, Frédéric: *Bazille's Studio* 153, 174, *175*
Bellini, Giovanni: *Woman (?Venus) at Her Toilet* 12, *12*
Bellotto, Bernardo: *View of the Rio dei Mendicanti and the Scuola di San Marco, Venice* 153, 170, *170–71*
Benjamin, Walter: 'Arcades Project' 120
Bernard of Clairvaux 47
Bibiena family 149
Blavatsky, Helena 52
Bloch, Carl: *After the Bath: A Young Girl Knocking at the Fisherman's Window* 101, *101*
Bonnard, Pierre: *The Open Window* 4, 81, 112, *113*

Boucher, Marie-Emilie 78
Bourges, France: Palais Jacques Cœur 81, 94, *94*
Boursin, Maria ('Marthe') 112
Breton, André 135
Brücke, Die (The Bridge) 143
Brunelleschi, Filippo 9
bull's-eye windows 26, *26*, *27*, 62, *63*, 68, *69*
buon fresco 92

C

Caillebotte, Gustave
    Interior, Woman at the Window 81, 102, *102*
    Man on a Balcony, Boulevard Haussmann 81, 103, *103*
Campin, Robert
    (workshop of) Annunciation Triptych (Merode Altarpiece) 9, *10*
    (follower of) *The Virgin and Child before a Firescreen* 81, 84, *84*, *85*
Caravaggio, Michelangelo Merisi da: *The Calling of St Matthew* 47, 70, *71*
Carpaccio, Vittore: *St Augustine in His Study* 66, 67, *67*
Carus, Carl Gustav
    Studio Window 18, *19*
    Window at Oybin by Moonlight 128, *129*
Chartres Cathedral, France 50, *51*
Christo (Christo Javacheff): *Four Store Fronts Corner* 81, 120, *121*
Cœur, Jacques: palace in Bourges 81, 94, *94*
Cornell, Joseph: *Untitled (Window Box Construction)* 17, *18–19*
cubism 17

D

Dada 17
Dahl, Johan Christian: *View of Pillnitz Castle* 127, *127*
Dale, Chester 56
Dalí, Salvador
    Figure at a Window 130, *131*
    The Sacrament of the Last Supper 56, *56–57*
David, Jacques-Louis: *Oath of the Tennis Court* 47, *72–73*, 73
De Chirico, Giorgio 60
Delaunay, Robert: *Windows* 17, 20, *118*, 119
Delvaux, Paul: *The Window* 125, 134, 135, *136*
Diamond, Harry 106, *107*
Dobuzhinsky, Mstislav: *Man in Glasses* 81, *90–91*, 91
Dou, Gerrit
    Old Woman at a Half-Door 96
    Old Woman with Jug at a Window 96, *97*
Duchamp, Marcel: *Fresh Widow* 16, *17–18*
Dufy, Raoul: *Window on the Promenade des Anglais, Nice* 22, 23, 44, *45*
Dürer, Albrecht
    illustration of perspective device *8*, 9
    St Jerome in His Study 62, *63*

E

Eddy, Don: *New Shoes for H* 81, 122, *123*
Egg, Augustus Leopold: *The Travelling Companions* 23, 42, *43*
Eliasson, Olafur: *The Daylight Pavilion* 20–21, *21*
Eyck, Jan van
    The Ghent Altarpiece (with Hubert van Eyck) 81, 86, *86*, *87*

Portrait of Giovanni Arnolfini and His Wife
23, 26, *26*, 27

F
Fauves 114
Fragonard, Jean-Honoré: *The Love Letter*
47, 78, *79*
Freud, Lucian: *Interior at Paddington*
106, 107
Friedrich, Caspar David 127, 128, 130
Window with a View of a Park 81, 111, *111*
Woman at the Window 125, 126, *126*, 127,
133

G
Giotto di Bondone: *The Annunciation to
St Anne* 47, 58, *58*, 59
Goethe, Johann Wolfgang von 128
Gogh, Vincent van: *Window in the Studio*
153, *176*, 177
Gris, Juan: *Still Life before an Open Window,
Place Ravignan* 17, 116, *117*
Grünewald, Matthias: *St Anthony and a
Devil* (from the Isenheim Altarpiece)
68, *68*, *69*
Guardi, Francesco: *The Doge Offers Dinner*
23, 34, *34–35*

H
Hammershøi, Vilhelm: *Sunbeams or
Sunshine. Dust Motes Dancing in the
Sunbeams* 153, *154*, 155
Hassam, Childe: *The Goldfish Window* 81,
108, *108–109*
Hockney, David: *Mr and Mrs Clark and Percy*
23, 24, *24–25*

Hoffmann, Josef 36
Hofmann, Hans 122
Hogarth, William: *The Marriage Settlement*
(from *Marriage à la Mode* series) 11, 81,
82, *82–83*
Hoogstraten, Samuel van: *A Peepshow
with Views of the Interior of a Dutch House*
11, 166, *167*
Hopper, Edward
Night Windows 80, 81, 104, *104–105*
Western Motel 20, 153, *178–79*, 179
Humboldt, Alexander von 128
Hunt, William Holman: *The Awakening
Conscience* 47, *48*, 49
Huxley, Aldous 125, 149

I
Impressionists 102, 108, 174

J
Jabès, Edmond 19
Jerome, St 62, *62*, 67, 156, *157*
Juvarra, Filippo 149

K
Kelly, Ellsworth 18

L
Leonardo da Vinci: *The Last Supper* 47,
54–55, 55
Lichtenstein, Roy: *Stretcher Frame with
Cross Bars III* 18, *18*
Lippi, Fra Filippo: *Portrait of a Woman with
a Man at a Casement* 125, 138, *139*
Lorenzetti, Ambrogio: *The Effects of Good
Government on Town and Country* 81, 92, *93*

M
Magritte, René
The Human Condition 17, 125, 136, *136*
In Praise of the Dialectic 124, 125, 136, *137*
Manet, Edouard 100, 174
Manet, Eugène 11, 100, *100*
Mantegna, Andrea: *The Death of the Virgin*
81, 88, *89*
Mantua, Ludovico II Gonzaga, Marquis
of 88
Matisse, Henri 12, 17, 107
Open Window, Collioure 114, *115*
Red Interior: Still Life on a Blue Table 14
Red Room (Harmony in Red) 13
Menzel, Adolph: *The Balcony Room* 23, 40, *41*
Michelangelo Buonarroti 146
Mies van der Rohe, Ludwig: Seagram
Building, New York 146
Mocenigo, Alvise Giovanni, Doge 34
Moll, Carl: *My Living Room (Anna Moll at the
Desk)* 36, *37*
Monchaty, Renée 112, *112*
Monet, Claude 174
The Red Cape 125, 140, *141*
Morisot, Berthe: *Interior, Isle of Wight* 11,
81, 100, *100*
Munch, Edvard
Melancholy (Laura) 11, *11–12*
Moonlight 144
Moonlight I 12, 125, 144, *145*

N
Nazarenes, the 64
Neusüss, Floris (with Renate Heyne):
Homage to William Henry Fox Talbot: His

'Latticed Window' in Lacock Abbey as a Photogram ... 153, *160*, 161, *161*

O

'one-point' perspective 9
Overbeck, Friedrich 64

P

Palladio, Andrea/Palladianism 32, 82
perspective *8*, 9, 62
Pforr, Franz: *Sulamith and Maria* 64, *65*
Picasso, Pablo 12, 17, 56
   The Studio 15
Piranesi, Giovanni Battista: *Carceri d'invenzione* 125, *148*, 149
Pliny the Elder 8
Pompeii: House of the Vettii *7*, 8
Pozzo, Andrea: painted canvas with illusionistic architecture in the Church of Saints Flora and Lucilla, Arezzo *164*, 165
Precisionism 20, 180

R

Redon, Odilon: *The Window* 52, *53*
Renaissance, the 9, 12, 62, 153, 156
Renoir, Pierre Auguste 174
Robert, Hubert: *Project for the Transformation of the Grande Galerie of the Louvre* 153, 172, *172*, *173*
Rondinone, Ugo: *Clockwork for Oracles* 19, *20*
Rørbye, Martinus: *View from the Artist's Window* 81, 110, *110*
Rothko, Mark: *Red on Maroon (Mural, Section 4)* 125, 146, *147*

S

Saenredam, Pieter: north transept ... of St Odulphuskerk, Assendelft *152*, 153, *162–63*, 163
Saint-Denis, abbey church of, Paris 47
Sainte-Chapelle, Paris 153, 158, *158*, *159*
Savinio, Alberto: *Apparition (The Annunciation)* 60, *61*
Schmidt-Rottluff, Karl 125, *142–43*, 143
Segal, George: *The Curtain* 95, *95*
Sheeler, Charles: *New York No. 2* 20, 153, 180, *181*
Shiota, Chiharu: *House of Windows* 20, 125, 150, *151*
stained glass 47, 50, *50*, *51*, 52, 153, 158, *158*, *159*
Suger, Abbot 47
Sunnerberg, Constantin *90*, 91
surrealist movement 17, 130, 135

T

Talbot, William Henry Fox 161
Theosophical Society 52
Titian (Titiano Vecellio): *Venus of Urbino* 23, *30*, 31, *31*
trompe l'œil 32, 153, 165

U

Urbino, Guidobaldo della Rovere, Duke of 31

V

Vauxcelles, Louis 114
Vermeer, Jan 6
   The Astronomer 47, 74, *75*
   The Geographer 74
   Girl Reading a Letter at an Open Window *46*, 47, 76, 77, 78
   The Girl with the Wine Glass 28
   The Glass of Wine 23, 28, *28*, *29*
   The Little Street 153, *168*, 169
Veronese, Paolo: *Stanza del Cane* 23, 32, *33*
Vitruvius Pollio, Marcus 7, 8, 32, 172

Z

Zielcke, Leopold: *The Artist's Studio in His Apartment at Friedrichstrasse 228* *38*, 39
Zimmerbilder 23, 39, 40

Picture Credits

© ADAGP, Paris and DACS, London 2011/Digital image 2011 © Art Resource, New York/Photo Scala, Florence: 22, 44; © ADAGP, Paris and DACS, London 2011/Image © The Metropolitan Museum of Art, New York/Art Resource, New York/Photo Scala, Florence: 132; © ADAGP, Paris and DACS, London 2011/ National Gallery of Art, Washington, D.C., USA/Giraudon/The Bridgeman Art Library: 136; © ADAGP, Paris and DACS, London 2011/National Gallery of Victoria, Melbourne, Australia/Felton Bequest/The Bridgeman Art Library: 124, 137; © ADAGP, Paris and DACS, London 2011/Phillips Collection, Washington, D.C., USA/The Bridgeman Art Library: 4, 113; akg-images: jacket back (tl, br), 19, 37, 41, 53, 90–91, 111, 126, 141, 168, 176; akg-images/ Cameraphoto: 58, 59; akg-images/ Electa: 93; akg-images/Erich Lessing: jacket back (bl), 12, 51, 82–83, 97, 100, 103, 127; akg-images/Paul M.R. Maeyaert: 94; akg-images/Joseph Martin: 159; © 2008 Carsten Andersen. Reproduced with the permission of Studio Olafur Eliasson, Berlin: 21; © Vito Arcomano/SuperStock: 7; © Peter Barritt/SuperStock: 158; © Birmingham Museums and Art Gallery/The

Bridgeman Art Library: 43; Chartres Cathedral, Chartres, France/The Bridgeman Art Library: 50; © Christo and Jeanne-Claude, Four Store Fronts Corner, 1964–65. Photo: Wolfgang Volz/laif/Camera Press: 121; Currier Museum of Art, Manchester, New Hampshire. Museum Purchase: Currier Funds, 1937.2: jacket back (tr), 108–109; © DACS 2011/akg-images: 134; © DACS 2011/Photo: akg-images: 142–43; © DACS 2011/Photo Scala, Florence: 61; © Salvador Dalí, Fundació Gala-Salvador Dalí, DACS, 2011/National Gallery of Art, Washington, D.C., USA/The Bridgeman Art Library: 56–57; © Salvador Dalí, Fundació Gala-Salvador Dalí, DACS, 2011/Photo: Fundació Gala-Salvador Dalí: 131; © Don Eddy: 123; © The Estate of Roy Lichtenstein/DACS 2011/Photo: akg-images: 18; © The George and Helen Segal Foundation/ DACS, London/VAGA, New York 2011/ Photo: Smithsonian American Art Museum/Art Resource, New York/ Photo Scala, Florence: 95; Germanisches Nationalmuseum, Nuremberg, Germany/The Bridgeman Art Library: 38; © David Hockney. Collection: Tate Gallery, London/Photo: Tate, London 2011: 24–25; © The Joseph and

Robert Cornell Memorial Foundation/ DACS, London/VAGA, New York 2011/ The Menil Collection, Houston. Photographer: Hickey-Robertson, Houston: 17; Hans-Peter Klut/BPK, Berlin/Photo Scala, Florence: 77; Hans-Peter Klut/BPK, Bildagentur für Kunst, Kultur und Geschichte, Berlin/Photo Scala, Florence: 46; © L & M Services B.V. The Hague 20110812/Digital image: The Museum of Modern Art, New York/Photo Scala, Florence: 118; © The Lucian Freud Archive/Photo © Walker Art Gallery, National Museums Liverpool/Bridgeman Art Library: 106; The Metropolitan Museum of Art, New York/Art Resource, New York/Photo Scala, Florence: 10, 79, 139; © Munch Museum/Munch-Ellingsen Group, BONO, Oslo/DACS, London 2011/ Photo Scala, Florence: 11, 145; Munson Williams Proctor Arts Institute/Art Resource, New York/Photo Scala, Florence: 181; Musée d'Unterlinden, Colmar, France/Giraudon/The Bridgeman Art Library: 68, 69; Museum Georg Schäfer, Schweinfurt: 65, 129; The Museum of Modern Art, New York/ Photo Scala, Florence: 80, 104–105; The National Gallery, London/Photo Scala, Florence: 26, 27, 84, 85, 156, 157, 167;

National Gallery of Denmark,
Copenhagen/© SMK Photo: 101, 110;
Floris Neusüss: 160, 161; Ordrupgaard,
Copenhagen/Pernille Klemp: jacket
front, 154; The Philadelphia Museum
of Art/Art Resource, New York/Photo
Scala, Florence: 117; Neil Phillips/
Alamy: 99; Photo Scala, Florence:
30, 31, 33, 34–35, 63, 66, 67, 71, 75, 86,
87, 89, 164, 172, 173, 175; Photo Scala,
Florence/BPK, Bildagentur für Kunst,
Kultur und Geschichte, Berlin: 28,
29, 148; Photo Scala, Florence. Courtesy
of the Ministero Beni e Att. Culturali:
54–55, 152, 162–63, 170–71; © Ugo
Rondinone, courtesy of Sadie Coles HQ,
London, and Galerie Eva Presenhuber,
Zürich/Photo: Charles Mayer/Institute
of Contemporary Art, Boston: 20; © 1998
Kate Rothko Prizel and Christopher
Rothko/ARS, New York and DACS,
London/Tate, London 2011: 147; Chiharu
Shiota © DACS 2011/Photo: Sunhi Mang:
151; © Succession H. Matisse/DACS 2011.
Image courtesy of National Gallery of
Art, Washington, D.C., USA/Collection
of Mr and Mrs John Hay Whitney
1998.74.7: 115; © Succession H. Matisse/
DACS 2011. Photo: akg-images: 14;
© Succession H. Matisse/DACS 2011.
Photo Scala, Florence: 13; © Succession
Marcel Duchamp/ADAGP, Paris and
DACS, London 2011/Digital image
© 2011 The Museum of Modern Art,
New York/Photo Scala, Florence: 16;
© Succession Picasso/DACS, London
2011/Tate, London 2011: 15; White
Images/Photo Scala, Florence: 48,
72–73, 102; Yale University Art Gallery/
Art Resource, New York/Photo Scala,
Florence: 178–79.

For Clara, Emilia and Zoë

Acknowledgements

I should like to thank Nicola Bailey, Claire Chandler, Alenka Oblak, Mark Ralph and Nick Wheldon at Merrell for their excellence and professionalism in producing this book; and Lars Kann-Rasmussen, Anders Kirketerp-Møller and Troels Rasmussen at VKR Holding for their unfailing enthusiasm and wise advice. I am, as ever, especially grateful to all the members of my family, big and small, for supporting and diverting me with such vim; and to my friends, especially Mr David Selwyn, for perennial encouragement and inspiration.

First published 2011 by

Merrell Publishers Limited
81 Southwark Street
London SE1 OHX

merrellpublishers.com

British Library Cataloguing-in-Publication Data:
Masters, Christopher.
Windows in art.
1. Windows in art.
I. Title
758.9'7-dc22

ISBN 978-1-8589-4554-5

Produced by Merrell Publishers Limited
Designed by Nicola Bailey
Project-managed by Mark Ralph
Indexed by Vicki Robinson

Printed and bound in Italy

*The publisher wishes to express its deepest gratitude to VKR Holding A/S
and, in particular, Mr Lars Kann-Rasmussen, without whose generous
support the publication of this book would not have been possible.*

JACKET FRONT AND SPINE
Detail of Vilhelm Hammershøi, *Sunbeams or Sunshine. Dust Motes
Dancing in the Sunbeams*, 1900 (see page 154)

JACKET BACK, CLOCKWISE FROM TOP LEFT
Detail of Jan Vermeer, *The Little Street*, *c*. 1658 (see page 168);
detail of Childe Hassam, *The Goldfish Window*, 1916 (see
pages 108–109); detail of Odilon Redon, *The Window*,
c. 1905 (see page 53); detail of Giovanni Bellini, *Woman
(?Venus) at Her Toilet*, 1515 (see page 12)

PAGE 4
Detail of Pierre Bonnard, *The Open Window*, 1921
(see page 113)

PAGE 22
Detail of Raoul Dufy, *Window on the Promenade des Anglais, Nice*,
1938 (see page 44)

PAGE 46
Detail of Jan Vermeer, *Girl Reading a Letter at an Open Window*,
c. 1658–61 (see page 77)

PAGE 80
Detail of Edward Hopper, *Night Windows*, 1928
(see pages 104–105)

PAGE 124
Detail of René Magritte, *In Praise of the Dialectic*, 1937
(see page 137)

PAGE 152
Detail of Pieter Saenredam, North transept and adjoining
areas of the choir and nave of St Odulphuskerk, Assendelft,
c. 1633 (see pages 162–63)